D0985085

FEMINIST REALISM AT THE *FIN DE SIÈCLE*

The Influence of the Late-Victorian Woman's Press on the Development of the Novel

Molly Youngkin

The Ohio State University Press
Columbus

Library of Congress Cataloging-in-Publication Data

Youngkin, Molly, 1970–
Feminist realism at the fin de siècle : the influence of the late-Victorian woman's press on the development of the novel / Molly Youngkin.
  p. cm.
Includes bibliographical references and index.
ISBN-13: 978–0–8142–1048–2 (cloth : alk. paper)
ISBN-13: 978–0–8142–9128–3 (CD-ROM)
  1. Feminism and literature—England—History—19th century.
2. English fiction—19th century—History and criticism. 3. Feminist fiction, English—History and criticism. 4. Journalism and literature—Great Britain—History—19th century. 5. Women and literature—Great Britain—History—19th century. 6. Feminism in literature.
7. Women in literature. 8. Realism in literature. 9. Modernism (Literature)—Great Britain.   I. Title.
PR878.F45Y68 2007
823.'809352042—dc22
                        2006026277

Cover design by DesignSmith.
Type set in Adobe Garamond.
Printed by Thomson-Shore, Inc.

9 8 7 6 5 4 3 2 1

Contents

Illustrations

Acknowledgments

Institutional support was key to the completion of this book. California State University, Dominguez Hills provided two course releases, without which I would not have finished this project. Also, the Sally Casanova Memorial/RSCAAP Grant provided financial support for an additional course release and an important trip to the British Library in the summer of 2004. My thanks to Selase Williams for his support of my applications for these grants, and thanks to Garry Hart, Ray Riznyk, and Ed Zoerner for facilitating funds related to the reproduction of images in this book. The Ohio State University provided institutional support during the early stages of this project. The English Department granted me the Edward P. J. Corbett Research Award and the Summer Research Fellowship; the Women's Studies Department provided the Elizabeth D. Gee Grant; and the Graduate School provided the Alumni Grant for Graduate Research and Scholarship, the Summer Research Fellowship, and the Presidential Fellowship. Thanks to Susan Williams and Debra Moddelmog, who served as Director of Graduate Studies in the English Department, for their support of my applications.

I respectfully acknowledge other organizations that supported my work in various forms. Thank you to the librarians who assisted my research at the British Library, the National Library of Ireland, the Cincinnati Public Library, the Special Collections at Arizona State University, The Ohio State University, and UCLA. Thanks also to Robert Langenfeld, William Scheuerle, Kitty Ledbetter, Jennifer Cognard-Black, and Elizabeth MacLeod Walls, all of whom encouraged the publication of my work in other venues. Portions of chapter 1 of this book appeared in "'All she knew was, that she wished to live': Late-Victorian Realism, Liberal-Feminist Ideals, and George Gissing's *In the Year of the Jubilee*," *Studies in the Novel*, v. 36, no. 1, Spring 2004. Copyright © 2004 by the University of North Texas. Reprinted by permission of the publisher. Portions of chapter 4 appeared in "George Moore's Quest for Canonization and *Esther Waters* as Female Helpmate," *ELT: English Literature in Transition, 1880–1920* 46.2 (2003): 117–39; "'Independent in Thought and Expression, Kindly and Tolerant in Tone': Henrietta Stannard, *Golden Gates*, and Gender Controversies at the *Fin de Siècle*," *Victorian Periodicals Review* 38.3 (2005): 307–26; and "Selected Letters: Henrietta Stannard,

Marie Corelli, and Annesley Kenealy," *Kindred Hands: Letters on Writing by Women Authors, 1860–1920,* ed. Jennifer Cognard-Black and Elizabeth MacLeod Walls, University of Iowa Press, 2006.

Figures 1 through 5 images were produced by ProQuest Information and Learning Company as part of American Periodical Series Online. Inquiries may be made to: ProQuest Information and Learning Company, 300 North Zeeb Road, Ann Arbor, MI 48106-1346 USA; telephone 734.761.4700; email info@il.proquest.com; Web site www.il.proquest.com. Thanks to ProQuest Learning Company for permission to reprint these images. The cover image, Albert Moore's *A Reader,* was provided by Manchester Art Gallery, Mosley Street, Manchester M2 3JL, telephone 0161 235 8888, Web site www.manchestergalleries.org.uk. I am grateful to Jo-Anne Hogan of ProQuest and Tracey Walker of Manchester Art Gallery for providing excellent assistance during the process of obtaining permission. I also want to acknowledge those at The Ohio State University Press who worked diligently to see this book to publication. A special thanks to Sandy Crooms, who worked with me with great enthusiasm throughout this process, and to Maggie Diehl, who carefully copyedited the manuscript.

In addition to the institutional and organizational support I received, many individuals encouraged my work in different ways. Thanks to Peter Bracher and Barry Milligan, who were the first to spark my interest in nineteenth-century British literature. Also, great appreciation goes to Marlene Longenecker, James Phelan, Clare Simmons, and David Riede, who read portions of this project in its early stages and provided ongoing support in the transition from dissertation to book. A special thanks to Marlene, who suggested the title *Feminist Realism at the Fin de Siècle.* I also want to acknowledge Teresa Mangum, Sally Mitchell, Jennifer Phegley, Talia Schaffer, Beth Sutton-Ramspeck, and the many members of RSVP (The Research Society for Victorian Periodicals) and the VICTORIA listserv, who made suggestions for revision and answered questions that arose while I worked on this project. And I would like to acknowledge my colleagues at Dominguez Hills, some of whom offered advice about publication matters and all of whom offered intellectual camaraderie and friendship during the writing process. Finally, deep gratitude to my parents, Betty and Bill Youngkin. Their belief in my writing ability is longstanding, and they regularly listened to and discussed my flow of ideas as the project progressed. They were involved in the writing of this book on a weekly, and sometimes daily, basis, and I thank them for their belief in me and the project.

INTRODUCTION

The Woman's Press at the *Fin de Siècle*

On October 27, 1888, Henrietta Müller—who had already participated in the nineteenth-century women's movement by attending Girton College, organizing women's trade unions, and improving working conditions for women through her position on the London School Board—founded the *Women's Penny Paper* (see figure 1), an eight-page paper with a "progressive policy" and a plan to "speak with honesty and courage" about issues important to women. This paper, which claimed to represent all different types of women and to be "open to all shades of opinion, to the working woman as freely as to the educated lady, to the conservative and the radical, to the Englishwoman and the foreigner" (Anonymous, "Our Policy" 1), would become, in 1891, *The Woman's Herald* (figure 2) and, later, *The Woman's Signal* (figure 3). Throughout its run, which ended in 1899, the paper served as an important outlet for Müller and other activists to express their ideas about the advancement of women.

Four years after the founding of the *Women's Penny Paper*, Margaret Shurmer Sibthorp—a member of the Theosophical Society and later one of the founders of the League of Isis (a group advocating the ideas of Frances Swiney about sexuality and motherhood)—introduced another periodical, *Shafts,* with a similar approach and agenda. Drawing on the image of a woman holding a bow and shooting shafts, or arrows, of wisdom, truth, and justice into the atmosphere (figures 4 and 5), Sibthorp called on women of all classes to help in the fight for emancipation "so that the bow of our strength may not lose power" and "so that all who write and all who read may join in the great work to be done" ("What the Editor" 8). With the goal of women's emancipation in mind, both *Shafts* and *The Woman's Herald* adopted a weekly format to pursue this goal and became active voices in the feminist movement throughout the 1890s. Only after a full decade of publishing articles to forward the cause of women would the writers for these two periodicals lay down their pens.

1

WOMEN'S PENNY PAPER

The only Paper Conducted, Written, and Published by Women.

EDITED BY
HELENA B. TEMPLE.

"Seventy years ago a man might rise to high positions in Parliament or the State and take no notice whatever of the humbler classes. THEY HAD NO VOTES AND COULD BE SAFELY NEGLECTED." *(W. E. Gladstone, October 26th, 1889.)*

Offices—86, STRAND, W.C.
Registered at the G.P.O. for transmission abroad.

No. 88. Vol. II.]   JUNE 28, 1890.   [PRICE ONE PENNY.

Interview.

MRS. MONA CAIRD.

SO much has been said and written about the famous Mrs. Mona Caird that is misleading, that a true account of her will be of interest. I was fortunate enough to find the popular authoress at home, and willing to be interviewed for the *Women's Penny Paper*, in which she takes a very great interest and warmly wishes it all possible success. Whatever may be Mrs. Mona Caird's views upon marriage, she certainly is a wife who knows how to make home attractive in the matter of decoration, and her drawing-room is not only pretty, but as unlike the majority of London drawing-rooms as it is possible to imagine. The cosy corners by the fireside with the windows over the mantelpiece are delightful resting-places; the room has a sense of repose and quiet content which are very inviting.

Of her early days Mrs. Mona Caird declared she had little to tell. "As a child I rebelled against the current thoughts. It was not natural to me ever to take things as I found them. My life as a girl was very secluded on account of my father's ill-health, and personal influence, therefore, played little part in my development. I had literally to 'scramble up.' All the influence of my immediate surroundings I resisted obstinately. Had I yielded to it, I should have been beloved by the British Matron, and should have been regarded as the chosen adviser of the *Young Person*."

"What made you first take to writing?" I asked.

"I always wrote, even as a child; it was an outlet for my thoughts, but I was discouraged in my efforts as soon as these seemed to become absorbing. My literary work was, therefore, done under adverse circumstances, amidst the very greatest difficulties. The usual idea prevailed that a girl's only career was matrimony and a life of domesticity whether it suited her or not."

"But," I answered, "it is just upon this question of the marriage state I would ask your real views! Do you believe that men and women should be allowed to marry and separate as easily as they would meet for a week or so in a country house?"

"My idea of marriage is that it should be a Free Contract entered into by those who perfectly understand what they are doing, and who are aware of all the responsibilities which are entailed. The force of Society matches, in which the girl is as much bought and sold as any slave, are utterly abhorrent to me. I do not think the world at present is sufficiently educated to understand the idea of the new marriage, *which is a far more elevated one than the present bond*. When men and women are differently educated, when women are allowed to meet more freely, when our girls are rendered no longer dependent for their very existence upon men, then it will be possible to realise *a better and truer* state of things. I do not advocate any startling change at present, for I do not believe any Free Marriage is possible until the proposed contract is free in fact as well as in name; but because my idea may not be practicable at present it does not follow it will always be so; till it comes I would educate men and women to a better and higher view of the estate and its responsibilities."

"But do you not think men would be likely to leave their wives when they became older and less attractive if the marriage bond were easily dissolved?"

"No; I believe, with proper education, chivalry would be far greater than at present; the very fact that the marriage could be dissolved more easily would often lead to greater happiness and constancy in the married state. We are contradictory by nature, and the fact that we cannot undo a thing will make many wish immediately to do so."

"You have been much misrepresented by the world at large," I said.

"That is the fate of all who propagate any new ideas. In reality *I am as much in favour of life-long marriages as anyone*, but they should be free and not enforced, and if a man and woman found that they had, after all, made an unfortunate mistake in their union, and that by reason of incompatibility of temper, or other causes, life together was impossible, I certainly believe it would be far better in every way to allow them to dissolve such a mistaken contract, rather than to force them to live on for the rest of their lives a terrible existence in which neither soul nor body could be free. Under the blessing of the Church many a horrible outrage is committed. Girls marry under conditions in which they have no opportunity of gaining any true knowledge of the man they wed; they are rushed into these marriages by Society mothers and ambitious fathers, and then left uncared-to to their fate."

It was impossible to hear Mrs. Mona Caird talk and not be convinced that she earnestly believes what she advocates. If all men and women could attain the high ideal she has formed, the marriage contract might be a very different one, and might perhaps be allowed to rest upon Love and Conscience. At present, as she says, the world is not pure enough. Sensuality and money rule the world, and love, alas! often plays but a small part in our marriage ceremony. I asked Mrs. Mona Caird her views on Women's Suffrage.

"Of course I am ardently in favour of the vote for all women, irrespective of condition and circumstances. I am a Liberal in politics, and I would not shut women out from any profession or career in which it were possible for them to succeed. Men and women should have equal rights in every respect, and the same laws should apply equally to both. What is wrong in the woman is wrong in the man; there should be no fear or favour. Until she be recognised there can be no real progress."

"Were you influenced by anyone in forming your views?"

"No, not particularly. I knew so few whose intellect I respected. My views were pronounced at an early age. John Stuart Mills, I think, was the first to help me to bring these thoughts and feelings into form by his writings. Shelley, also, had a strong influence over me, and the modern scientific writers, Tyndall, Huxley, Herbert Spencer, and, of course, Darwin. I came in contact with no leading minds, except in their writings, but these were more than sufficient education."

Here the entrance of tea and of Mrs. Caird's husband put a stop to our conversation.

In compliance with my expressed wish she shewed me her own special sanctum.

"I have not had the privilege of my own study long," she said, "but I now do all my work here."

The room and furniture were painted in white enamel, a commodious writing desk with numberless drawers revealed the law of order, while the bookcases were well filled with books.

"Here are my own books," said Mrs. Mona Caird, and handed me *One that Wins, When Nature Leadeth,* and her latest, *The Wing of Asrael.* The latter is published by Trübner and Co., who also published her two Westminster articles. Chapman and Hall are the publishers of the last, *Morality of Marriage.*

Mrs. Mona Caird has undergone the Sun Cure in Austria, and her very graphic account of her experiences was published in the *Pall Mall Gazette.*

Mrs. Mona Caird has, since my visit, contributed some very interesting articles to our paper upon the Suffrage for Women, in which she clearly states the position.

Her husband is the son of Sir James Caird. She has one son, a fine,

---

Figure 1

Front cover, *Women's Penny Paper* (June 28, 1890): 421. Image published with permission of ProQuest Information and Learning Company. Further reproduction is prohibited without permission.

AUGUST 17, 1893.

The Woman's Herald

Motto
FOR GOD and HOME and EVERY LAND

Edited by LADY HENRY SOMERSET and EDWIN H. STOUT.

Sarah Grand:

A STUDY.

"SARAH GRAND," as the author of "Ideala" and "The Heavenly Twins," who tries to disguise—somewhat transparently—her personality, is one of the most valuable recruits which the cause of woman has gained in recent years. She has made her mark, and is now free of the camp—a trusted comrade who can be relied on in the highest of high places not to fail or to flinch. But although Sarah Grand has done good and noble service by boldly challenging Society to say why men should not bring to the marriage altar as unspotted a record as they demand from their brides, she is but a neophyte. Her best work is still to come. Hitherto she has studied the world from the outside, in books, in maiden meditation fancy free. The supreme note that will yet make her books powerful and searching as a two-edged sword has still to be sounded. But we shall have it before long, and although it may sadden us it cannot fail to purify our hearts with the pathos of its passionate undertone.

Sarah Grand, as all may see from the accompanying portrait, is still in the bloom of her youth's prime. Married very early, she has travelled much and suffered not a little. But her life work is still to be done. What shape it will take it is difficult at this moment to say. Life is the great shaper of our destinies, and Sarah Grand, even more than most people, needs the Providence that shapes our ends, rough hew them as we may. There is a good deal of the dreamy abstraction of "Ideala" about her creator, and there is also a spice of Angelica, minus, unfortunately, the tomboy element which saved Angelica. But the adventurous curiosity which made Angelica put her finger into so many cogwheels, to see how it would feel to test by experiment the force of explosives, of the real nature of which she seems to be as innocent as a baby is of the properties of dynamite, taught that Heavenly Twin something of the realities of life; and Sarah Grand, like all the rest of us, will graduate in the same school. If a little transfusion of blood could be effected, so as to graft something of Mrs. Josephine Butler's healthy womanhood, saint-like faith, and apostolic fervour upon the

"SARAH GRAND."
From a Photograph by H. S. Mendelssohn.

somewhat despairing nervelessness of Sarah Grand, the gain resulting would almost be sufficient to justify the passing of an Act of Parliament legalising such a vivisectional experiment. For Sarah Grand, like many of those whose experience in youth had had too much of the frost that chills the budding ideal, has not too much faith either in God or in Man. It will come, no doubt, as she grows and the sun shines and her inner nature develops; but at present she diets herself upon what Mr. Morley called the "ground-bottle glass" of Positivist lectures, and looks out from a somewhat dreary standpoint upon what seems an orphaned world. The kindling inspiration of a great enthusiasm, that would transform everything, has still to come. But come it will.

Meanwhile, Sarah Grand is working along, and there is great safety and great consolation in work. Her magazine article in The Humanitarian upon the Morals of Manners and Appearance is pre-eminently sane and sensible. No one can say how much the cause of women has suffered from the neglect of the art of making the best of yourself, which characterised some of the early pioneers. Some foolish women think it is a kind of homage to advanced principle to wear a decayed hat and a dowdy jacket. To wear a smart frock and to look as nice as you can seems to be bowing in the temple of Rimmon. All that is mischievous nonsense. Reverse the position, and imagine that men were a disfranchised, unrecognised class. What would women think if the advocates of male enfranchisement were to regard the cultivation of physical strength and manly vigour as treason to the cause of man? If the men who pleaded for citizenship were sickly, effeminate, hollow-chested, bandy-legged weaklings, they would never so much as gain a hearing, however much they might demonstrate the indisputable justice of their course. What strength is to the man beauty is to the woman. Physical strength is a very brutal thing, no doubt; it is certainly much coarser and less refined than the art of beauty. All this and much more of the same sound sense "Sarah Grand" insists upon in her recent article. It is a good sign. When people begin to take pains to mend their fellow-creatures by practise as well as by precept they have set their faces Zionwards, and they are not far from the way of salvation.

Figure 2

Front cover, *The Woman's Herald* (Aug. 17, 1893): 401. Image published with permission of ProQuest Information and Learning Company. Further reproduction is prohibited without permission.

THE
WOMAN'S SIGNAL

A Weekly Paper for all Women

ABOUT ALL THEIR INTERESTS, IN THE HOME AND IN THE WIDER WORLD.

EDITED BY
MRS. FENWICK MILLER.

VOL. V., No. 109.   JANUARY 30, 1896.   [Registered as a Newspaper.]   One Penny Weekly.

Character Sketch.

JOHN STRANGE WINTER.

Most of us can remember when a clever little story, totally unlike anything that had before been done, and entitled "Bootles' Baby," burst upon the world, and created an immediate reputation for a writer. It was not, however, the first work that its author had published under the same pen name. The first book that had appeared bearing the signature of "John Strange Winter," was called "Cavalry Life." It was not supposed for one moment by any of the readers or critics of these stories of army life, that the author was a woman. It is quite amusing to read the criticisms upon those early works, filled as they are with compliments, not only to the author's stories and literary art, but also to "his" accurate descriptions of army life, and the *manliness* of "his" mind. Here, for instance, is what the *Morning Post* says:—

"The author elects to call his books 'light.' They are no doubt invariably entertaining and humorous; but he can also be pathetic in no ordinary degree. His intimate knowledge of the inner life of barracks renders his tales of soldiers and their ways accurate, whilst they are without exception bright and amusing."

"Bootles' Baby" appeared first in *The Graphic* in 1885. It was an immediate success there, and a yet greater one when it appeared in a shilling volume on the bookstalls. But there are two interesting facts to be told about that apparently sudden and easy success. The author who to the public eye thus leaped to fame at a bound, had in fact been working obscurely, but with untiring industry, for exactly ten years before. Her first work was published in 1874, and in the intervening period, before her success was scored, this energetic and resolute writer had produced no fewer than forty-two stories, several of them of three-volume length. All were published in various periodicals, but without making any particular mark; yet she had

taken untiring pains, and spent unstinted toil upon their production. The "staying power" thus shown should be a lesson to aspiring young authors, who imagine that they are to succeed at once, and if they do not do so are discouraged and depressed. Furthermore, not only was John Strange Winter's first success thus the reward of a long and arduous apprenticeship, but even with regard to "Bootles' Baby" itself, courage and hope were necessary. This little tale, which was to prove one of the most distinct literary successes of our time, was rejected by no fewer than six editors before it was taken by Mr. Arthur Locker for *The Graphic*.

It is this same "staying power" that has

MRS. ARTHUR STANNARD.
(From photo by Alfred Ellis, 20, Upper Baker Street, W.)

enabled the author to go on steadily, maintaining her position by a succession of works, not presuming on the fame she had gained to cease exercising the qualities by which she gained it.

One of the first questions that interviewers always ask the author is, how she came to adopt the name under which she publishes? The explanation is simple. It is the name of one of the characters in "Cavalry Life," and was placed upon the title-page as the name of the author, because the publishers insisted that there was no chance of success for a military book known to be written by a woman; in which view they were probably quite right.

How did she come to know enough about this exclusively masculine life to be able to write books about it that military men themselves at once received as accurate and vividly representative? The answer is found in her early life and training. Her father, the Rev. J. Palmer, was for some time an officer in the Royal Artillery, his father, grandfather, and great-grandfather having all been in the Service also. Mr. Palmer, however, left the army and took orders; but "once a soldier always a soldier," in a way; and John Strange Winter's youth was passed in the almost exclusively military society that gathered round her father's home while he was Rector of St. Margaret's, York.

She is one of those sensible women who make no secret of their age. She was born exactly forty years ago on the 13th of this January. She was married in 1884 to Mr. Arthur Stannard, a civil engineer, who was for some time associated in work with General Gordon. Mrs. Stannard's marriage is quite one of the successes of her career. Never was there a more fortunate match. Mr. Stannard is an excellent man of business and manages all his wife's financial affairs. He is also of the most gracious manners and urbane disposition, and aids her to attach and keep the troops of friends whom her bright intelligence and unaffected good-nature, no less than her literary celebrity, gather around them.

Figure 3

Front cover, *The Woman's Signal* (Jan. 30, 1896): 109. Image published with permission of ProQuest Information and Learning Company. Further reproduction is prohibited without permission.

Figure 4

Front cover, *Shafts* (Nov. 3, 1892): 1. Image published with permission of ProQuest Information and Learning Company. Further reproduction is prohibited without permission.

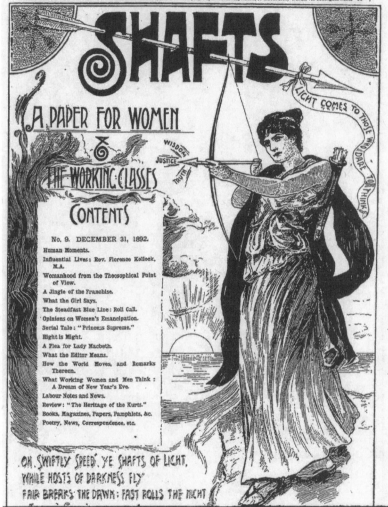

Figure 5

Front cover, *Shafts* (Dec. 31, 1892): 129. Image published with permission of ProQuest Information and Learning Company. Further reproduction is prohibited without permission.

This book centers on the feminist agenda of the late-Victorian woman's press and argues that *Shafts* and *The Woman's Herald* in particular focused on literary representation as a method to advance the cause of women. Along with articles about local politics, key figures within the movement, and nonliterary events and issues, these two periodicals reviewed the works of both women writers and male authors, and they articulated a consistent "feminist realist" aesthetic that not only advanced a cause but also helped transform the novel from Victorian to modern. Influenced by John Stuart Mill's writings on individual liberty and the difficulty women had in achieving such liberty due to cultural conditions, *Shafts* and *The Woman's Herald* insisted on realistic representation of "woman's agency" because woman's agency was a key concept in the development of individual liberty. They also encouraged representations that balanced the difficult conditions women faced with the triumphs of some women over these conditions. To triumph over these conditions, fictional women needed to assert agency in the same manner real-life women did: they needed to experience a transformation of *consciousness* to realize their condition, articulate their condition through *spoken word,* and use *concrete action* to change their condition. In fact, both periodicals had mottos emphasizing one or more of these methods: *Shafts* declared, "Light comes to those who dare to think" on its front cover, and *The Woman's Herald* ran the banner, "Speak unto the people that they go forward."

As Teresa Mangum has shown in her discussion of "middlebrow" feminism in *Married, Middlebrow, and Militant: Sarah Grand and the New Woman* (1998), feminism is both a political and an aesthetic category, and writers such as Grand practiced what Mangum calls "literary feminism," which sprung from "a commitment to an aesthetics based on education, ethics, and activism" (7). *Shafts* and *The Woman's Herald* articulated a similar commitment and developed a systematic reviewing apparatus that placed strong emphasis on both the connection between literary representation and social change and the connection between content and form within literary representation. According to the book reviews published in *Shafts* and *The Woman's Herald,* which were written by a range of women and men committed to the cause, literary representations of woman's agency employed three distinct narrative strategies roughly corresponding to the three methods of assertion: *internal perspective* to indicate transformations of consciousness, highly developed *dialogue* to illustrate women's use of spoken word, and *descriptions of characters' actions* to show how women acted as well as thought and spoke. Successful representations of woman's agency balanced all of these narrative strategies, and, when authors managed to combine all three, the result was a decidedly feminist heroine. In articulating this "feminist realist" approach, as I like to refer to the literary aesthetic found in these periodicals, reviewers for *Shafts* and *The Woman's Herald* broadened the ongoing discussion about realism, a discussion that spanned much of the century and set a particular standard for authors to meet. Not only did authors need to consider the principles of mid-century high realism (as seen in the work of Dickens and Trollope) and late-century variations of realism (such as French naturalism and Jamesian psychological realism), but they had to negotiate this emerging school of feminist realism.[1]

This book surveys the work of eight important male and female authors of the *fin de siècle*—Thomas Hardy, "Sarah Grand" (Frances Bellenden-Clarke McFall), George Gissing, Mona Caird, George Meredith, Ménie Dowie, George Moore, and Henrietta Stannard ("John Strange Winter")—most of whom had direct knowledge of the aesthetic articulated by these periodicals. It illustrates how these authors incorporated feminist realism into their novels: each of the first three chapters focuses on a different aspect of expressing agency and includes representative examples from selected authors. The final chapter shows how effectively combining all three aspects and presenting successful representations of women shaped literary reputations during the 1890s and beyond. By incorporating feminist realism into their novels, these authors helped push the development of the novel from Victorian to modern, since this new aesthetic placed stronger emphasis on consciousness and subjective experience than previous realist aesthetics had. While feminist periodicals valued representations of women presenting the fullest expression of agency possible, they also articulated a causal relationship between consciousness and the other two methods; that is, feminist consciousness often led to expressions of agency through spoken word and action. By incorporating a literary aesthetic that privileged consciousness over spoken word and action, these authors anticipated the centrality of subjective experience in the modernist novel.

Influencing my argument are certain assumptions about the woman's press and the two periodicals that provide the evidence for my argument. First, I identify these periodicals, and the philosophy they espouse, as specifically *liberal* feminist rather than more generally "feminist" because underlying their analyses of women's issues and literary representations of women is the equality doctrine, the belief that the best route to emancipation for women is the achievement of equal political and legal rights. This form of feminism is perhaps best understood in contrast to difference-based forms, such as conservative feminism and radical feminism. In the mid-nineteenth century, difference-based feminism was most evident in conservative feminism, which was informed by the evangelical movement and in which woman's biological difference was celebrated and constituted a justification for the separate spheres doctrine. This form of "feminism" was best represented by Queen Victoria herself and was then furthered by women such as Sarah Stickney Ellis, author of *The Women of England* (1839) and other guides for women's conduct emphasizing domestic duties, and Eliza Lynn Linton, most famous for her attack on the New Woman in a series of articles titled "Wild Women," published in *The Nineteenth Century.* Whether or not a conservative approach to women's issues should be considered "feminist" is debatable, but as literary historians have come to understand the complexity of the burgeoning women's rights movement, this form of "feminism" has gained credibility. The important point here is that liberal feminism differs significantly from conservative feminism, since the equality doctrine demands that the separate spheres philosophy no longer apply.

In the late nineteenth century, there was another form of difference feminism from which liberal feminism differed. This form cannot be called radical feminism because it lacked the strong analysis of cultural difference defining twentieth-century radical feminism. Still, as it was sometimes found in tandem with liberal feminism in some late-nineteenth-century periodicals, it anticipated radical feminism of the twentieth century, in which woman's difference, especially her ability to live separately from and independently of men, was celebrated. Moreover, some recent literary critics have relied on this form of feminism to justify an alternative literary canon, in which the work of women writers is central. For example, in *Subversive Discourse: The Cultural Production of Late Victorian Feminist Novels* (1995), Rita Kranidis relies on the "feminist" criticism of Adeline Sergeant, Fabian Society member and author of *Esther Denison* (1889), to show the way in which difference feminism was developing out of "the left" as well as "the right" in the late nineteenth century. In "George Meredith's Views of Women by a Woman" (1889), which appeared in *The Temple Bar,* Sergeant argues that while Meredith's female characters are preferable to those drawn by most male authors, his ideas about the role of women in the future are less than liberating. According to Sergeant, while Meredith believes that women should strive to become "equal" to men, this goal echoes men's standards, where women end up only the "rib of Adam" (Sergeant 210–11). Sergeant believes that a better approach is to recognize woman's differences—physical, intellectual, and temperamental—since the "sooner women grant that there are moral and mental as well as physical differences between the sexes, the sooner will their freedom be achieved—the freedom to live their own lives, and satisfy the individual needs of their several natures" (213). This approach to the advancement of women has none of the traditional moral judgments of conservative feminism, but it does have an emphasis on biological difference that separates it from liberal feminism of the late nineteenth century.

In describing the liberal feminist agenda of *Shafts* and *The Woman's Herald,* then, I use the term "liberal feminist" to denote a type of feminism that focuses on the political and legal rights of women without necessarily adopting the stance on sexual morality advocated by conservative feminists or the separatist vision espoused by predecessors of twentieth-century radical feminism. Here forward, I will use the term "liberal feminist" sparingly; instead, I will refer to these periodicals, and the philosophy they promote, as "feminist," with the assumption I am referring to a liberal-feminist perspective.

My second assumption concerns the term "woman's agency." This term needs some explanation because two major issues could be raised about it. First, the *woman* in "woman's agency" suggests that there is some type of action, an expression of independence and selfhood one might say, that is unique to women and that all women share. I do not advocate the essentialist stance suggested by this statement; I do believe, however, that given the historical context in which the novels I examine were written, a discussion of the *concept* of woman's agency is appropriate. The novels I examine were written during a time in which few people understood that gender is socially constructed, and, even as the Victorian notion of separate spheres was breaking down, the notion of the Victorian woman as pure, motherly, and submissive to her husband was replaced with other essentialist concepts, for example, the single woman asserting new-found sexual independence, which was based to some degree on the notion of woman's innate passion. Here and throughout this book, I am looking at the essentialist concept of woman's agency from a non-essentialist point of view. I use quotation marks when referring to woman's agency specifically as a term, but I drop the quotation marks elsewhere, with the understanding that I am not advocating essentialism.

The term "woman's agency" also raises an issue about the relationship between "artistic representation" and "historical reality." In particular, one might ask whether it is possible for a fictional character to "assert agency" and also whether, when I discuss a fictional moment when a female character asserts agency, I am referring to a woman's resistance to cultural norms that support the subordination of women or her resistance to specific narrative strategies. These two questions point out the fact that, while language is not the only site for expression of agency, a woman's resistance often happens through language, and language is the very basis of representation. The following model may be of help in understanding the space in which I wish to work, a space in which the interdependence between representation and the cultural status of real-life women can be emphasized rather than placed into rigid spheres. I work under the assumption that two "worlds" exist: the "historical world," in which real-life Victorian women sometimes resisted certain cultural norms, and the "story world," where we find the representation of such acts of resistance. As readers, we are aware of the difference between these two worlds and understand that it is not possible for a fictional character to assert agency in the historical world, but it is possible for her to do so within the story world. Further, while the story world is not the same as the historical world, the conditions of the historical world can be represented by the author in the story world. Thus, when a fictional character performs an act of resistance within the story world, she resists cultural norms that support the subordination of women rather than specific narrative strategies.[2]

My last assumption involves the three methods of asserting agency (consciousness, spoken word, and concrete action) and their corresponding narrative strategies. These methods and strategies are worth glossing briefly, so readers understand how I am using these terms and how they often appear in literary works. *Consciousness* is best represented by the narrative strategy of internal perspective (or "focalization," as narratologists call it), which involves tracking shifts in vision within narratorial discourse, especially shifts from the narrator's vision to characters' visions but also shifts from one character's vision to another character's.[3] A narrator's or character's vision can simply reflect what he or she sees, but the feelings of the narrator or character also often appear, indicating the narrator's or character's thought processes, or "consciousness." Still, it is important to acknowledge that consciousness alone does not necessarily result in assertion of agency according to the aesthetic articulated by *Shafts* and *The Woman's Herald*. In fact, it is *increased* consciousness, especially the awareness that one's personal life is connected to the political sphere, that is necessary for feminist assertion of agency. Typical scenes in which increased consciousness is represented through internal perspective are "awakening" or "epiphany" scenes, when a female character experiences new awareness about her cultural status; it is often after this awakening that she decides to speak out or take action.

The second method through which characters assert agency—*spoken word*—is best represented by the narrative strategy of dialogue, especially moments in dialogue in which characters engage competing ideologies about the cultural role of women. My methodology is influenced by the work of Mikhail Bakhtin, whose "Discourse in the Novel" suggests that assertion of agency is most likely to occur at "heteroglossic" moments in the novel. Assertion of woman's agency often occurs in moments when the female protagonist, desirous of speaking up about the difficult conditions of her life, is able to mount resistance to language that attempts to categorize and vilify her. In late-Victorian novels, these conversations often occur when a woman is accused of a sexual "fall" or when a woman is negotiating with her family about her role in the home and the community.

Finally, the third method of expressing agency—*concrete action*—is best represented by the narrative strategy of description of characters' actions. According to both the feminist ideal of the 1890s as well as current feminist ideals, the way for women to change their subordinate position is through action. From the anti-crinoline campaign waged in the 1890s to the arrests of suffragettes in the early 1900s to pro-choice marches in the 1980s, concrete action has often provided the foundation for feminist resistance. When female characters in literary works resist cultural norms that support their subordination through action, they participate in this feminist tradition. Most often, women in late-Victorian novels take action related to their position within the family: unhappy wives leave their husbands despite the social stigma; single daughters leave their parents to work in the city rather than wait at home for a marriage proposal; and, occasionally, women even leave home for positions in organized movements.

These narrative strategies, while representing a traditional way of analyzing character, become more transgressive when considered in light of recent discussions of woman's agency, especially poststructuralist perspectives on this issue. The difficulty of finding a way to "do feminist criticism" in the poststructuralist world is expressed well by Judith Butler in "Contingent Foundations: Feminism and the Question of 'Postmodernism'" (1992), in which she argues that, while it is assumed that all political criticism must uphold the existence of the subject, it is possible to do political criticism by questioning such assumptions (1–2, 8). Poststructuralist feminist criticism, then, involves an understanding of subjectivity as the-subject-who-acts-is-already-acted-upon; no subject's actions can be independent of actions that have come before, and, therefore, intentionality is displaced (10). That said, to see the subject as such does not mean that one cannot discuss agency—only that one must think about it in different terms: when subjects feel "excluded," as women often do, it is because they are a part of a system of "domination" rather than because they lack individualized power (13–14).

Butler offers a new way to approach feminism, but even she recognizes a potential problem with her analysis: it locates any possible expression of agency wholly within the deployment of language. In her closing example about the ways in which masculinist language about rape is used to overdetermine the actions possible for women, Butler refutes other critics' charges that she ignores the conditions, especially "material violence," under which women live, but her refutation of these charges acknowledges her dependence on language as the site for assertion of agency (17–18). For Butler, language itself acts: "The very terms by which the violation is explained enact the violation, and concede that the violation was under way before it takes place as a criminal act" (19). While Butler gestures at the connections between language and action, and while her discussion in this closing example seems to suggest that she understands the importance of the subject's consciousness in carving out a space for agency in the post-structuralist world, she does not adequately address the connection between thought, language, and action.[4]

Likewise, Amanda Anderson, in *Tainted Souls and Painted Faces: The Rhetoric of Fallenness in Victorian Culture* (1993), has shown how difficult it is to reconcile feminist criticism's need for the self-determined subject with poststructuralist perspectives accepting the death of the subject. After presenting her argument that representations of fallen women in Victorian literature are markers of the Victorian middle-class's need for models of selfhood that place too much emphasis on self-determination, Anderson turns, in her afterword, to a discussion of poststructuralist theories about subjectivity. While Anderson finds poststructuralist critiques of the self-determined subject to be useful (201–2), she believes that such criticism "can itself end up reifying subjectivity in its more extreme constructionist formulations" (203), and she clearly differentiates her own perspective on subjectivity from other poststructuralist approaches, including Butler's (205–6). Anderson draws on the work of people interested in "lived experience" or autobiography, and she argues that we need models of selfhood that acknowledge both social construction and the subject's participation in such constructions. Writes Anderson, "[W]e need to elaborate conceptions of subjectivity and social interaction that remain constant with the normative principles that guide practices of interrogation and transformation" (203).

Anderson's alternative, a revised version of Habermas's theory of communicative action, offers yet another way to begin reconciling the constructed aspects of subjectivity and the space in which the subject takes part in this construction, since in this model the subject (which in fiction would be the characters in the story, especially the female protagonist) participates in social constructions of the self by way of "mutual understanding," an element already present in language. Just as systems of domination work to "undermine, distort, or even foreclose" the opportunity for dialogue, according to Anderson, language also contains the potential for dialogue that creates change through "recognition and respect" (207). In offering this alternative, Anderson gives us a way to continue to discuss agency, but, like Butler's model, her model relies heavily on only one possible site for expressing agency: language. Still, Anderson's model does offer more recognition of the relationship between language and thought, since Habermas's theory of communicative action focuses on "mutual understanding," a concept that extends beyond the realm of language to that of thought. In fact, Anderson claims,

> Habermas's account of the relationship of reciprocity and recognition that are presupposed in any action oriented toward reaching understanding disallows the radical rupture between ethics and epistemology . . . [His] discourse ethics insists that the higher level of argumentation required in any self-reflexive democratic process is an extension of the more primary mode of action that is oriented toward reaching understanding. (222)

By historicizing traditional feminist assumptions about subjectivity and methods of asserting agency, I embrace poststructuralists' critiques of traditional approaches to identity issues, but I also show how poststructuralist theory must more thoroughly explicate its own assumptions about the postmodern subject, especially the assumption that language is the primary site for expression of agency.

With these assumptions in mind, we can turn to the two specific aims of this study: to analyze previously ignored evidence about the debate over realism and to reconsider the transition from the Victorian novel to the modernist novel in light of this evidence. In bringing forward the evidence found in *Shafts* and *The Woman's Herald,* my aim is to complicate readers' understandings of the term "realism," which previously has been defined too narrowly and with insufficient acknowledgment of a feminist influence. Recent studies of nineteenth-century British realism have worked to show how realism is *not* the narrow genre we often assume: a highly detailed, external description of society that does not engage the inner life of the mind.[5] Still, these studies have not investigated late-century forms of realism, especially feminist realism, as fully as they might. In the latter part of the century, authors engaged a wide range of variations on mid-century realism, including French naturalism and psychological realism, and discussion of Gissing's and Henry James's work in particular has shown how engagement with these variations on realism opened up the definition to some degree. Yet even in its late-century variations, realism often appears as a genre that does not account adequately for women's experiences in the world. Some forms, especially naturalism, may lead to even further objectification of women and their bodies. As Naomi Schor states in *Breaking the Chain: Women, Theory, and French Realist Fiction* (1985), the "classic" naturalist text works to "contain female libido" to the degree that Schor is "led to conclude that the binding of female energy is one of (if not) the enabling conditions of the forward movement of the 'classic text.' Realism [naturalism] is that paradoxical moment in Western literature when representation can neither accommodate the Otherness of Woman nor exist without it" (xi).

Nevertheless, the 1890s New Realists, led by Hardy, sought to redefine the term in such a way that at least some controversial subject matter might be more directly addressed in literature. As I will discuss in further detail in chapter 1, Hardy's comment about the need to explore "the relations of the sexes" in "Candour in English Fiction" (1890) helps set the tone for questioning traditional assumptions about realism in the late century. Yet, as Rita Kranidis shows in *Subversive Discourse,* the New Realists may have been more interested in using the New Woman to comment on wider societal issues than they were driven by feminist principles (108–9), and Kranidis highlights some important ways in which feminist discourse was appropriated by the New Realists.

While I admire Kranidis's work, especially her discussion of the way discourse influences the cultural production of novels, she seems to split the New Realists and the New Woman novelists into two separate and distinct groups, and my aim in this study is to show how more fully intertwined they were. Jane Elridge Miller's *Rebel Women: Feminism, Modernism and the Edwardian Novel* (1997) is helpful here because Miller explains that the generally male-dominated New Realists and the generally female-dominated New Woman novelists gravitated toward each other because both shared an interest in the realistic portrayal of human life through frank discussion of sexuality, but she also recognizes that anxiety about the role of feminism in literature made some New Realists distance themselves from the New Woman novelists (12). Still, the New Realists had an interest in retaining the feminine audience that had ensured the success of the mid-Victorian novel, and they recognized that New Woman writers appealed to this audience, which was itself being transformed by the changes in society regarding the status of women (18). Likewise, the New Woman novelists recognized that the New Realists employed narrative strategies that held authority with critics who had denigrated the work of women writers. As a result, the New Woman novelists appropriated the formal conventions of the New Realists (14, 17), and the New Realists incorporated the content of New Woman novels into their work (22, 33).

Ultimately, the two groups came to share as many similarities as they did differences, and these similarities help clarify the degree to which both male and female authors contributed to the debate over realism, as well as the transition from Victorianism to modernism.

In thinking about how we might view realism in a more complex manner, I also find the work of George Levine, author of *The Realistic Imagination: English Fiction from Frankenstein to Lady Chatterley* (1981), to be useful, since Levine argues that the term "realism" needs radical redefinition. Levine—whose concern is not feminist influence on the term but the misinterpretation of the term by poststructuralists (who have unfairly characterized realists as upholding a view of the world overly concerned with "truth")—sees an intriguing interplay between realism and antirealism (or "the monstrous") in much nineteenth-century literature. From Levine's perspective, realism is not an effort to avoid the indeterminacy of human experience (and hence a form of literature antithetical to modernism) but an attempt to engage this indeterminacy (and hence a precursor of the emphasis on subjective experience seen in modernist literature). Nineteenth-century realists engage indeterminacy by trying to reconcile the monstrous with the more "civilized" lives nineteenth-century society dictated they should live, and of nineteenth-century realism Levine writes:

> It was not a solidly self-satisfied vision based in a misguided objectivity and faith in representation, but a highly self-conscious attempt to explore or create a new reality. . . . In the integrity of its explorations, realism increasingly imagined the limits of its power to reform, the monstrous possibility of the unnameable, the likelihood that the monstrous lurked in its very desire to see and to make the world good. (19–20, 22)

This acknowledgment that there might be a more complicated relationship between realism and antirealism points us toward a more flexible definition of realism and encourages us to consider feminist influence over the term.

By developing a more flexible definition of realism, we can reconsider our assumptions about the development of the novel, especially the transition from Victorianism to modernism. This transition is often assumed to rest on the development of antirealist narrative strategies, and some critics argue that it is the antirealist strategies used by women writers that should be credited with transforming the novel at the turn of the century. For example, Sally Ledger, in *The New Woman: Fiction and Feminism at the Fin de Siècle* (1997), argues that modernism is a form of "women's writing" because of its nonlinear qualities, and the protomodernist narrative strategies used by some late-Victorian women writers contributed to the transition from Victorianism and modernism. Ledger focuses on the work of "George Egerton" (Mary Chavelita Dunne Bright), whose short stories put special emphasis on the interior thoughts of women, using a technique that anticipates modernist stream-of-consciousness. Contrasting Egerton's "Wedlock" with Hardy's *Jude the Obscure,* Ledger argues that the technique employed by Egerton allows her to represent the experiences of women in ways Hardy and other New Realists could not, since they were using conventional narrative techniques. In drawing attention to Egerton's technique, Ledger clearly lays out the transition from Victorianism to modernism, but she concludes that modernist narrative technique is more feminist than late-Victorian realist technique. While Ledger acknowledges that Egerton's work might be better classified as "feminine" than "feminist" (192), in the end her suggestion that literature has the potential to become fully feminist only in the modernist period sets aside the achievements of the realist work of the 1890s, by both women and men, and its contribution to feminism.

Talia Schaffer, too, has emphasized the differences between male authors and women writers of the *fin de siècle* and has argued that women writers, particularly the female aesthetes, had a stronger hand in the transition from Victorianism to modernism than other groups of writers. In *The Forgotten Female Aesthetes: Literary Culture in Late-Victorian England* (2000), Schaffer focuses on female aesthetes such as "Ouida" (Marie Louise de la Ramée), Alice Meynell, and "Lucas Malet" (Mary St Leger Kingsley Harrison), as opposed to the New Woman writers, because their interest in aestheticism rather than realism put them in a better position to move literature in a new direction (35–37). Aestheticism, Schaffer reasons, is inherently antirealist (49, 70), and she shows how aestheticist narrative strategies such as the epigram, fragmented prose, and avant-garde discourse were used first by women writers rather than the male authors who typically receive credit for them (244). For example, the epigram was invented by Ouida and appropriated by Meredith and Oscar Wilde (138, 151), and Malet's *Wages of Sin* (1890) was appropriated and rewritten by Hardy in *Jude* (217). Ultimately, Schaffer sees the female aesthetes as underappreciated but responsible for much of the transition from Victorianism to modernism. While Schaffer points out the important innovations made by women writers, who certainly have been marginalized by twentieth-century configurations of the canon, her argument does not address the vital role of realist narrative techniques that emphasize consciousness in modernism. Further, her argument rests on a narrow definition of modernism— that it was "a rebellion against Victorian strictures" (247)—but modernism should also be defined according to its prominent

narrative strategies, especially attention to the representation of consciousness via innovative narration.

Lyn Pykett offers what seems to be a better articulation of the complexity of the transition from Victorianism to modernism, especially in terms
of the role of both male and female authors and their use of realist narrative strategies. In "The Cause of Women and the Course of Fiction"
(1995), she discusses Mona Caird's position as a marginalized woman
writer whose novels were "self-conscious aesthetic artifacts" and influential
in the development of modernism (140). While Pykett accurately criticizes the masculinist underpinnings of the modernist aesthetic and the
role of this aesthetic in the marginalization of women writers, she does not
set Caird against late-Victorian male authors in order to prove her place in
the literary canon. Further, she emphasizes that it is the *realist* narrative
strategy of internal perspective, used to show increased consciousness, that
is key to the development of the modernist novel. As Pykett explains,
Caird's *Daughters of Danaus* and New Woman novels from the 1890s are
different from the 1860s sensation novel because they emphasize the *psychological* conditions of woman's entrapment rather than simply the
mechanics of the entrapment (134), and this focus on the psychological,
which is shown through the realist narrative strategy of internal perspective, makes the New Woman novel key in the transition from
Victorianism to modernism.

While Pykett confines her discussion to Caird's work in "The Cause of
Women," she lays out similar issues on a much broader scale in
Engendering Fictions: The English Novel in the Early Twentieth Century
(1995). Here, she encourages readers to "rethink modernism" and move
away from the notion that modernism requires a "complete break with the
past, and particularly with the nineteenth century" (3). Instead, Pykett
sees the beginning of modernism as difficult to pinpoint, in part because
it was determined by a critical process extending well into the twentieth
century (10) but also because it grew out of late-Victorian debates about
gender in which the shifting cultural status of women (exemplified by the
New Woman) became a symbol of both regeneration and renewal (53). In
terms of literary technique, this period produced writing that was innovative yet still rooted in techniques of the past. Writes Pykett:

> Like its modernist successors, much New Woman fiction broke with
> or modified the representational conventions of realism. Instead of
> re-presenting a normative view of a prior reality, the New Woman
> fiction either offered a different view (that of the woman-as-
> outsider), or constructed a new version of reality shaped to a
> woman's desires. . . . The New Woman writing also broke with con-

ventions of narration. In place of the wise and witty sayings, and the moral and social guidance of the omniscient narrator, we find a decentered narrative, and (particularly in marriage-problem novels) a polyphonic form in which the multiplicity of voices and views on current issues are juxtaposed. (57)

Not only does Pykett recognize how the content of the New Woman novel contributed to the development of modernism, but she links content and form to show how New Woman novelists pushed the boundaries of realism as part of this transition at the *fin de siècle.*

Like Pykett, Ann Ardis, in *Modernism and Cultural Conflict, 1880–1922* (2002), argues for a more gradual transition from Victorianism to modernism and recognizes the contribution of New Woman fiction to this transition. In making this argument, Ardis exposes the way in which "the men of 1914"—Joyce, Pound, and Eliot—presented modernism as a literary movement that left behind the subversive elements of the late-nineteenth century, including New Woman fiction, rather than acknowledging them as predecessors. "What *other* aesthetic and political agendas were either erased from cultural memory or thoroughly discredited as the literary avant garde achieved cultural legitimacy . . . ?" asks Ardis. "How are the edges, the margins, and even the limitations of modernism revealed once we start paying attention to the ways this literary movement intersects with, borrows from, and reacts against other cultural enterprises?" (7). Ardis takes up the case of New Woman fiction and how it shaped modernism in chapter 4 of *Modernism,* "Mapping the Middlebrow in Edwardian England"; she shows how Pound in particular set up a binary opposition between Victorian realism and modernism—a binarism in which modernism is all that realism cannot be (115). Still, a writer such as Netta Syrett, who situated herself among the New Woman writers of the 1890s by publishing in the famous "Keynotes" series in the 1890s, "talked back" to Pound by continuing to write feminist fiction in the early-twentieth century (118). Syrett's fiction, explains Ardis, "undermine[d] the bourgeois ideologies commonly associated with literary realism even as she employe[d] its strategies of narration" (126). Syrett connected Victorian realism and modernism in a way not acknowledged by Pound and his compatriots, in part because of her feminism.

I am indebted to Pykett and Ardis for their ideas about the development of the novel, but my study adds a new layer to our understanding of the transition from Victorianism to modernism by focusing on a different contributor to this transition: the late-Victorian woman's press. By focusing on this press, this book also draws on the work of other critics interested in Victorian periodicals and the development of a feminist sensibility in these periodicals. Kate Flint's *The Woman Reader, 1837–1914* (1993) brought attention to feminist periodicals, including *Shafts,* when few others were writing about them. Flint writes that *Shafts* was among those feminist periodicals that constructed a distinctly different model of the woman reader than the mainstream press had, seeing her *not* as a reader who needed to be protected and controlled but as one who should expand her knowledge beyond those topics traditionally assumed appropriate for women (150–51). While this shift in the construction of the woman reader begins in the 1860s, with *The Englishwoman's Review* and *The Victoria Magazine,* Flint notes the lack of attention to (and occasional concern over) fiction reading in these periodicals, and she argues that it was only after the founding of *Shafts* that the woman's press took women's fiction reading seriously. "Not until the appearance of the liberal feminist *Shafts* (1892–9)," writes Flint, "does one find literary criticism which both selects particular books relevant to the interests of forward-thinking women, such as the letters of Geraldine Jewsbury to Jane Welsh Carlyle, or, indeed, *The Heavenly Twins,* and which suggests that women may have different priorities from men in their methods of reading and in the aspects of texts which they stress" (151–52). My study rejects the idea that there were more differences than similarities between women's and men's reading (and writing), but Flint's inclusion of *Shafts* in her study is largely responsible for my introduction to the periodical.

Like Flint, Hilary Fraser, Stephanie Green, and Judith Johnston, in *Gender and the Victorian Periodical* (2003), focus on the development of a feminist sensibility in the periodical press, beginning in the 1860s and extending through the 1890s. They argue that by the late 1880s the feminist sentiment in England was strong enough that the mainstream press had to acknowledge the growing body of women writers and readers (146). Though Fraser, Green, and Johnston concentrate more on the contributions of 1860s periodicals such as *The Englishwoman's Journal* and *The Victoria Magazine* than the contributions of 1890s periodicals to a feminist sensibility, they briefly discuss *The Woman's Herald,* referring to it as a paper that, under the editorship of Florence Fenwick Miller, "embraced women's issues in the broadest sense, including art, technical education, women in religion, notes on bills before parliament, recipes, and poetry" (166). Still, Fraser, Green, and Johnston do not discuss the paper under its earlier editors, when book reviews and articles about specific authors were featured more regularly.

Finally, Jennifer Phegley, in *Educating the Proper Woman Reader: Victorian Family Literary Magazines and the Cultural Health of the Nation* (2004), examines depictions of the woman reader in four mid-century family literary magazines (*Harper's Magazine, The Cornhill Magazine,*

Belgravia, and *Victoria Magazine*) and argues that each magazine created new roles for the woman reader. While Phegley does not discuss how the influence of these magazines continued into the late century, her discussion of *The Victoria Magazine* indicates how the woman reader was transformed into the woman critic via a literary aesthetic that anticipated the aesthetic articulated by *Shafts* and *The Woman's Herald.* My study might be seen as a sort of sequel to Phegley's study, since it shows how a feminist realist aesthetic continued into the *fin de siècle.*

I also am indebted to the numerous critical studies about the 1890s New Woman, including Gail Cunningham's *The New Woman and the Victorian Novel* (1978), Ann Ardis's *New Women, New Novels: Feminism and Early Modernism* (1990), and Ann Heilmann's *New Woman Fiction: Women Writing First-Wave Feminism* (2000). Cunningham set the stage for recovery of lesser-known women writers of the 1890s by showing how their writings influenced the work of what Cunningham calls the "major" authors of the period: Hardy, Meredith, and Gissing. While Cunningham's study clearly focuses on the better-known male authors, her attention to writers such as Grand, Caird, and Dowie signaled that critics should take the New Woman novel seriously. Her work was particularly important given the publication of Elaine Showalter's *A Literature of Their Own* in 1977, which discussed many of the same women writers but ultimately labeled them as too intent on a cause and judged them less important than the "female" authors of the early twentieth century, who returned to the "art" of literature and developed a more complex aesthetic than the "feminist" writers of the 1890s had.

With the door open to take the New Woman novel seriously, critics such as Ardis and Heilmann have focused on the ways in which this novel became a site of representing a range of important social issues of the period. Ardis, in *New Women, New Novels,* lays out the cultural context for her argument that the New Woman novel contributed to the rise of modernism. She explains that the New Woman was both an "agent" and a "representative" of "social change," who then became the object of denunciation by those who were anxious about change (10–11). By putting canonical works in conversation with less canonical ones, such as Hardy's *Tess of the d'Urbervilles* (1891) with Olive Schreiner's *The Story of an African Farm* (1883), she shows how specific novels became "effective cultural agents" (60). Ardis connects her discussion of the New Woman novel to the overall development of the novel, arguing that "the history of the New Woman and the New Woman novel did not end at the end of the nineteenth century" (168). Further, she recognizes the contributions of realist writers of the 1890s to the transition from Victorianism to modernism when she writes that "issues of female identity fueled tremendous experimentation with narrative form in the 1890s," even though these writers have not been remembered as fully as those typically credited with "originating" modernism (169–70).

Heilmann, too, emphasizes the cultural impact of the New Woman, explaining that the New Woman "stood at once for the degeneration of society and for that society's moral regeneration," and, through the "intense and prolonged critical debate she engendered," she "shaped central aspects of British literature and culture from the late-Victorian age through the Edwardian period and beyond" (1–2). Like Ardis, Heilmann puts male and female authors in conversation with each other, with more emphasis on the contributions of overlooked women writers than Cunningham was able to provide twenty years earlier. Heilmann departs from Ardis by keeping the emphasis on the social mission of the New Woman novel, claiming that the novel was not as responsible for the transition to modernism (8–9). However, she recognizes that the New Woman novelists' use of specific narrative strategies in combination with content emphasizing a particular social mission brought a new tone to literature. Not only did these novelists "challenge" readers to "engage in a diversity of perspectives" through their "reflection of multiple female subjectivities," but also, "by making women characters the focus of the narrative voice, writers first and foremost appealed to the contemporary readers to adopt a (multiplicity of) female viewpoint(s) as opposed to the conventional male vantage point which shapes so much of even oppositional Victorian literature" (9). In highlighting this new tone in literature, Heilmann acknowledges the more gradual transition from Victorianism to modernism I advocate in this book.

Together, the studies by Cunningham, Ardis, and Heilmann enhance our understanding of why canonical male authors wrote as they did in the 1890s, and these studies are responsible for recovering the reputations of at least two of the lesser-known women writers discussed in this book. (Heilmann in particular has continued this effort with the recent publication of *Sex, Social Purity, and Sarah Grand,* four volumes of documents regarding Sarah Grand and her work.) Further, these studies also deserve acknowledgment because they show how the New Woman novel became a site for discussion of gender issues at the *fin de siècle,* and this achievement is especially important because the connection between literary representation and social issues is central to the feminist realist aesthetic I consider in this book. Ultimately, I engage a major literary problem of the turn of the century: how did we get from Victorianism to modernism, and what role did feminist realism play in this development? It played an immensely important role in that it pushed the novel toward new concepts without turning its back on the novel's roots in realism. To better understand the role of feminist realism, we should turn to a more detailed discussion of the content of *Shafts* and *The Woman's Herald*, especially how the feminist realist aesthetic was articulated by these two periodicals.

🐝

Although Henrietta Müller was the founding editor of the *Women's Penny Paper*, editorship changed hands several times over the course of the 1890s. Müller, who took on the editorial pseudonym "Helena B. Temple," saw the paper through its first name change, to *The Woman's Herald*, in 1891. In 1892, however, when Müller decided to travel to India, other women stepped in and served in the position of editor: first Mrs. Frank Morrison and then Christina S. Bremner. In February 1893 the temperance activist Lady Henry Somerset took over the editorship and changed the name of the paper to *The Woman's Signal* in January 1894. Annie E. Holdsworth joined Somerset as co-editor until October 1895, when the suffrage leader Florence Fenwick Miller began editing the paper; she saw the paper through the end of its run in 1899. While some women in the publishing industry saw Somerset's editorial control as a significant change,[6] and while it is true that less attention was given to literary issues once Somerset became the editor, I find enough consistency in the book reviews and literary articles in the paper, especially in terms of the feminist realist aesthetic, to think and write about the *Women's Penny Paper, The Woman's Herald,* and *The Woman's Signal* as one entity in this book. I refer to all three papers as *The Woman's Herald* in the main text of this book, except when it seems necessary to distinguish between the three. I do distinguish between the three in the bibliography of this book, so readers have the information needed to trace sources properly.

Shafts, on the other hand, existed under only one name and one editor for its entire run, and it seems that the sole editor, Margaret Sibthorp, found her initial inspiration in the pages of *The Woman's Herald*. In 1898, when a dispute about the history of *The Woman's Herald* arose between Sibthorp and Fenwick Miller, then the editor of *The Woman's Signal,* Sibthorp writes passionately about the inspiration Müller's paper provided her:

> [I]t was full of power and grand outreaching; it was edited and super-intended by a woman of unique force of character; it never aimed at anything short of the emancipation of woman, socially, industrially, educationally, and politically. . . . All women owe a deep debt of gratitude to *The Woman's Herald*. It was a pioneer, it *led the way,* and it left the world of women's hopes and struggles toward freedom, many

paces ahead of the point it had reached when the journal was started. ("Two Women's" 79)

In *Shafts*, one certainly sees the same commitment to the emancipation of
women found in Müller's paper. At the top of her first editorial column in
Shafts, "What the Editor Means," Sibthorp places a quote from Ibsen that
highlights the power of women and working men to transform the world:
"The revolution in the social condition now preparing in Europe is chiefly
concerned with the future of the WORKERS and the WOMEN. In this
I place all my hopes and expectations, for this I will work all my life and
with all my strength" (8). And in the column itself Sibthorp iterates the
paper's commitment to women and the working class and details the various feature columns that will express this goal: "What the Girl Says," a
column about girls' thoughts and thoughts that women remember having
as girls; "Steadfast Blue Line," which highlights "all that has been done, or
is now being done by women"; and "What Working Women and Men
Think." She calls on women "specially" to contribute to the paper, so the
goals of the paper and the movement will be achieved.

While both periodicals ran a wide range of articles and were not strictly literary magazines, literature was discussed on a regular basis. This
commitment to literary criticism sets *Shafts* and *The Woman's Herald*
apart from some earlier women's magazines, such as *The English Woman's
Journal* (later the *The Englishwoman's Review*) which Phegley characterizes
as committed to a feminist agenda but not necessarily interested in developing a feminist literary criticism (159–60).[7] Yet *Shafts* and *The Woman's
Herald* did share a commitment to feminist literary criticism with *The
Victoria Magazine,* and Phegley attributes this commitment in *Victoria* to
Emily Davies's editorial efforts (175). Davies, who served as acting editor
beginning in May 1863, and then as book-review editor beginning in
February 1864, used George Eliot's reviews in *The Westminster Review* as
her model and "developed a decidedly gendered definition of realism that
required not only verisimilitude, complex characters, and a moral purpose (all commonly recognized components of the form), but also female
characters who could serve as role models for strong, intelligent women"
(176).

Certainly, this model is similar to that used by *Shafts* and *The Woman's
Herald,* though *Victoria* emphasizes whether female characters are good
role models or not, whereas the later periodicals spend more time articulating how strong, intelligent women can assert agency. While there are
moments when *Victoria* gestures at the three-step method of consciousness, spoken word, and action by discussing whether a particular character speaks out or not, or by highlighting the actions a woman does or

does not take, there is not the consistent application of the three-step method found in the reviews in *Shafts* and *The Woman's Herald*. For example, *Victoria's* review of George Meredith's *Emilia in England* in 1864 focuses on whether or not Meredith's female characters are realistic. The reviewer praises Meredith for his creation of the heroine Emilia, whose character is "beautiful and original in a very high degree," and also Lady Charlotte, who is "powerfully drawn" and "true to the life." However, the reviewer criticizes his creation of the Pole sisters, who are "meant to be typical rather than individual" but who fail as characters because "there is no class of women moving in society whose type of character is fairly represented by the Poles" (Anonymous, "Literature" 184). The reviewer gestures at the issue of women's speech and action by stating, "Girls who stoop to the sort of petty competition for supremacy which the Poles carry on with the Tinleys, would in their private conferences be confabulating over frivolous questions of adornment, or dilating on the gossip and scandal current in their circle" (184), but the reviewer does not systematically cover all three methods of asserting agency as many of the reviewers for the later periodicals do. We undoubtedly see the foundation for a feminist realist aesthetic—that literary representations of women should parallel real-life women and there should be positive role models for women in literature—but not the specifics of how women might create social change by modeling their own assertions of agency after those of literary heroines, as we see in the later periodicals. Further, *Victoria* tends to critique poor representations while *Shafts* and *The Woman's Herald* tend to praise good ones, a trend likely reflecting the lack of feminist novels in the 1860s and the more plentiful supply in the 1890s.

Still, *Shafts* and *The Woman's Herald* are similar to *Victoria* in that literary representation and social change are intertwined, to the degree that discussion of literature often saturated the papers. A typical issue included at least one substantial book review or article about literature, and in *The Woman's Herald* interviews with women writers dominated the cover stories. An index of cover stories from 1888 to 1892 shows that the periodical ran cover stories about Elizabeth Barrett Browning, George Eliot, Jean Ingelow, Harriett Martineau, George Sand, Beatrice Potter, Harriett Beecher Stowe, Mona Caird, and a number of lesser-known women writers. In addition, both periodicals ran stories on literary topics that often discussed earlier historical periods of literature or specific topics found in literature. For example, *Shafts* published articles on Lady Macbeth and other Shakespearian women, on poets who praised women in their work, on ways to choose books for young women, and on the influence of modern literature on the advancement of women's rights. *The Woman's Herald* ran similar articles, such as "Browning's Women," "George Eliot's

Heroines," and "Women Writers in '93," and it published short stories by contemporary women writers, especially Olive Schreiner and Frances E. Willard. Finally, both papers often indicated how women writers might be seen as the inspiration for real-life work and action. Sometimes an article about a nonliterary topic was infused with literary references, as in Effie Johnson's two-part essay "Self-Education" which described the history and importance of self-education for women and in which Johnson drew espe-cially on the poetry of Elizabeth Barrett Browning to encourage women to further their knowledge of the world. *Shafts*, too, had many literary refer-ences: the paper featured quotations from writers the staff admired, some-times under the heading "Choice Morsels from Choice Pens," and these quotations were often used to fill white space. For example, in the December 10, 1892 issue, Ibsen's statement, "In these days it is you, women, who are the pillars of society," helped fill the space left at the bot-tom of a page.

Exact numbers regarding readership of the two periodicals are difficult to determine and are not cited in David Doughan and Denise Sanchez's very important bibliography of feminist periodicals, *Feminist Periodicals, 1855–1984* (1987), but under Florence Fenwick Miller's editorship of *The Woman's Herald*, 500 copies went to suffrage societies (Crawford 414), and it seems likely that women who were members of other women's societies were readers of the periodicals, since both ran regular columns about the activities of these societies. *Shafts* ran meeting notes from the Pioneer Club, and *The Woman's Herald* ran notes from a variety of local liberal associations as well as county councils, which may have created a reader-ship base. Circulation to other periodicals also is evident. One finds praise but also criticism of *Shafts* in Henrietta Stannard's magazine, *Golden Gates*, which she edited from 1891 to 1894. "We have been favoured with the first number of a penny weekly journal entitled *Shafts*. . . . [M]uch of the paper is well written, but then so are scores of other journals which are well established, and which are written to suit the popular tastes. *Shafts* would be a splendid pennyworth for Girton girls, and for the average blue-stocking, but we fear that the British workman will not rush to read it" (Anonymous, "Notes" 449). *The Englishwoman's Review* also ran notices about the introduction of *Shafts* into the market (Anonymous, "Reviews" 61) and the change in name of *The Woman's Herald* to *The Woman's Signal* (Anonymous, "Reviews and Notices" 52).

While distribution to other periodicals and to women's societies seems to have built a readership base, Sarah Grand believed there was a negative side to the strong connection between the periodicals and some of the women's societies. She claimed, in a letter to William Blackwood, that one member of a suffrage society had given Margaret Sibthorp £1000 to start

Shafts and she too was offered £400 to "write for the cause." Grand rejected the money because she "felt they would have bound me to be the faithful servant of a party, and my ambition is to be an artist" (Heilmann and Forward, *Letters* 34). Elizabeth Crawford, in *The Women's Suffrage Movement: A Reference Guide 1866–1928* (1999), confirms that these periodicals received money from suffrage societies in exchange for covering their cause. Beginning in 1889, *The Woman's Herald* agreed to print a column from the Central National Society for Women's Suffrage for a price of £52 per year (429). Still, the book reviews in both papers were distinctly literary, and one does not have the sense that these pieces were unduly influenced by specific people or groups.

Nevertheless, it is important to recognize the potential biases of particular reviewers and the connections they might have had with the authors whose works they reviewed. Some of the reviews are unsigned and cannot be analyzed for bias, but many are signed. When reading M. E. (Mary Eliza) Haweis's review of Hardy's *Tess of the d'Urbervilles* in *The Woman's Herald,* for example, we should keep in mind that Haweis and Hardy were acquaintances and shared a common concern about the vivisection of animals. In June 1894, Haweis invited Hardy to one of the many "at homes" she hosted over the years, which usually consisted of a lecture on a particular topic and a meal or tea. He agreed to attend, though he had previously turned down a request from her to give a lecture himself, and Elizabeth Robins confirms Hardy's presence at one of Haweis's "at homes" in 1894 (Hardy, *Collected Letters* 2:36, 2:59, 5:349). Still, Haweis was an established writer, having written books on women's dress and beauty in the 1870s, and she would go on to write *A Flame of Fire* (1897), a book with a feminist angle in that it intended to show how women continued to be subordinated to men via the institution of marriage (Haweis, "Foreword" iv). While Haweis's acquaintance with Hardy may undermine her credibility as reviewer of *Tess,* her experience as a writer and as an active member in the women's community affirms her credibility.

In addition to tracking the relationships between reviewers and authors, it is important to track the regularity with which reviewers wrote for the periodicals, since one can see a consistent aesthetic across the reviews written by regulars. Margaret Sibthorp is the most obvious example (she wrote many of the articles in *Shafts*), but perhaps the more interesting example is Gertrude Kapteyn, who wrote more than one review for *Shafts* and whose reviews are some of the most thorough in terms of the feminist realist aesthetic. Kapteyn remains elusive, and little is known about her outside the pages of *Shafts,* but, in addition to her book reviews of Moore's *Esther Waters* and Meredith's *Diana of the Crossways,* she wrote articles on the Norwegian writer Björnstjerne Björnson and on the topic "moral education," which seems to have led Kapteyn and others to start a series of classes for children to introduce them to ethical issues (Young 370).

Most of the authors whose works are discussed in this book had some knowledge of these periodicals, and there is evidence that some of them read specific reviews of their own work. For example, Gissing read the review of *The Odd Women* that ran in *The Woman's Herald* and was pleased with what he found (*Collected Letters* 120). Stannard and Caird obviously knew about these papers, since both authors were interviewed by *The Woman's Herald* and wrote at least one article for the paper. Caird also wrote articles for *Shafts*, and, as previously noted, Stannard mentions *Shafts* in her magazine, *Golden Gates*. There is little doubt that Grand knew about the periodicals, since she was interviewed by *The Woman's Herald* and was a member of the Pioneer Club (Crawford 127), and Hardy probably knew of the review of *Tess* through his friendship with Haweis. Meredith knew John Stanley Little, who wrote an article for *The Woman's Herald* about Meredith's work, so it is possible he knew of the paper as well (Meredith, *Letters* 1020). It is difficult to know whether Moore and Dowie knew of or read the articles in the two periodicals; I have no specific evidence they did, but they may have, through friends and their general knowledge of the publishing world. The literary community in London in the 1890s was small, so it is likely that all of these writers knew of the periodicals, even if they did not read them regularly.

In order to illustrate more specifically how *Shafts* and *The Woman's Herald* articulated a feminist realist aesthetic, we should turn to some of the literary articles and reviews that ran in the two papers. Perhaps the most important of these articles is M. H. (Mary) Krout's "Women in Fiction," which ran in the September 21, 1893 issue of *The Woman's Herald*. In this article Krout sketches out a literary tradition devoted to the accurate representation of women, and she directly states that accurate representation means depicting women who can think, speak, and act for themselves. Before Jane Austen, Krout argues, the typical heroine was "a creature all tears and sensibility," but beginning with Austen the heroine with more than a "rudimentary brain," and even "intelligence," began to develop. Still, the ideal—the woman who "thought and spoke and conducted herself in fiction as a flesh-and-blood creature would have been apt to do in like surroundings and under like circumstances" (485)—did not appear until the middle of the century, with Charlotte Brontë's *Jane Eyre*. Of Brontë, Krout writes, "She gives us, for the first time, a heroine wholly lacking beauty, but abundantly provided with brains, a woman who charms and holds where mere physical attraction would have been power-less" (485). After *Jane Eyre,* Krout explains, some writers have continued to write women who can illustrate only "human idiocy," but others have con-tributed to the new ideal of the intelligent woman who speaks up and acts on her own behalf. George Eliot, Mary Ward (also known as Mrs. Humphry Ward and the author of the 1894 novel *Marcella*), and George Meredith are among those Krout admires for their representations of women characters. Eliot shows both the "perfection" and "imperfection" of "womanhood," and Ward illustrates that women are "no longer puppets in the hands of exponents of any given school"; still, Meredith is "the great-est of all novelists," since he "comprehend[s] woman in her full mentality and her spirituality" (485). In detailing the way the nineteenth-century heroine developed and the ways in which contemporary authors represent-ed women as thinking, speaking, and acting for themselves, Krout defines well the specifics of the feminist realist aesthetic.[8]

Other articles in *Shafts* and *The Woman's Herald* highlight particular methods of expressing agency, and the chapters of this book are arranged around these specific methods. For example, chapter 1 focuses on the rep-resentation of increased consciousness in the work of Sarah Grand and Thomas Hardy, using Edith Ward's "Shafts of Thought" which appeared in the inaugural issue of *Shafts* and indicates the feminist belief in the power of thought to change the world. In the article Ward presents a pseu-doscientific argument for the idea that thoughts travel between people in the same way microbes, or germs, travel through the atmosphere. Within this context, as I discuss further in chapter 1, we can understand why fem-inists came to value thought so highly and how consciousness became an important element in the feminist realist aesthetic.

In addition to using articles that consider specific methods of asserting agency, I use reviews of specific novels to illustrate how *Shafts* and *The Woman's Herald* assessed works of literature according to their aesthetic and also how these reviews might shape our own twenty-first-century readings of these novels. While *Shafts* and *The Woman's Herald* praise authors for partial fulfillment of the feminist aesthetic, they prefer complete fulfillment of this ideal, and, occasionally, reviews reveal that authors had met this goal.

It is worthwhile to examine briefly two of the reviews that discuss suc-cessful novels because doing so will help us understand what constitutes complete fulfillment of the ideal. In the first issue of *Shafts,* the writer "Dole" reviews George Meredith's *Diana of the Crossways* as part of an arti-cle about Meredith's commitment to the women's movement. In the arti-cle, titled "Mr. George Meredith on Women's Status," Dole compares Meredith to J. S. Mill, asserting that Meredith is "a friend of woman's liberty quite as hearty as J. S. Mill" (8). In fact, Dole has enough admiration for him to state, "Since Mill died, no man's heart has felt so strongly, nor man's brain expressed with equal force and wit the disabilities of women" (8). Dole then analyzes Meredith's work, admiring him for his ability to combine artistic style and socially aware content, a·central tenet in the feminist aesthetic. Meredith's novels, according to Dole, are books with both "narrative form" and "philosophical treatises on life" (8), and, as the review shows, his novels highlight all three aspects of woman's agency. Meredith "lays great stress on the intellect of women," which suggests that consciousness is key in his representations, and Meredith allows readers to hear women's "internal sentiments," a more general word for internal perspective (8). Further, Dole tells us that Meredith "does not admire" the "Womanly Woman," who "occupies herself merely in picking up the dropped stitches of other people, or in lubricating the wheels of her domestic machinery," suggesting that Meredith values action rather than submission on the part of women. He even suggests women are capable of fighting in war, confirming that physical action is important to him. Finally, Dole indicates that Meredith understands the importance of spoken word for the modern woman, since his "beautiful rebel" Diana "rebukes" those women who are content to cave in to the oppressive conditions of the present (8).

This definition of agency, and its correspondence with particular narrative strategies, can also be found in the reviews written for *Shafts* by Gertrude Kapteyn, including her review of George Moore's *Esther Waters*. Kapteyn's discussion of *Esther Waters* serves as an excellent model of a review that discusses specific narrative strategies in detail. While Kapteyn does not use the analytical language of current literary critics but a more characteristic nineteenth-century style of discussing books, she does make clear the effectiveness of Moore's use of internal perspective, dialogue, and description of characters' actions. Of Moore's use of internal perspective, Kapteyn writes about the "impressiveness" of Esther's "first realization of the terrible consequences of her weakness" after she becomes intimate with her lover (24), a comment suggesting that Moore has effectively captured the consciousness of Esther at a particular moment in the story. Kapteyn also points out Moore's use of dialogue as a strategy for representing assertion of woman's agency: she refers to the resistance Esther puts up to cultural norms that support the subordination of women in a conversation with Fred Parsons, the Brethren lay minister who tries to "save" Esther by marrying her and adopting her child (25). Finally, Kapteyn suggests Moore's skill at describing characters' actions, stating that his relay of specific actions taken by Esther is "perfect in his picturing of [her] unfaltering perseverance" (25).

Of course, one charge that might be leveled against the feminist realist aesthetic employed by *Shafts* and *The Woman's Herald* is that it is too "prescriptive," akin to the "images of women" criticism of second-wave feminism, and this is a valid objection, since the reviewers sometimes seem narrow in their judgments. To understand why feminist criticism can sometimes be prescriptive but also avoid this problem, it is useful to turn to a second-wave feminist statement regarding critical goals and practices. Cheri Register's "American Feminist Literary Criticism: A Bibliographical Introduction," one of six essays in the 1975 anthology *Feminist Literary Criticism: Explorations in Theory*, lays out specific criteria for successfully feminist literature, and these criteria are remarkably similar to those advocated by feminist periodicals of the 1890s. According to Register, the text must first be "authentic," not necessarily "politically orthodox" but certainly a "realistic representation of 'female experience,' 'feminine consciousness,' or 'female reality'" (12). Further, the text must be judged credible by the "female reader, who is herself familiar with 'female reality'" (13). While Register recognizes that this particular judgment test is "dangerously narrow," since there is no one reality all women experience, she believes that this form of criticism starts with readerly identification and then moves to more productive analysis, such as analyzing the importance of a woman's reality in a particular text even if it is not similar to the reader's own experience (13). Having set out these criteria for prescriptive feminist criticism, Register then identifies five specific objectives of feminist criticism. It should "serve as a forum for women," especially by providing perspectives not usually seen through works written by men; "help achieve cultural androgyny" by cultivating social values not normally recognized by mainstream culture; "provide role-models" by representing women who do not emulate only traditional feminine roles; "promote sisterhood" by encouraging women to support each other in their endeavors to change oppressive societal norms; and "augment consciousness-raising" by illustrating the connection between literary representation and real-life issues without being overly didactic (19–23).

What is striking about the similarities between feminist criticism of the 1970s and feminist realism of the 1890s is the emphasis on realistic representation and the balance between the critical and utopian aspects of this aesthetic. Just as second-wave feminist critics wanted to see both an exposure of cultural conditions that supported the subordination of women *and* the dismantling of these conditions through alternative representations of women, so did feminist critics of the 1890s, who were aware of the need for a twofold approach to creating change for women. Further, it is striking that while Register is quite specific about the goals of feminist criticism, she explicitly states that successful works of literature need not be "politically orthodox" and should not be overly didactic. The same appears to be true for the aesthetic employed by *Shafts* and *The Woman's Herald*. While the reviewers certainly make judgments about literature based on specific principles, especially *how* agency should be asserted, their reception of works attempting to represent this agency was highly flexible. Primarily, they wanted to see authors *attempt* to use the feminist realist aesthetic; even if their success was limited, reviewers were eager to give authors credit for their attempts.

I do not advocate "prescriptive" criticism, but, like Register, I believe a feminist criticism that evaluates the representation of women without becoming didactic and inflexible is beneficial to literary criticism as a whole. Most forms of so-called political criticism run the risk of becoming too prescriptive; as long as the practitioners remain flexible, such pitfalls can be avoided. Further, as a reader who believes in feminist ideals, I acknowledge my own tendency to read according to similar criteria, especially readerly identification. At times my analysis of particular texts overlaps with that of 1890s feminist critics; for example, when discussing Moore's *Esther Waters,* my analysis is both strengthened and informed by that of Gertrude Kapteyn. Throughout this study I adopt the stance of a critic using the feminist realist aesthetic and distinguish works that fulfill the feminist realist ideal from those that do not. Rather than suppress my own feminist ideals in my analysis of texts, I have let them remain apparent, with the hope that doing so will show the connections between feminisms of different historical periods.

Chapter 1 of this book shows how *Shafts* and *The Woman's Herald* highlighted consciousness in their discussions of woman's agency; it focuses on Thomas Hardy and Sarah Grand, perhaps the most recognized male and female writer of the 1890s respectively, and their attempts to incorporate feminist consciousness into their novels. It examines their best-known works—Grand's *The Heavenly Twins* (1893) and *The Beth Book* (1898) and Hardy's *Tess of the d'Urbervilles* (1891) and *Jude the Obscure* (1895)— and shows how they incorporated consciousness by focusing on the internal perspectives of female characters. While Grand's novels more often centered on female characters and their thoughts from the outset and were praised by *Shafts* and *The Woman's Herald* for doing so, Hardy also received praise for his commitment to representing woman's agency in part because feminist periodicals hoped to gain his support for their cause.

Chapter 2 makes it clear that expression of agency through spoken word was as important as consciousness for *Shafts* and *The Woman's Herald,* and it details how, for some authors negotiating feminist realism, spoken word served as the dominant method. This chapter examines George Gissing's *The Odd Women* (1893), which directly engaged feminist discourse through the intentionally single Rhoda Nunn and which was praised by feminist periodicals for its use of spoken word. It also examines Mona Caird's *Daughters of Danaus* (1894), which featured extensive philosophical debates about the rights of women and which was admired for its attention to the speech of female characters. While Gissing does meet the feminist ideal regarding spoken word, Caird achieves a better balance of increased consciousness and spoken word in *Daughters of Danaus,* and *Shafts* and *The Woman's Herald* recognized Caird as the more successful author.

Chapter 3 highlights the sentiment of the feminist periodicals that expressions of woman's agency could not be complete without action. It examines articles focusing on this method, and it discusses the work of George Meredith, author of *Diana of the Crossways* (1885) and *The Amazing Marriage* (1895), and Ménie Dowie, author of *A Girl in the Karpathians* (1891), *Women Adventurers* (1893), and *Gallia* (1895). Both authors concentrate closely on feminist actions, but Meredith received more attention from *Shafts* and *The Woman's Herald* than Dowie did, in part because Dowie was seen as holding extreme views on gender issues, which put feminists in an uneasy position. While Dowie was mostly ignored (and occasionally ridiculed) by the woman's press, Meredith was held up as a model for other authors, both male and female, to emulate.

Chapter 4 indicates that, ultimately, both *Shafts* and *The Woman's Herald* looked for novels incorporating all three methods of asserting agency, and authors who fulfilled this ideal had the opportunity to capitalize on their success and improve their literary reputations. When George Moore's *Esther Waters* (1894) was praised for fulfilling the ideal, Moore took specific steps to ensure that readers would remember his novel and its author beyond his own lifetime. On the other hand, Henrietta Stannard, who wrote under the pseudonyms "Violet Whyte" and "John Strange Winter," might have improved her literary reputation by more thoroughly engaging the feminist realist aesthetic in her novel *A Blameless Woman* (1894), which had many of the markings of a New Woman novel but ultimately was not remembered as one. I examine why one author was successful in improving his literary reputation via feminist realism while another was not successful in improving hers.

Throughout these chapters I argue for the inclusivity of the feminist realist aesthetic as articulated by *Shafts* and *The Woman's Herald.* While the aesthetic was discerning, feminist periodicals needed writers, both female and male, to support their cause; as long as a writer attempted to incorporate one or more of the three methods of expressing agency, the periodicals drew attention to the strengths of the writer's work rather than focusing on its weaknesses. This inclusivity, I believe, contributes to the way in which the transition from the Victorian to the modernist novel occurred. In the afterword I argue that the aesthetic articulated in *Shafts* and *The Woman's Herald* contributed significantly to the debate over realism at the end of the nineteenth century, since it advocated serious consideration of the representation of woman's agency and, by focusing on woman's consciousness, anticipated the thought-oriented aesthetic of modernist writing. The feminist realist standard, which praised authors for incorporating any of the three methods but saw expression through spoken word and action as springing from increased consciousness, acknowledged consciousness more fully than previous realist aesthetics and thus helped transform the novel from Victorian to modernist at the *fin de siècle*.

CHAPTER I

"They are learning to think . . . for themselves": Consciousness Raised

For *Shafts* and *The Woman's Herald,* consciousness was key to transforming the cultural status of real-life women in the 1890s; in fact, increased consciousness about the cultural conditions women faced was the first step women might take in embracing feminist ideals. As Mary Krout writes in "Women in Fiction," heroines who had brains as well as beauty, who were "learning to think . . . for themselves," were to be admired greatly, and writers who created these female characters were contributing to social change (485). Margaret Sibthorp, the editor of *Shafts,* agreed that thinking was the first step in women's emancipation, and in her first editorial column she emphasized the idea that *thought* had the potential to change the world. Writing of the paper's commitment to freedom of thought and diversity of opinion, she states:

> Life on this planet is not a condition of the *status quo;* its inevitable law is ceaseless evolution—ceaseless evolution in the conditions of existence, in thought, in beliefs, in aspirations. Such a state of things naturally gives rise to conflicting opinions. The attempt to coerce opinion, to force multitudes of living intelligent creatures to think in one groove, to believe one thing, has been productive of disastrous results in the past, and is productive of grave evils even now, though the advancing thought of many is making itself felt; is creating newer and brighter light to aid and guide human judgment. ("What the Editor" 8)

For Sibthorp, the cause of individual liberty, which was important to many feminists, is strongly connected to freedom of thought, especially the freedom to hold opinions distinct from the status quo.

35

How thought specifically operates in the process of social change is detailed in "Shafts of Thought," another article in the inaugural issue of *Shafts,* where Edith Ward discussed thought in pseudoscientific terms. Equating the movement of thought in the world to the movement of microbes, or germs, in the atmosphere, she writes, "The belief that every human soul is creating by its inmost thoughts an active influential force which goes forth for good or evil . . . is one of the most solemn creeds that the world has ever known. . . . [W]e are on the verge of discoveries which will prove that thought creates on the ethereal plane vibrations which travel until they are neutralized by transformation on the material plane" (2). What becomes of these thoughts, Ward explains, depends on their reception (they either find "congenial soil for development" or they are "sterlised according to their character, good or bad"), and this process has "terrible significance" because it means that all people are partially responsible for the acts of others. If we send out negative thoughts and someone else commits a crime or commits a harmful deed because of them, we are equally responsible for the action.

Though Ward's pseudoscientific explanation of thought-influence seems extreme now and is perhaps less committed to diversity of thought than Sibthorp's article is, it does help explain why feminists of the 1890s put so much emphasis on consciousness—they viewed thought as a way to transform the world and reflect their own values. In fact, Ward distinguishes women as pioneers in thought-influence. Referring to the image of the woman that graced the front cover of *Shafts,* Ward writes that there now is "active work on many lines for the good of humanity, but of none more than of woman as the mind-influencer in the cause of purity and justice. The female figure who hurls the shafts of light into the dark places of sin, injustice, and ignorance, typifies the position in which every human soul stands, whose thoughts are pure and true, and whose will is strong to follow the path of duty" (2).

Although Ward does not address the role of the writer in this design, her concluding paragraph, with its emphasis on "women and men engaged in active work" (2), suggests that the writer does have a role, and in *Shafts's* review of Sarah Grand's *The Heavenly Twins,* which ran approximately six months after Ward's "Shafts of Thoughts," the anonymous reviewer credits Grand with doing precisely the work of thought-influence advocated in Ward's article. Writes the reviewer:

> [S]o skilfully has the clever author brought her art to bear upon each chapter, incident, and individual character combining to make up the wondrous whole, that readers are under the pleasing delusion that they make their own deductions. . . . Has the writer intended all

this, or has she imparted to each character and incident some of her own marvellous creative force, so that thoughts and deductions flow from all continuously, with immortal power. . . . The personalities [in the novel] . . . create within us thoughts that breathe and burn, thoughts that grow, stretching forth as they take into themselves the nourishment here supplied. (Anonymous, "Reviews: Heavenly" 268)

Here, the reviewer implies that Grand, as an author, participates in the process of sending out thoughts that can transform the world by imparting these thoughts to her characters, which are then passed on to readers. By putting strong emphasis on the continuity of thought between author, characters, and readers, this review highlights the degree to which feminists of the 1890s valued consciousness as an integral part of changing the world for the better.

This chapter focuses on Sarah Grand and her contemporary Thomas Hardy as representative examples of late-Victorian authors' attempts to incorporate feminist consciousness into their novels. As perhaps the most recognized male and female writer of the decade respectively, Hardy and Grand were central figures in articulating the New Realism of the 1890s, and both wrote about previously taboo subjects regarding sex and gender. In their best-known works of the decade—Grand's *The Heavenly Twins* (1893) and *The Beth Book* (1898) and Hardy's *Tess of the d'Urbervilles* (1891) and *Jude the Obscure* (1895)—they incorporated feminist consciousness by focusing on the internal perspectives of female characters. While Grand more often focused on women's thoughts from the outset in her novels and was praised by *Shafts* and *The Woman's Herald* for doing so, Hardy also received praise for his commitment to representing woman's agency. Although Hardy's representation was not fully consistent with the feminist realist ideal, *Shafts* and *The Woman's Herald* gave Hardy credit for his effort, in part because it seems as though the periodicals recognized the need for well-respected writers to lend their support to the feminist cause. This willingness to praise both Grand and Hardy, despite some failings on Hardy's part, points to an important feature of the feminist realist aesthetic: it was as inclusive as possible, and, as long as authors made some attempt to represent woman's agency, they received accolades from the reviewers.

In "Candour in English Fiction," published in 1890 as part of a symposium in *The New Review*, Hardy carves out a space for himself and others interested in broadening the definition of realism at the end of the nineteenth century. Responding to the criticism that English fiction of the period suffers from a "lack of sincerity," Hardy defines a new "sincere school of Fiction," which will realistically represent life of the period (15–16). Hardy's emphasis on representing the life *of the period* is important, since he can then assert that "the relations of the sexes" are part of this life and a legitimate subject for realist fiction (16–17), and, in *Tess of the d'Urbervilles* and *Jude the Obscure,* he puts this theory into practice. In *Tess,* readers learn the story of a young woman's attempt to help her family survive financially, only to be seduced and abandoned by two different men, and in *Jude* readers learn about the struggle of two cousins whose love for each other is unacceptable within their own community. Though mainstream reviewers, who shaped significantly the opinions of the general public, were taken aback by Hardy's representation of the relations of the sexes in these two novels, feminist periodicals of the 1890s recognized the importance of Hardy's contribution.[1]

Like Hardy, Grand faced criticism for her willingness to tackle taboo subjects, such as syphilis in *The Heavenly Twins.*[2] While Grand's writing was not accepted by the mainstream press, sales of *The Heavenly Twins* (more than 20,000 copies in one year) indicate at least some acceptance by the general public. And even Hardy, who was reluctant to associate himself too fully with progressive women for fear he might be linked favorably to the suffrage issue, believed that Grand should be admired for her "bold writing." In fact, in September 1893 he recommended that his friend and sometimes literary collaborator Florence Henniker take up her pen with the same boldness exhibited by Grand:

> If you mean to make the world listen to you, you must say now what they will all be thinking and saying five and twenty years hence: and if you do that you must offend your conventional friends. 'Sarah Grand,' who has not, to my mind, such a sympathetic and intuitive knowledge of human nature as you, has yet an immense advantage over you in this respect—in the fact of having decided to offend her friends (so she told me)—and now that they are all alienated she can write boldly, and get listened to. (*Collected Letters* 2:33)

Furthermore, Grand's nonfiction essays are now viewed as having contributed significantly to the debate over gender and sexuality in the 1890s. The majority of Grand's essays have been reprinted in *Sex, Social Purity, and Sarah Grand,* edited by Ann Heilmann and Stephanie Forward (2000), and "The New Aspect of the Woman Question" regularly appears in collections of nonfiction writings from the 1890s, such as Sally Ledger and Roger Luckhurst's *The Fin de Siècle: A Reader in Cultural History c.*

1800–1900 (2000) and Carolyn Christensen Nelson's *A New Woman Reader: Fiction, Articles, and Drama of the 1890s* (2000). "The New Aspect of the Woman Question," which ran in *The North American Review* in 1894, is Grand's most famous essay, since it introduces the "New Woman," who has been quietly waiting for men to recognize her intellectual abilities but has been overlooked in favor of less intelligent women. Grand writes of the women who are currently recognized by men:

> Both the cow-woman and the scum-woman are well within range of the comprehension of the Bawling Brotherhood, but the new woman is a little above him, and he never even thought of looking up to where she has been sitting apart in silent contemplation all these years, thinking and thinking, until at last she solved the problem and proclaimed for herself what was wrong with Home-is-the-Woman's-Sphere, and prescribed the remedy. (29–30)

In making this statement, Grand declares not only that the New Woman exists but that she is a *thinking* woman, one who has been reflective for some time but now has turned her thinking into action.

Ultimately, both Hardy and Grand were labeled as writers with a "purpose," a label Hardy strongly rejected on the basis that art and politics did not mix. Hardy consistently refused requests from suffrage societies for his support for their cause, including one in 1892 from Alice Grenfell, secretary of the Women's Progressive Society and an occasional contributor to *The Woman's Herald,* who wanted Hardy to serve as the society's vice president (Hardy, *Collected Letters* 1:266). Even when asked to support his favorite cause, the ethical treatment of animals, he often refused, citing his duty as an author to keep art separate from politics (2:135–36). Still, Hardy did occasionally break his rule about keeping art and politics separate, especially so he could support antivivisection efforts. He allowed the pig-killing chapter from *Jude* to be reprinted in a Society for the Protection of Animals publication (2:97), held an antivivisection meeting at his home (2:157), notified the Society for the Prevention of Cruelty to Animals when he thought animals were being mistreated at the Alhambra Theatre (3:213), wrote a letter about the cause to *The Humanitarian* (4:90, 96–97), and even served on the Committee of the Council of Justice to Animals (4:143).

Grand, too, resisted the label of writer with a purpose, no doubt because she understood the negative implications of it but also because, like Hardy, she was committed to realistic representation in her work above all else. Grand believed there were boundaries between art and politics which artists had to uphold. As already mentioned, she refused the money that progressive women offered her to write for the cause, and she regularly articulated the ways in which her own work was intended to be realist rather than polemic. One example of Grand's insistence about realistic representation can be found in her preface to *Our Manifold Nature*, a collection of short stories that appeared in 1894. In this preface Grand states that her stories are "simply what they profess to be—studies from life" (iii), and she objects to those critics who define realism so narrowly that the writer must "garnish" the representation in the same way an actor must "paint his face to make it look natural in the glare of the footlights" (v). At the end of this preface, Grand insists that while she is certainly doing something different from traditional realists, she is still writing within the realm of realism.

While Hardy and Grand shared a commitment to realistic representation of the relations of the sexes in their writing, it should already be evident that there are differences in their respective positions on gender issues. In her articles Grand places greater emphasis on the importance of transforming one's consciousness in order to enact social change, a factor not mentioned in Hardy's nonfiction writing. In addition to focusing on *thinking* women in "The New Aspect of the Woman Question," Grand consistently focuses on this topic in the other articles she wrote during the 1890s. In "The Modern Girl," also published in *The North American Review* in 1894, Grand argues for the inherent intelligence of girls and the need to allow girls to develop this intelligence as fully as possible, and in "The Modern Young Man," published in *The Temple Magazine* in 1898, Grand discusses the modern girl's male counterpart but iterates her commitment to the intelligence of girls. One advantage women have over men, Grand argues, is that they are open to change, eager to improve themselves, and willing to accept their imperfections. The result is that once women have the opportunity to use their intelligence, they use it well. "[B]y degrees her influence is expanding our knowledge of life, and carrying it on to the point at which it may become useful to herself and beneficial to the race" (60). Grand believed that women were turning thought into action and would have an effect on the rest of the world through their thoughts and resulting actions.

However, in "On Clubs and the Question of Intelligence," published in *The Woman at Home* in 1900, Grand recognizes that women and girls still need encouragement to develop their thoughts and turn them into action. While Grand believes society has become more concerned with the development of women's intelligence (94), some women and girls still are reluctant to take on the responsibility of shaping public life. Grand recommends they educate themselves in this role by joining women's clubs, which offer women the opportunity to "enlarg[e] their minds by social intercourse" (95) and girls the opportunity to participate in a "bracing mental atmosphere" (99). Writes Grand, "Conversation runs on topics of the day, on politics, literature, and art; and they must make an effort to interest themselves, to learn, to keep up with the rest, or they find themselves left behind, nonentities" (99). In other words, at the turn of the century, women and girls need to step up and put to use their inherent intelligence.

While Grand writes about all three methods of expressing agency in her essays, it is evident that, for her, the three methods are progressive: that is, consciousness comes first, followed by speech and action. In several of her essays from the mid-1890s, Grand articulates this progressive movement, primarily by talking about the difficulty with which women move from consciousness to speech and action. In "The New Aspect of the Woman Question," Grand makes it clear that women have been thinking about the problems of gender relations in their own culture for some time, but they have just begun to speak and act on the matter (30), and in "The Modern Girl" Grand writes that "silence may conceal thought, but does not stifle it" (43), highlighting again the need for movement from consciousness to action. In addition, Grand indicates that the woman writer often has the same problem of moving from consciousness to another method of expressing agency, particularly writing, which might be seen as the writer's equivalent of speech. In "Marriage Questions in Fiction," published in 1898 in *The Fortnightly Review,* Grand reviews Elizabeth Chapman's book *Marriage Questions in Modern Fiction* and speaks of this struggle. Citing Chapman's book as one in which the leap from thought to writing has been achieved, Grand states: "Our minds are for ever reaching out after something, something elusive, something which hovers on the confines of thought, but is not to be coaxed into focus; that something which it would make such a difference to be able to say to ourselves and convey to others" (79). Still, while the "power of expression" sometimes "eludes" the writer, Grand believes that when the expression finally does come, it is "rapture" (79). In choosing a word such as "rapture" to describe the transition from thought to writing/speech, Grand emphasizes the passion with which she believes in the abilities of women to create social change.

Grand's primary concerns—the struggle of women to create social change and her own struggle as a writer to find expression for her thoughts—dovetail nicely in the foreword to the 1923 edition of *The Heavenly Twins,* in which Grand says she wrote the novel because the ideas were there, floating around in the culture, and she simply acted as a medium for ideas that already were part of the collective consciousness.

I did not choose my tool; it was given to me. I did not, that is to say,

dropping metaphor, choose the *motiv* of this book; the *motiv* chose
me. I broke silence, as one breaks silence at any time, on the impulse
to speak, or rather, in my case, and to be exact, on the urgency to
write which comes to the writer who has something to say. The
Zeitgeist determined my subject matter. Again and again has it been
written or said to me: "You have put into words what I have always
felt and longed to express but could not." Sooner or later the
thoughts and feeling of the inarticulate, seeking expression, select a
medium, and I happened to be the medium on whom the ideas in
the air laid hold. (Grand, "Foreword" 400–401)

In presenting herself as simply a medium for expression of ideas already
present in the culture, Grand shows that while expression of agency is an
individual journey in which women change their own lives by moving
from consciousness to speech and action, it also is a collective journey in
which women speak for and with each other in order to create social
change.

More directly than Hardy, then, Grand argues for woman's consciousness
as key in depicting the relations of the sexes, and, if we turn to Grand's
Ideala, The Heavenly Twins, and *The Beth Book,* we can see the ways in
which feminist consciousness is represented in her work. I begin with
Ideala, the story of a woman whose difficult marriage to a man with a
roaming eye and a tendency toward violence prevents her from achieving
feminist consciousness until she leaves the marriage. *Ideala* establishes the
foundation for Grand's emphasis on consciousness in *The Heavenly Twins*
and *The Beth Book* but does not fit the feminist realist ideal entirely
because of its use of first-person narration through the eyes of a male character. I then turn to the two other novels, which come closer to the feminist realist ideal because of their use of third-person narration, where there
is more room for unmediated internal perspective of female characters.
Theoretically, *The Beth Book* comes closest to achieving this ideal because
it features a heroine who successfully moves from consciousness to action
through speech rather than through writing. Still, as my analysis shows,
The Beth Book does not fulfill the ideal completely, since the novel ends
with the heroine accepting a life in which she probably will not continue
to assert agency. Still, early-twenty-first-century readers with feminist
ideals can appreciate the ending of *The Beth Book* once they understand
how it illustrates Grand's commitment to speech rather than writing as the
facilitator for feminist action.

As will become evident in my analysis, the connection between what Grand wrote in her novels and what she wrote in her nonfiction essays is strong, and Grand often introduces her fiction through nonfiction commentary. In *Ideala,* she does so via a preface, which indicates that the novel is about the development of the mind of the main female character, Ideala, especially the stages of this development under difficult conditions (iii). Grand wants readers to look not for "perfection" in Ideala's mind but for the way her mind goes through a "transitional" maturation process. By paying attention to this transitional process, which reveals all the flaws of the mind as it develops, we can learn from Ideala's experience and apply her experience to our own lives. Writes Grand, "[W]hy exhibit the details of the process? you may ask. To encourage others, of course. What help is there in the contemplation of perfection ready made? It only disheartens us. . . . The imperfections must be studied, because it is only from the details of the process that anything can be learned" (iii). The preface, then, prepares us for the fact that woman's consciousness will be central to this novel but this consciousness is still in a developmental state.

In fact, Ideala is initially characterized as someone who lacks consciousness, and much of the novel is about her attempt to discover her own sense of self as well as understand her place in society. However, because she is involved in an unhappy marriage, as are many of Grand's characters, there is not much she can do for society until she works out her own problems. Key to the development of her mind after she suffers great cruelty from her husband is meeting Lorrimer, a man who works at a nearby mental hospital and who allows Ideala to come to the hospital to read and talk when she wishes. Here, Ideala finds the peace of mind she cannot find at home, and eventually she falls in love with Lorrimer. Interestingly, Lord Dawne, the male narrator who idealizes Ideala but also genuinely cares for her, characterizes Ideala's relationship with Lorrimer as one in which she is *losing* consciousness rather than gaining it (103–4), but Ideala herself does not define their relationship in quite the same way. She sees the relationship as one that gives her clarity of thought: "I was wandering in some such mental mist," she explains to Dawne when he confronts her about the relationship, "lost and despairing, when Lorrimer came into my life, and changed everything for me in a moment, like the sun. Would you have me believe that he was sent to me then only for an evil purpose?" (154).

Clearly, Ideala's perspective is different from Dawne's, and she even tries to convince Dawne that she should leave her husband and run away with Lorrimer. Though Dawne disapproves of Ideala's involvement with Lorrimer, at this point in Ideala's development, she can most effectively combat the social conventions that have put her through an unhappy marriage by ensuring her own happiness—by establishing that she is a "free agent" capable of making her own decisions without thinking about the wider community (164).[3] Still, this emphasis on individual liberty prevents Ideala from moving from increased consciousness to action to change the cultural status of women. It is only after Ideala ends her relationship with Lorrimer and goes to China with a group of missionaries, where she learns about the struggles of the Chinese women to survive in a culture that prevents them liberty of action by binding their feet, that she experiences feminist transformation. Upon Ideala's return from China, it is clear that her definition of consciousness has changed dramatically and is more distinctly community-oriented. When asked about her plans upon her return to England, Ideala draws a parallel between the oppression of women in China and the oppression of women in England. She explains to Dawne and her other friends:

> Certainly the Chinese women of the day bind their feet. And yet they do a wonderful thing. When they are taught how wrong the practice is, how it cripples them, and weakens them, and renders them unfit for their work in the world, they take off their bandages. . . . When I learned that, and when I remembered that my countrywomen bind every organ in their bodies . . . [i]t seemed to me that there was work enough left yet to do at home. (183)

In responding to the question about the type of work she will do, Ideala makes it clear that *increased consciousness* is key to changing the world, and feminist action should be aimed at changing conditions for all women, not just for herself. Says Ideala, "Women have never yet united to use their influence steadily and all together against that of which they disapprove. They work too much for themselves, each trying to make their own life happier. They have yet to learn to take a wider view of things, and to be shown that the only way to gain their end is by working for everybody else" (188). Though Dawne initially worries about the prospects for Ideala's "recovery," as he puts it, he eventually comes to believe that her "labors will eventually make themselves felt with a good result in the world" and that she is an example of someone who has developed well and cannot go back to "the old, purposeless life" she once had (189–91). In the end Ideala symbolizes the growth of a healthy mind, and she also seems to have made the transition from focusing on the transformation of her own consciousness to action that might transform the wider world.

In *Ideala*, then, Grand lays the important foundational work for arguing that consciousness is key to a woman's development. While our understanding of Ideala's progress is obscured somewhat by the first-person narration of Dawne, it is clear that Grand values consciousness in a way other writers of the 1890s do not. In *The Heavenly Twins,* the story of three women struggling to overcome society's expectation they will be submissive wives and mothers, Grand continues to emphasize consciousness as an important step in feminist transformation, and the narrative of Angelica, one of the three women, serves as an especially strong example of such transformation. Still, the novel also shows that consciousness alone does not guarantee feminist transformation. Sometimes representations of women's agency through consciousness result in exposure of the cultural conditions that *prevent* women from expressing agency rather than creating positive role models for real-life women to emulate, and the story of Evadne, the second of the three women, is one such example. While both Angelica and Evadne gain awareness of their marginalization in Victorian culture, and while Angelica is able to speak up and take action at least some of the time, Evadne cannot move successfully from awareness of her cultural status to speech and/or action that might make her life better. Nevertheless, since *The Heavenly Twins* is written mostly in third person, it offers a more reliable narrative about the struggles of various women than *Ideala* does, even if not all of the women successfully assert agency.

Third-person narration allows for a certain degree of narrative freedom, since the narrative perspective can shift easily from one character to another. Further, when the internal perspectives of female characters are emphasized early in a novel, there is at least the impression that there is a greater possibility these characters will assert agency than if their internal perspectives are not emphasized early on. Similar to other novels from the 1890s featuring female characters, *The Heavenly Twins* begins with the possibility Evadne will assert agency, since the story opens with emphasis on her internal perspective. "At nineteen," the narration reads, "Evadne looked out of narrow eyes at an untried world inquiringly. She wanted to know. She found herself forced to put prejudice aside in order to see beneath it, deep down into the sacred heart of things. . . . It was a need of her nature to know" (3). The key phrase here is "She wanted to know," since "to want to know" is comparable to desire. Evadne desired to know, and this desire, we are told by the narrator, is what defines Evadne as an active, thinking girl from the beginning of the novel. Over the course of the first few chapters, this characterization of Evadne is reinforced, primarily through the narrator's internal perspective but without interruption from the perspectives of other characters, such as Evadne's father, whose perspective would do much to diminish a characterization of Evadne as thoughtful, since he believes girls are inferior to boys. Like Gissing's *Jubilee,* which I discuss in a later chapter and in which the competing ideologies of a girl and her father are central to the plot, Grand's novel begins with the focus on the girl, not on the authority figure who tries to control her, and, by keeping the focus on the girl, the narrator suggests that Evadne will not be subject to her father's control.

In addition to keeping the focus on Evadne through internal perspective, the narrator, by focusing on the connection between consciousness and action, also suggests that Evadne will assert agency. In the opening of the novel we are told by the narrator that thought often leads to action, and in the case of Evadne action is "inevitable" (3). This tendency in Evadne is confirmed when early in the novel Evadne saves the life of Angelica's twin, Diavolo, after he accidentally plunges a penknife into his thigh and cuts his femoral artery. While everyone else is caught up in the confusion of the moment, Evadne's quiet observation and quick thinking lead her to place her thumb over the cut and keep Diavolo from bleeding to death (10). While this example is not one in which the leap from thought to action involves feminist action, Evadne's leap is described as "the quiet power of the girl" (11), which suggests that she at least might have the potential to take feminist action at some later point.

Still, Evadne's feminist development is complicated by her relationship with her father. While Evadne manages to draw her own conclusions about the ideas he expresses, despite her father's belief that women do not have brains (5–6, 11), she does not speak out against her father's ideas. Instead, she takes to writing in a Commonplace Book as a method for reacting against his ideas and for constructing her own ideas. She especially uses the Commonplace Book to process the books she reads under her father's direction, including *Roderick Random* and *Tom Jones,* which he believes are "true to life in every particular, and not only to the life of those times, but of all time" (20). Evadne, on the other hand, believes these books are "putrid" and perhaps even "poisonous," evidence of the "self-interest and injustice of men, the fatal ignorance and slavish apathy of women" (20), and she writes these opinions in her book. Still, the narrator thinks that Evadne would have benefited more fully had she talked about these books with other people rather than just writing about them, and this comment by the narrator speaks to the issue of *why* expression of agency according to the feminist ideal is threefold—a combination of consciousness, *speech* (not *writing*), and action. While the Commonplace Book gives Evadne a place to articulate her thoughts, the narrator believes she is "bold to a fault with her pen," replacing the "free discussion" that "would doubtless have been an advantage to Evadne at this impressionable period" with a more private method of resisting her father's patriarchal ideas (20).

The privileging of speech over writing here is important because it runs through Grand's work and is helpful in understanding why the feminist aesthetic includes speech but not necessarily writing. Speech might be seen as a necessary step in the process of feminist transformation—a kind of facilitator, as Grand implies in *The Heavenly Twins,* for the movement from consciousness to action. Writing can also serve as a facilitator for this movement, and in some of the other novels of the 1890s female characters do write about their marginalization as a way to facilitate action against cultural norms that support the subordination of women. For example, both Nancy Lord in Gissing's *Jubilee* and Diana Merion in Meredith's *Diana of the Crossways* write the stories of their struggles with romantic relationships, and both find inspiration through this writing. Still, Grand chooses to privilege speech over writing in both *The Heavenly Twins* and *The Beth Book,* where Beth first writes her resistance but then gives up writing to become an orator. One reason for this privileging might be that speech is always circulated, whereas writing is not necessarily circulated.

Unfortunately, the early possibilities for expression of agency by Evadne in *The Heavenly Twins* do not come to fruition. Pressured into marrying a man who will not allow her to progress in her development, Evadne's mind stagnates. She stops writing in her Commonplace Book, and, while she initially expresses her opinions in the company of others, she is constantly pressured by her husband to suppress these opinions. Further, Evadne's husband, Colquhoun, begins to control other outlets for her thoughts; at one point, he requests that she not write or speak publicly about the social issues in which she is interested. Evadne reluctantly agrees, and the effect is damaging, since she no longer has a method for facilitating the movement from thought to action. "As her mind grew sluggish, her bodily health decreased, and the climate began to tell on her. . . . [S]he was skin and bone, and the colour of death" (349–50). Once the development of Evadne's mind is lost, so is her ability to assert agency and fulfill the feminist ideal.

While Evadne's life spirals downward, life improves for Angelica, since she continually maintains an active mind and moves from thought to action. In "The Tenor and the Boy" section of the novel, Angelica disguises herself as her twin brother Diavolo, and while wearing this disguise she begins an intellectual friendship with a man nicknamed "The Tenor." This friendship ends only after Angelica falls into a river, loses her disguise, and inadvertently discloses that she is a woman (446). Unlike Evadne, who cannot figure out how to keep her mind stimulated while married to Colquhoun, Angelica does what is needed to keep her mind active. Disguised as her brother, she can have the intellectual conversation and freedom of movement she craves but cannot have in the body of a woman. John Kucich, in "Curious Dualities," attributes the effectiveness of this section of the novel to its antirealist narrative style, but I believe this section of the novel is successful not strictly because it is antirealist but because it features Angelica moving from consciousness to action.

As Teresa Mangum points out in *Married, Middlebrow, and Militant,* Angelica's decision to write speeches about women's issues, which her husband delivers in Parliament, is yet another "disguise" she puts on in order to survive in a culture that will not grant her complete independence. Here, Angelica's disguise is that of "wife," Mangum explains, and she uses her husband's position in Parliament as a way to articulate her own beliefs (139). What is interesting about this decision, in my mind, is that it highlights once again Grand's tendency to privilege speech over writing. While Angelica's speech writing is more effective than remaining silent, Angelica might have been more successful in asserting agency toward the end of the novel had she opted to speak her resistance instead of writing it for someone else to speak. As we know from the narrator's assessment of Evadne's use of the Commonplace Book to challenge patriarchal values, speech is the better choice. Still, it is arguable that Angelica chooses to write because it is the only viable option she has. The culture in which she lives will not allow her to speak in a venue where she might affect the opinions of others, so she chooses the next-best option. Also, given the narrative context in which Angelica makes this decision, we might develop a more sympathetic reading of Angelica's decision to speak through her husband, since she makes this decision after experiencing a personal crisis, the death of the Tenor. After his death, Angelica says she is "tired of action" and "tired of thinking too," despite the fact that thoughts continue to run through her head (525), so she makes her decision to speak through her husband at a time when she would prefer to do nothing at all. In this context her decision seems to be a step forward in her own personal development rather than a step back, since she continues to make the move from consciousness toward action, even if she chooses a less-than-ideal way of facilitating this move.

In fact, Angelica finds she cannot help but act independently. In addition to writing speeches for her husband to deliver, she takes up crossdressing again so that she can move about with the same kind of physical freedom men have. She is caught by Lord Dawne (the narrator from *Ideala* who resurfaces in this novel) and must answer to his shock over her actions (530–32). Her conversation with him focuses on the double standard for men's and women's actions, and talking about this issue gives Angelica a sense of release similar to the one she feels when she wears her disguise. Eventually, she also is able to tell her husband about her relationship with the Tenor and receives acceptance from him. As the final book of the novel ends, Angelica finds a way to participate in the world, albeit through writing speeches for her husband rather than through playing her violin, as she once hoped to do (541, 567).

Of course, Angelica's story is one of compromise, but her compromise is not as extreme as the one made by Evadne, who struggles to find the will to live at the end of the novel. Interestingly, Evadne's struggle is strongly tied to her inability to take action in her own life, and, as is the case in *Ideala,* readers encounter a male character, Dr. Galbraith, who seems to assert a more strongly feminist position than most of the female characters in the book. As other critics have pointed out, Galbraith certainly objectifies Evadne through the medical gaze,[4] but he sympathizes with Evadne's struggle to take action once he understands how cruel Colquhoun was to her and how he prevented her from facilitating the movement from consciousness to action. Once Galbraith is cognizant of Evadne's past and how it has affected her mind, his goal becomes helping her recover the impulse to act, a goal in line with the feminist ideal. "And now the difficulty was: how to help her? How to rouse her from the unwholesome form of self-repression which had brought about her present morbid state of mind. . . . How to draw her from the dreary seclusion of her *Home in the Woman's Sphere* and persuade her that hours of ease are only to be earned in action" (645–46).

Evadne's struggle, and Galbraith's role in it, highlight once again Grand's interest in examining the movement from consciousness to action, though, as some critics have noted, the ending, in which Galbraith and Evadne are still searching to find a way for Evadne to embrace action, is less than satisfying for many readers, especially those who hold feminist ideals.[5] Especially difficult to accept is the fact that the novel does not even end with Evadne's thoughts on her own struggle but with Galbraith's interpretation of her thoughts. Still, within the context of Grand's ideas about the complex relationship between thought and action, it would be unfair to read the ending as necessarily patriarchal because throughout his narrative Galbraith has urged Evadne to adopt a feminist approach to life. Within this context the ending becomes infinitely more interesting, if not wholly satisfying. By examining Grand's use of narrative strategies to represent different methods of expressing agency in *The Heavenly Twins,* a more nuanced reading of the end of the novel emerges.

Still, at the time *The Heavenly Twins* was published, some mainstream reviewers saw Grand's use of the narratives of three different women (Edith Menteith, who contracts syphilis from her husband and dies, is the third) to be problematic, since the storyline constantly jumps back and forth between the narratives, and in *The Beth Book* (1898) Grand seems to have tried to correct this problem by focusing on *one* woman's development rather than the development of three different women. By focusing solely on Beth, whose story of an unhappy marriage to a controlling man is very similar to Evadne's story, Grand avoids the scattered effect some critics felt when reading *The Heavenly Twins.* Nevertheless, focusing on one woman's

development from beginning to end creates a different problem for
Grand: a perceived *overemphasis* on consciousness and a lack of consistency in the actions Beth takes.[6] Even late-twentieth-century critics have
complained about lack of consistency in Beth's character, especially when
at the end of the novel Beth seems to turn away from feminist ideals by
envisioning herself as "saved" by a Tennysonian knight, who turns out to
be Arthur Brock, a man Beth nursed back from illness while sacrificing her
own health. As Terri Doughty, in "Sarah Grand's *The Beth Book:* The New
Woman and the Ideology of the Romance Ending" (1993), puts it:

> [T]he very open-endedness of Beth's romance with Arthur is in itself
> disturbing, as it seems to dissolve serious problems in a solution
> compounded of Tennyson, love, and sunshine. . . . If Arthur is
> Lancelot, then Beth must be the Lady of Shalott; the latter's weaving
> is related to Beth's own artistic endeavours. This does not auger well
> for Beth—for once the Lady saw the knight and left her art, she lost
> her creative vision and died. (192)

I, too, struggle to find a way to reconcile Beth's reliance on Brock and
its damaging effect on her transformation process. Nevertheless, our
understanding of the importance of consciousness to Grand helps mitigate
this reaction in our own early-twenty-first-century feminist readings. I
read other references to Tennyson's "Lady of Shalott" in the novel more
positively than I might without the context of Grand's ideas about turning thought into action, and detailing my reading of these references
should provide insight into alternative ways to read the ending.

The first time Beth envisions the Tennysonian knight coming to save
her is in the midst of a spell of "madness," which is induced by her husband's cruelty and which Beth tries to write herself out of, much in the
same way Angelica tries to escape from her misery by cross-dressing. Beth,
who is described by one nineteenth-century reviewer as "Angelica and
Evadne rolled into one" (Anonymous, "Some Books" 464), sets up a secret
room in the attic of her house, a place where she can escape the reality of
her marriage and write in peace, but this solution proves ineffective in
staving off madness. Yet, as soon as Beth sees the knight, who has come to
save her, she realizes the "horrid spell" is over (433). In fact, she feels that
she has "recovered her self-possession, her own point of view," and the narrator characterizes this moment as one that begins the process of restoring
Beth's mind to its former state (434). For Beth, living with her husband,
Dan, has been like living as the entrapped Lady of Shalott did, and, while
Beth has her writing just as the Lady had her weaving, no amount of writing Beth does (not even the letters to her family) can release her from the

prison Dan has built for her. While being saved by the knight does not offer much hope according to feminist ideals of today, it does offer hope for Beth, for once she is outside Dan's prison, the equivalent of the tower in Tennyson's poem, she may be able to speak about her experiences and to facilitate the movement from thought to action through speech rather than writing. In addition, what Beth gains from her vision of the knight is the restoration of her mind, the exact thing Evadne cannot achieve in *The Heavenly Twins,* no matter how much help she has from Galbraith.

In some ways the knight is Beth's equivalent of Evadne's Galbraith. She is dependent on him, as Evadne is on Galbraith, but both men represent a better life than the lives the women have led previously with men less sympathetic to feminist principles. The problem with the end of *The Beth Book* is not Grand's use of the Lady of Shalott image but the fact that she does not do enough to convince her readers that Arthur Brock could be the equivalent of Lancelot or Galbraith. While Arthur vows to find Beth after he learns she sacrificed her own hair in order to pay for his care (516), there is no evidence Arthur will be supportive of Beth in the same way she has cared for him. In fact, Arthur seems to hold antifeminist views: after Beth cuts her hair, he characterizes her as looking like part of the "unsexed crew that shriek on platforms" (509). Given his negative perception of the modern woman, it is hard to imagine that Arthur will support Beth in her newfound role as feminist orator. Had Grand provided different character development for Arthur, the end of the novel might be read as a positive part of Beth's feminist maturation: Arthur would become an assistant in Beth's facilitation of the thought-to-action process through speech, as Galbraith is for Evadne in *The Heavenly Twins.*

While Grand's commitment to representing woman's consciousness cannot be doubted, considering Hardy's work in light of the feminist ideal of consciousness-raising results in more ambiguous findings. Certainly, one cannot argue with the idea that Hardy has a strong interest in consciousness since an emphasis on "the gaze," one person thinking of and desiring another, is incessant in his novels. Yet Hardy's commitment to assertion of agency by female characters is less clear, as is his commitment to representing the increased consciousness of women. Diane Sadoff, in "Looking at Tess" (1993), argues for assertion of agency by Tess through her return of the male gaze and consent to participate in a "system of looks." On the other hand, Kaja Silverman, in "History, Figuration, and Female Subjectivity in 'Tess of the d'Urbervilles'" (1984), falls more firmly on the side of little or no agency for Tess, arguing that the male narrator is responsible for the usurpation of Tess's story. Further, Bernadette Bertrandias, in "Jeux de focalisation et problematique de la figuration dans *Tess*" (1988), points out that, narratively speaking, it is the limited degree of Tess's consciousness rather than the abundance of it that stands out to readers. Tess's internal perspective is overlooked in favor of the internal perspectives of other characters, and Tess ultimately loses the role of focalizer in the novel to the male characters, Alec and Angel, and the narrator, whose discourse suggests that Tess has little power against the larger forces of Fate.

Still, in novels such as *Tess of the d'Urbervilles* and *Jude the Obscure,* there are subversive moments in which women do assert agency, but these moments are more likely to occur through a method other than that of increased consciousness. I find the most subversive moments in the "confession" scenes in these novels, when the female characters use spoken word to try to change their male partners' views on the relations of the sexes. For example, Tess patiently listens to Angel Clare's confession of his sexual indiscretion and then makes her own confession, revealing her seduction by Alec d'Urberville. Tess asks Angel to accept her as his wife, despite her status as a fallen woman and, in asking for this acceptance, suggests that Angel adopt a less conventional perspective on the relationship between husband and wife. In *Jude,* Sue Bridehead confesses her unhappiness in her marriage to her husband, Phillotson, and uses the language of the New Woman to convince Phillotson to let her leave the marriage.

Before considering in depth the two confession scenes, we first should consider Tess and Sue as focalizers,[7] since we can see the inadequacy of consciousness as a method of expressing agency in Hardy's novels. From the beginning of both novels, internal perspective is dominated by narrators with a subtle but consistent control over the telling of the story. While Hardy's narrators tend not to be overly intrusive in presenting stories, they do infuse straightforward description with subtle commentary, often in the specific characteristics of people or places. *Tess* begins, for example, with a description of John Durbeyfield's "rickety" legs, which create a "bias in his gait" (31), and *Jude* begins with the description of several characters, all of whom are taking actions that reflect something about their characters on the day the schoolmaster Phillotson leaves the village.

From a feminist perspective, what is interesting about the openings of *Tess* and *Jude* is that female characters either are passed over as focalizers, as in the case of Tess Durbeyfield, or do not become focalizers until well into the novel, as in the case of Sue Bridehead. While it might be argued that Sue should not appear early in the novel, given the title's suggestion that the focus is on Jude, we know from Hardy's letters that he thought about the novel as a woman-centered work during the composition process.[8] That Hardy made the choice to withhold Sue and her internal perspective for nearly one-third of the story indicates that he had at least some ambivalence about presenting woman's consciousness prominently. In contrast to Sue, Tess is present from nearly the beginning of the novel, yet Hardy again falls short of the feminist realist ideal about this narrative strategy by passing over Tess as focalizer of impressions of her father, John Durbeyfield, in the second chapter of the book (38). Hardy's decision to pass over Tess as focalizer is important, for had he made her a focalizer, the way in which the story develops might be, perhaps would have to be, different. To give Tess thoughts and feelings early on, regardless of what they might be, would lay the foundation for a character who might assert agency more often and more successfully, according to the feminist assumption that consciousness is necessarily the first step in meaningful transformation.

Despite the lack of internal perspective by Tess and Sue early in the novels, their internal perspectives do become important at certain moments in their stories, though in very different ways. The first significant evidence of Sue's internal perspective occurs immediately following Jude's attendance of a church service, where he hopes to catch sight of Sue. Through narration emphasizing Jude's internal perspective, Hardy tells of Jude's attempt to see her, inserts a line break, and begins again, this time recounting an earlier incident in which Sue walks in the country by herself (138–41). This account establishes Sue and her internal perspective as independent from Jude and his perspective, and this independence of mind proves to be important later in the novel when Sue is characterized as a New Woman, likely to resist cultural norms that support the subordination of women. In strong contrast, Tess's internal perspective becomes significant in relationship to rather than separate from Angel Clare's. The shifting back and forth between Tess's and Angel's internal perspectives in chapter 19, when the two are working at the dairy farm and slowly growing to love each other, mirrors the development of Tess and Angel's relationship. When they come to love each other, their internal perspectives become so intertwined that at the end of chapter 19 the narrator's commentary reveals that their actions ("They met continually; they could not help it" [145]) and their internal perspectives ("they seemed to themselves the first persons up of all the world . . . as if they were Adam and Eve" [145]) have completely merged. Once Tess begins to focus on romance, her internal perspective is possible only in conjunction with her male partner's.

While internal perspective plays the important role of establishing the relationships between female characters and their romantic partners, and while the first instance of Sue's internal perspective anticipates to some degree her later resistance to cultural norms, these instances of internal per-

spective rarely play a direct role in the resistance of these female characters. Instead, resistance occurs through spoken word, so we must turn to
the confession scenes for evidence of resistance. My analysis of these scenes
is influenced by Mikhail Bakhtin's concept, from "Discourse in the
Novel," of heteroglossia: assertion of woman's agency through dialogue
often occurs in the moments when female characters are able to mount
resistance to language that attempts to categorize and vilify them,
moments I like to see as first "heteroglossic" and then potentially subversive, when the opportunity opened up by heteroglossia can turn into more
concrete displays of resistance, in defiance of the social apparatuses
described by Michel Foucault in *The Archaeology of Knowledge, Discipline
and Punish,* and other works. But it is also true that these heteroglossic
moments do not always become fully subversive; it depends on the way in
which female characters use language and to whom they speak.

After Tess tells the story of her "fall" to Angel, a story the narrator tells
us contains "no exculpatory phrase of any kind," the reaction from Angel
Clare is one of shock and then disgust. "Am I to believe this?" he says to
Tess. "From your manner I am to take it as true. O you cannot be out of
your mind! You ought to be! Yet you are not. . . . My wife, my Tess—
nothing in you warrants such a supposition as that?" (232). When Tess
tries to employ the "language of sympathy," a type of language well-
established by the late-Victorian period, Tess asks Angel to "[f]orgive me
as you are forgiven!," but Angel only replies, "O Tess, forgiveness does not
apply to the case! You were one person; now you are another. My God—
how can forgiveness meet such a grotesque—prestidigitation as that"
(232).[9] While Tess's initial reaction to Angel is to defer to her husband and
his "language of logic," as we might classify the language he uses to oppose
her language of sympathy, once Tess realizes that her deference to Angel
will not work, she becomes more assertive. Taking advantage of a moment
in which a number of ideologically inflected languages are at play (in addition to Angel's language of logic, we find the languages of religion, innocence, experience, duty, and desire, among others), Tess pleads with Angel:
"What have I done—what *have* I done! I have not told of anything that
interferes with or belies my love for you. You don't think I planned it, do
you? It is in your own mind what you are angry at, Angel, it is not in me.
O, it is not in me, and I am not that deceitful woman you think me"
(235).

Despite Tess's attempt at asserting agency through spoken word, Angel
refuses to forgive her, primarily because he, despite rejecting cultural
norms such as traditional religious values, is still wedded to norms that
support the subordination of women. At the end of the conversation
between Angel and Tess, the narrator confirms that what readers witness

is an example of competing languages and ideologies. Though the narrator believes that Angel possesses a "back current of sympathy," which Tess might have uncovered, Tess's confidence is so poor she cannot resist Angel's stronger discourse anymore (244). The heteroglossic moment has passed, and Tess's opportunity to change Angel's mind is gone. Later, Tess does have another opportunity to change his mind—when the couple separates at the end of their ruined honeymoon and Angel heads for Brazil while Tess returns home—but she again fails to shape Angel's ideas about their future. Still, as the narrator points out, "If Tess had been artful, had she made a scene, fainted, wept hysterically, in that lonely lane, notwithstanding the fury of fastidiousness with which he was possessed, he would probably not have withstood her" (255).

Though the narrator seems not to advocate the type of speech and action we would label "feminist," since to make a scene, faint, and weep hysterically is more stereotypically "feminine" than it is feminist, his perspective does suggest that Tess has strategies she does not use here. Further, Tess has enough awareness about the power of sympathy to change the cultural status of women, and she later plans to use the same language of sympathy she used with Angel to try to convince his parents that they should forgive and accept her. However, the Clares' absence from home when Tess goes to speak to them (294–95) and an encounter with Angel's brothers and Mercy Chant, in which they speak disparagingly of poor people (296), prevent Tess from asserting the feminist agency needed to change the perception of herself and the status of fallen women in the larger community. These scenes indicate that Tess understands the power of spoken word and is prepared to use this method but fails to do so because she does not have the increased consciousness needed to believe in her grounds for resistance. Further, it is clear that the heteroglossic moments necessary for a woman to assert agency effectively disappear before Tess can assert agency in any concrete way.

What is striking about Tess's journey to the vicarage and her encounter with Mercy and Angel's brothers is the silence that overtakes her during the course of her journey. Whereas Tess imagined she would use spoken word to convince others that Angel should not be allowed to simply desert her and go to Brazil, her journey turns out to be just the opposite, with Tess speaking only to herself in the end (297). Once Tess reverts to silence, physical actions become her only method of resistance, and the novel culminates in Tess killing Alec d'Urberville and fleeing the scene of the crime. While the killing of d'Urberville should be seen as an act of resistance, it cannot be seen as one that is effective in changing the cultural status of Tess or a wider community of women. When Tess later resists Alec's control over her by killing him, her punishment is severe, showing that extreme forms of resistance, such as the taking of another life, may have immediate results but ultimately fail because they cannot improve the cultural conditions under which women live.

Sue Bridehead's confession to her husband in *Jude the Obscure* provides a similar example of how in Hardy's work female characters *attempt* to assert agency through spoken word rather than through increased consciousness. Upon returning to Phillotson after attending the funeral of Jude's aunt and after confessing to Jude that she is miserable in her marriage, Sue begins her resistance by asking her husband, "would you mind my living away from you?" (284). This question begins a conversation in which Sue's use of the language of the New Woman is central to her argument for going to live with Jude. Acknowledging that her request is "irregular," she argues that "[d]omestic laws should be made according to temperaments, which should be classified. If people are at all peculiar in character they have to suffer from the very rules that produce comfort in others!" (285). She states that these laws are no good, especially "when you know you are committing no sin," and by making such a claim Sue questions both legal and religious doctrines of the nineteenth century. She tries to establish a different moral code, one based not on religion or current law but on the principle of individual happiness and equality for women, when she says to Phillotson, "Why can't we agree to free each other? We made the compact, and surely we can cancel it—not legally, of course; but we can morally, especially as no new interests, in the shape of children, have arisen to be looked after" (285).

Sue then adopts language that is even more thoroughly New Womanish, since she claims J. S. Mill as her authority for ending the marriage contract: "She, or he, 'who lets the world, or his own portion of it, choose his plan of life for him, has no need of any other faculty than the ape-like one of imitation.' J. S. Mill's words, those are. I have been reading it up. Why can't you act upon them? I wish to, always" (286). Despite Phillotson's indifference to the ideas of Mill ("What do I care about J. S. Mill!" he says to Sue at this point in the conversation), Sue's resistance through spoken word has an effect on her husband, and he eventually agrees to let Sue live separately within their own home. Still, Sue's New Womanish language has only a limited effect because it is ultimately a physical action, jumping out a window when Phillotson accidentally enters her bedroom one night, that convinces her husband that Sue was right to ask for permission to leave the house entirely. Nevertheless, it is fair to say that Sue's early attempt at convincing Phillotson of the logic of separating has some effect on his decision to let her go since Phillotson himself adopts Sue's language in order to convince his friend Gillingham that he made the right decision. Claiming that "it is wrong to torture a fellow-creature" and that he does not want to be an "inhuman wretch" by forcing Sue to remain with him, Phillotson says to Gillingham:

> [S]omething within me tells me I am doing wrong in refusing her. I, like other men, profess to hold that if a husband gets a so-called pre-posterous request from his wife, the only course that can possibly be regarded as right and proper and honourable in him is to refuse it, and put her virtuously under lock and key, and murder her lover per-haps. But is that essentially right, and proper, and honourable, or is it contemptibly mean and selfish? (293)

Like Sue, Phillotson seems to accept the idea that there is a moral code based on some principle other than the current law or religious beliefs, and Phillotson iterates this to Gillingham after Sue has left the house when he says, "I was, and am, the most old-fashioned man in the world on the question of marriage—in fact I had never thought critically about its ethics at all. But certain facts stared me in the face, and I couldn't go against them" (299).

Sue's resistance gives readers a clear instance of assertion of woman's agency, but, as is typical in Hardy's novels, expressions of woman's agency rarely serve as the last word. Sue's own awareness of the larger communi-ty's views about her relationship with Jude prevent her from living free from shame after she leaves Phillotson, and this shame is most apparent in two scenes: the scene in which Sue and Jude are fired from their job repair-ing the Ten Commandments sign in a church and the scene in which Sue bemoans to Father Time the miserable conditions of her life. In the church scene Sue asserts none of the language of the New Woman she has used successfully in the past; here, the only language she can muster is that of self-pity: "How could we be so simple as to suppose we might do this!" she says to Jude. "Of course we ought not—I ought not—to have come!" (373). Then, in the scene with Father Time, which occurs after Sue and Jude are unable to find lodging for the entire family because they are not married, there is more evidence of Sue's loss of confidence. When Father Time says to Sue, "It would be better to be out o' the world than in it, wouldn't it?," Sue can only answer, "It would almost, dear" (406). Instead of explaining to Father Time the injustice of the way the family is treated, Sue allows him to think that he and his siblings are at fault, and this leads to his suicide and the murder of his siblings (408).

In both novels attempts at asserting agency through spoken word are ultimately undermined by competing languages, languages infused with ideologies that support the subordination of women. Sometimes these lan-guages are used overtly and clearly in dialogue with the fallen woman or

New Woman, while at other times it is simply the woman's awareness of this competing language that results in her lack of confidence. Part of the reason Tess fails to convince Angel and others of her purity is that she does not infuse her language with the ideology of religious repentance but uses language that only evokes pity, and part of the reason Sue cannot effectively combat language that vilifies her is that combating language means combating a religious ideology that has the support of strongly established institutions. But it is also true that Tess and Sue fail to transform ideas about the cultural status of women because they cannot attain access to those who might sympathize, as in the case of Tess, or because they voice their beliefs only to those with whom it is safe to speak frankly rather than to those in the wider community, as in the case of Sue.

Expression of woman's agency in Hardy, then, significantly complicates assumptions about methods of expression and their corresponding narrative strategies. In Hardy, consciousness on the part of female characters does not dominate, and when we turn to other methods of expressing agency, especially spoken word, we find that female characters' use of these methods has limited effectiveness. Still, Tess's and Sue's inability to use language effectively can be tied to social circumstances, and those circumstances, as feminist perspectives of the late nineteenth century show, are significant. What I want to emphasize here are *not* the inadequacies of Tess and Sue but instead the rhetorical choices made by Hardy. That Hardy's female characters do not possess increased consciousness in the same way Grand's characters do, that they do not use particular types of languages through which they might combat cultural norms that support the subordination of women, and that they do not take advantage of particular rhetorical situations when they do possess such language illustrate that Hardy made specific choices within a particular social context. In choosing neither to grant his female characters consciousness early on nor to combine increased consciousness with spoken word and/or action, Hardy limited the possibilities for assertion of agency according to the feminist realist ideal.

The differences in Grand's and Hardy's representations of woman's agency were recognized by *Shafts* and *The Woman's Herald*. Both acknowledged the emphasis on woman's consciousness in Grand's work, as well as Hardy's failure to fully capture it, but they did admire Hardy's attempt to challenge traditional realism and expose the difficulties women face in trying to assert agency, regardless of the method. *Shafts* acknowledged Grand's emphasis on consciousness in its review of *Heavenly Twins*. This review illustrates well the feminist realist agenda, since it opens with a discussion of the novel as one having a purpose but also possessing a certain degree of literary finesse. "It is a book with a purpose, and a decided purpose," writes the reviewer, "but so skilfully has the clever author brought her art to bear upon each chapter, incident, and individual character combining to make up the wondrous whole, that readers are under the pleasing delusion that they make their own deductions" (Anonymous, "Reviews: Heavenly" 268). The review highlights *Shafts*'s interest in consciousness when the reviewer writes of the deductions readers make when reading the novel:

> So numerous are the revelations that come to us, the lessons to be drawn, in flowing and outflowing to and from the other, that as we read we are amazed, and ask ourselves, Has the writer intended all this, or has she imparted to each character and incident some of her own marvelous creative force, so that thoughts and deductions flow from all continuously, with immortal power. (268)

Not only does Grand's work help readers think important ideas, but it seems as if Grand has infused her characters with important thoughts, to the degree that readers think the same way the characters do. While this assessment of Grand's novel does not use current literary terminology such as focalization or even internal perspective, it is thoroughly rooted in the consciousness-oriented discourse of "thought-influence," which I already have described in this chapter. Further, while the specific shifts in internal perspective in this novel are not described by the reviewer, the characters are described as particularly realistic, in part because they create certain thoughts within the reader. The characters "are not pictures, they are living creatures created by one who has learnt life's lesson; and in their turn they create within us thoughts that breathe and burn, thoughts that grow, stretching forth as they take into themselves the nourishment here supplied" (268).

Likewise, the review in *The Woman's Herald*, titled "Marriage and the Modern Woman; or, The Story of the Heavenly Twins," articulates well the feminist realist aesthetic, since it emphasizes the connection between literary representation of women's lives and the everyday experiences of real-life women. The review, which was divided into four parts and which ran weekly for a month, opens with praise: "To say that this is a remarkable book is to say little. It is a book which is a sign of the times. It raises and discusses with fearlessness, rare in the world of fiction, the most important of all questions which confront the modern woman. . . . 'Is any kind of man good enough to be my husband?" (Anonymous, "Marriage" 123).

Formerly, the reviewer continues, women believed that any man will do, but now that women are seeing, thinking, and acting for themselves, they can be more selective in choosing a spouse and can reject those who are "morally unfit" (123). The struggles women face when it comes to marriage is evident in the novel, since the novel possesses a "strong and almost cruel light" that exposes "the human sacrifices" made "before the altar of conventionality and custom" (123).

The reviewer also highlights consciousness: readers are guided through the entirety of Evadne's story, and close attention is paid to the sections about the development of her mind. For instance, the first installment contains a section on Evadne's early education, in which her mind is just beginning to develop, and the last installment takes up the issue of Evadne's state of mind after her husband dies and she marries Galbraith. In this installment the reviewer concludes with an assessment of the female characters in the novel. Of Angelica, the reviewer states that despite the upbeat tone of her story, there is an "undertone" of the "waste of a woman's life when she has no outlet or object before her adequate to her capacity and her power" (186). Of Evadne, the reviewer states that her "defect" as "a study of female character, is the lack of emotion of what may be called distinctively womanliness. There is in her the anatomy of a fine woman, but the flesh is withered, and the skin is dry and parched" (186). Based on what we know about Grand's emphasis on consciousness in her novels and nonfiction essays, this assessment of the female characters according to the way in which "emotion" of a character is presented, as well as the attention to a character's "capacity" and "power," indicates the reviewer's awareness of increased consciousness as an important method of asserting agency.

The review in *The Woman's Herald* also recognizes the importance of competing definitions of realism in the *fin-de-siècle* literary market and the unique contribution feminist realism makes by focusing on woman's consciousness. The review discusses not only the book itself but also the "Tom Jones controversy," which was concurrently running in *The Pall Mall Gazette*. The reviewer for the *Pall Mall* had stated that Grand would be better to "study life from Tom Jones's point of view" than the perspective she takes in *The Heavenly Twins,* and W. T. Stead responded to this claim, arguing that to suggest that Grand adopt the view of Tom Jones was to suggest that a woman become a promiscuous scoundrel in order to understand life. Such a suggestion would not be helpful to the improvement of gender relations, argued Stead, since it would result only in the degradation of both sexes rather than the improvement of either. Though many people replied to Stead, including the *Pall Mall* reviewer, *The Woman's Herald* sided with Stead on the issue and criticized the *Pall Mall* reviewer for its inability to see the double standard in *Tom Jones* (140). In taking Stead's side, *The Woman's Herald* suggested that there is more than one valid perspective in the world, and differing perspectives can be as realistic as those traditionally accepted by critics.

Despite some minor faults, *The Heavenly Twins* was viewed as a success by *The Woman's Herald*, and the paper gave Grand and her work significant space in the aftermath of the controversy over the novel. It ran articles about Grand as an author in the July 6, 1893 issue ("Two Women Who Write") and in the Aug. 17, 1893 issue ("Sarah Grand: A Study"), and the staff went back to *Ideala* and reviewed it, arguing that although the peculiarities of Ideala's character might seem odd to the reader, as the novel progresses, "one forgets the peculiarities, and can find little but sympathy and admiration for the many noble qualities of a very complex character." Further, the reviewer of *Ideala* states that the novel anticipates the "fearless denunciation of social evils" that receives "eloquent utterance" in *The Heavenly Twins* (Anonymous, "Our Library" 537).

Like *The Woman's Herald*, *Shafts* also ran other articles about Grand's work after its initial review of *The Heavenly Twins*. In an article titled "Knowledge Is Power," Mary Fordham applies what is discussed in *The Heavenly Twins* to real-life situations. She writes of a conversation she had with a young girl, in which she was surprised to find that the girl thought that Evadne was wrong to leave her husband rather than try to reform him. Fordham decries the current state of girls' thinking on the subject, stating that too many of them believe that it is acceptable to stay with promiscuous men, and too many excuse promiscuity on the basis that it is normal for men to "sow their wild oats" (137). Fordham argues that women must fight for an equal moral code for women and men, and mothers must exert their influence on their sons, so men, too, begin to believe in this code. Finally, Fordham returns to *The Heavenly Twins* and argues that Evadne was correct to leave Colquhoun, since "[t]o have lived with him would have been a wrong, not only to herself, but to the children" (137).

In these articles and in the reviews feminist periodicals ran in the mid-1890s, there is a sense that those who wrote for *Shafts* and *The Woman's Herald* were grateful to have Grand's presence in the literary market because she seemed to be writing for their cause. Still, feminist periodicals held Grand to a high standard when representing women's lives in literature, and the fact that Grand was a woman writer did not allow her to escape criticism from the woman's press. In the two articles about her position as author, *The Woman's Herald* suggests that Grand has not reached her potential yet and her best work was yet to come. One writer states that *The Heavenly Twins* is "only a transition stage in the evolution of its author's genius" and Grand is "not yet at her ripest" (Anonymous, "Two

Women" 309). The other writer echoes this sentiment, stating that Grand is "one of the most valuable recruits which the cause of woman has gained in recent years. . . . But although Sarah Grand has done good and noble service . . . she is but a neophyte. Her best work is still to come" (Anonymous, "Sarah Grand" 401).

Shafts did not criticize Grand directly in its reviews of her work or its articles about her, but they did print letters from readers illustrating the high standard to which Grand's work was held. In a letter that ran in the November 1893 issue, a reader writes that much of what is in *The Heavenly Twins* is "true," but the cause of women's rights will not be helped by Evadne's story. "I write in no sneering spirit, but I am honestly at a loss to see why her life should be proposed as a model for imitation— or even as an advance upon the life of the average woman whom she is to supersede" (Anonymous, "Correspondence" 167). This criticism points to one of the key issues surrounding the feminist realist aesthetic: is its primary goal to provide positive representations of women and illustrate how they assert agency using the three-step process, or to represent cultural conditions that prevent women from asserting agency, even if it means producing negative role models for women? *The Woman's Herald* also considers this issue in Grant Richards's article, "Women Writers in '93," in which Richards, known best for his role as publisher of George Bernard Shaw's plays, suggests that Grand spends too much time on "the woes of Evadne" (20). This criticism of Evadne may indicate that while Grand was employing the three-step process for expressing agency, her tendency to place so much emphasis on the conditions that prevented women from asserting agency discouraged some readers. Had there been a stronger combination of the three aspects of expressing agency, had Evadne been able to move from consciousness to speech and/or action, perhaps the reception of the novel would have been more positive.

Still, while there were occasional criticisms of Grand's tendency to expose cultural conditions rather than construct positive representations of women expressing agency, *The Woman's Herald* and *Shafts* generally were flexible enough to accept novels that *either* provided positive representations *or* exposed difficult cultural conditions. In addition, they were willing to suspend harsh criticism when they saw an author trying to fulfill even one aspect of woman's agency in his or her novels. This point— that the feminist realist aesthetic was remarkably flexible—becomes especially important when considering male authors whose works were reviewed in the papers, since, despite certain weaknesses in their novels, the works of male authors were praised by feminist reviewers.

Hardy serves as a fine example of a male author who was embraced by feminist reviewers, despite the fact that he did not fully achieve the feminist realist ideal. While Hardy's works received significantly less review space than did the works of Grand (there was a short review of *Tess* in *The Woman's Herald* and a lengthier review of *Jude* in *Shafts*), the reviewers of both periodicals found ways to praise Hardy for his representations of women, even as they criticized him for the weaknesses in these representations. These reviews are especially striking in contrast to reviews of the same novels in other periodicals. I contrast the review of *Tess* in *The Woman's Herald* to several mainstream reviews of the novel and also to another "feminist" review that happened to appear in a mainstream paper, and I contrast *Shafts's* review of *Jude* to Margaret Oliphant's more conservative review of the novel in *Blackwood's Edinburgh Magazine.*[10]

As mentioned earlier in this chapter, mainstream reviews of *Tess* had in common a dislike for Hardy's "unnatural" storyline, or his tendency to represent characters who did not reflect "civilized" society. Margaret Oliphant's review of *Tess* in *Blackwood's,* titled "The Old Saloon," is perhaps the best example because it confirms the negative opinions of the reviewers for *The Saturday Review* and *The Quarterly Review* but also adds a new objection: that stories focusing wholly on sexual behavior do not accurately represent late-Victorian life. Like *The Saturday Review* writer, Oliphant expresses a preference for more traditional forms of realism early in her review, commenting that although she has "a great many objections to make to Tess," she also recognizes the greatness of Hardy's skill in representing nature. Of *Tess* as a whole, Oliphant writes:

> [W]hat a living, breathing scene, what a scent and fragrance of the actual, what solid bodies, what real existence, in contrast with the pale fiction of the didactic romance! We feel inclined to embrace Mr. Hardy, though we are not fond of him, in pure satisfaction with the good brown soil and substantial flesh and blood, the cows, and the mangel-wurzel, and the hard labour of the fields—which he makes us see and smell. (204)

In other words, Hardy's depiction of the landscape is fine; it is other aspects of representations to which Oliphant objects.

According to Oliphant, the type of world Hardy represents is too narrow; instead, he should represent "a world which is round and contains everything, not 'the relations between the sexes' alone" (203). This remark clearly criticizes Hardy's claim in "Candour in English Fiction" that the relations of the sexes was a legitimate subject for fiction, and Oliphant sides with *The Saturday Review* and *The Quarterly Review* critics, pointing to the unbelievability of Tess's actions over the course of the novel as the major flaw of the book. Of Hardy's decision to have Tess return to Alec,

Oliphant writes, "We do not for a moment believe that Tess would have done it. Her creator has forced the rôle upon her, as he thinks (or says) that the God whom he does not believe in, does. . . . But whatever Mr. Hardy says, we repeat that we do not believe him" (212–13). In addition, the "real Tess," as Oliphant refers to the ideal character Hardy might have presented, never would have ended up in this situation in the first place, since she would have taken advantage of the opportunity she was given to escape Alec at the moment of her seduction (213).

Though the negative opinions of Oliphant and other critics are remembered now, clearly there were other opinions of Hardy's work in the critical discussion of the time. While *Shafts* did not review *Tess, The Woman's Herald* did, as did Clementina Black in *The Illustrated London News*. While *The Illustrated London News* was a decidedly mainstream newspaper and not a deliberately feminist periodical, Black herself had strong ties to the feminist community and occasionally wrote articles for or was featured in *The Woman's Herald*.[11] Known for her advocacy on working-class women's issues especially, Black often expresses a perspective in her reviews that is as feminist as those found *Shafts* and *The Woman's Herald,* and Black's review of *Tess* contrasts strongly to the reviews that ran in *The Saturday Review, The Quarterly Review,* and *Blackwood's.*

First, Black's review is deeply rooted in the feminist assumption that good books do not always have happy endings but instead draw attention to the difficult social conditions women face. Touting *Tess* as the "finest" novel Hardy has produced, Black paints the "conventional" reader as one who does not like to be challenged by the books he reads, but this is precisely what happens with *Tess:* the reader must use his "conscience" and reconsider the "traditional pattern of right and wrong." The traditional reader, writes Black, "detest[s] an open challenge of that traditional pattern, and *Tess of the d'Urbervilles* is precisely such a challenge" (186). Black then continues to say that, like Meredith's *Diana of the Crossways* (a novel also admired by many feminist reviewers), *Tess* is a book "founded on a recognition of the ironic truth" that the "most direct, sincere, and passionate" woman is often the "most liable to be caught in that sort of pitfall which social convention stamps as an irretrievable disgrace" (186–87).

In addition to establishing a distinctly different criterion for judging novels, Black's review acknowledges the various ways in which women assert agency, confirming the model *Shafts* sets up for the link between literary representation and the cultural status of real-life women. Black suggests, as I have, that it is Tess's confession to Angel, her spoken word, that establishes her "sincerity" as a character (187), a comment acknowledging the complexity of woman's agency in a way the more traditional, action-focused conceptions of woman's virtue, such as Oliphant's, do not. Finally,

Black rejects the usual tendency of critics to find Hardy's redemption in descriptions of rural scenery. Though the descriptions are "wonderful," Black writes that "characteristic as they are," they "are not the essence of the book. Its essence lies in the perception that a woman's moral worth is measurable not by any one deed, but by the whole aim and tendency of her life and nature" (187). This comment brings readers back to the point that a more complex understanding of woman's agency is essential to understanding Hardy's aim, something more conservative reviewers such as Oliphant could not see.

The review of *Tess* that ran in *The Woman's Herald*, written by Haweis, is more moderate than Clementina Black's: it acknowledges and even agrees with the more conservative view that Hardy's rural landscapes are his saving grace and his character building is not always consistent. "His perception of human character seems to me less decided, and a little warped in unexpected places," writes Haweis. "It is difficult to believe that so noble a woman as Tess would have really killed the feeble reptile that besmirched her life, after long shewing strength of brain, body and heart" (10). Still, Haweis seems to recognize that the weakness in Hardy's novel may be connected to the feminist realist ideal for expression of agency, since it is the inconsistency between Tess's strength of body, brain, and soul and her act of killing Alec d'Urberville that makes her character unbelievable—*not* her lack of virtue, as Oliphant suggests.

Further, Haweis also seems to recognize the connection between form and content, especially content focusing on the ability of women to change social conditions. In a rhetorically effective move, Haweis begins the review with the statement that the appearance of *Tess* at a time in history when it seems as though the prospects for women are improving is especially inspiring, and she then makes the connection between form and content clear, stating:

> There is not a syllable in 'Tess' about woman's physical equality with men; though in the sore winters of her husband's desertion Tess . . . worked as well as any man. . . . There is not a syllable in 'Tess' about the Suffrage, nor the right of heroic, magnificent, injured human creatures to be taken legal account of in the country they help to keep going. . . . It is merely the story of a girl's virtue bearing up like a rock against an ocean of natural disadvantages, from early neglect and uninstruction to the unbearable pains of desertion, starvation, insult, temptation, and repeated deceptions. (10)

Haweis's point—that although Hardy never states his agenda directly, he succeeds in articulating his point—shows the degree to which realistic representation of women's lives was important to feminist critics. Hardy shows women in strong positions, claims Haweis, rather than simply telling us about it, indicating that although the feminist definition of realism allowed for polemic, it also sought realistic form.

All in all, it is evident that the reviews written by feminist reviewers express a significantly more progressive opinion of Hardy's work and of the role of women in Victorian culture. This trend is also found in *Jude* criticism, which reveals the same contrast between the principles expressed by feminist reviewers and the more traditional principles expressed by mainstream reviewers. When *Jude the Obscure* was published at the beginning of November 1895, the mainstream reviews followed much the same pattern as those for *Tess:* the reviews generally were negative, and most commented on the extreme "gloom" of the novel (Gerber and Davis 67–71). Still, few reviews reached the level of negative criticism expressed by Oliphant in the now infamous "Anti-Marriage League," which grouped Hardy's novel with other novels of the mid 1890s (Grant Allen's *The Woman Who Did* and *A Splendid Sin* and Ménie Dowie's *Gallia*).

Oliphant begins the review by reminding readers of her earlier assessment of *Tess* in "The Old Saloon," and, expressing a slightly more favorable opinion of *Tess* this time around, she iterates that the rural scenery in *Tess* rather than the characters and their actions makes her admire Hardy. She then asserts that, unlike *Tess,* in which the rural scenery redeemed the novel, there is little to redeem *Jude* from the "grossness, indecency, and horror" it represents (138). Oliphant associates what Hardy does in *Jude* with the work of Zola, confirming that, for Oliphant anyway, the only acceptable form of realism is that which she has already narrowly defined as depictions of rural landscape and/or the display of free will on the part of humans. Though she acknowledges that Hardy is not as "disgusting," "impious," or "foul" as some followers of Zola, she suggests that Hardy comes as close to Zola's technique in *Jude* as a "Master" of fiction can. Further, Oliphant makes it clear that Hardy fails because he does not emphasize free will. Hardy's fate-based philosophy, where the actions of individuals cannot be linked to a logical moral consequence, irritates Oliphant to no end. In characterizing Jude and his story, Oliphant argues that Jude is "an attractive figure at his outset" because his aspirations to become educated and overcome the obstacles that stand in his way offer an opportunity for Hardy to represent humans attempting to improve themselves. Yet once Jude meets Arabella and Sue, says Oliphant, he "is made for the rest of his life into a puppet flung about between them." He is "always the puppet, always acted upon by the others" (139).

With this assessment of Jude—as one who would be more realistic had he been able to exert his free will throughout the novel—it is not surprising that Oliphant is even more critical when assessing the women in the story. Oliphant characterizes Arabella as a "fleshy animal" (139) and Sue as the "other" woman who "completes the circle of the unclean" and "makes virtue vicious by keeping the physical facts of one relationship in life in constant prominence" (140). Finally, she assesses all the women in the novel as negative, stating, "It is the women who are the active agents in all this unsavoury imbroglio" (140). By highlighting the women as "active agents," Oliphant institutes a strong qualification to her free-will philosophy. This philosophy works for Oliphant only when women act in a particular manner and uphold Oliphant's traditional expectations about the role of women. Since Hardy does not follow her model, she accuses him of challenging the appropriate way for human life to be represented in fiction.

Oliphant's review reveals the importance of the philosophical and ideological underpinnings of definitions of realism in the late nineteenth century, especially when her review is set next to those written by feminists, whose philosophical and ideological commitments emphasize more fully the role of social conditions on expressions of agency. In contrast to Oliphant's review, the assessment of *Jude* found in *Shafts* is significantly more sympathetic to Hardy, arguing that many critics have registered their opinions about the novel and most have overlooked the importance of the subtitle of the novel, "The Letter Killeth." In doing so, they have missed not only the irony and tragedy of the lives represented by Hardy but especially his genius in drawing the character of Sue. Writes the reviewer, the well-known suffragist Dora Montefiore, "[A]ll the characters are drawn with a master-hand; but in the case of Sue Bridehead the novelist has well nigh excelled himself. She is the type of the upward struggling woman, unconscious almost yet in her struggle, and feebly armed it may be against that terrible 'letter' which in the end shall kill her delicate ideal purpose" (12). Though Montefiore characterizes Sue as "unconscious almost" in her struggle, a comment suggesting Sue's lack of internal perspective, she does see Sue, at least initially, as a "highly developed" woman who is able to "inspire and lead" Jude (12). Still, when Sue's "fall" occurs, it is "ten times deeper than his and the 'letter,' the irresistible deadly 'letter' which ever holds woman in its cruelest grasp, dragged her down from the slight elevation she had painfully reached, to depths, lower than in her best moments she could have dreamt of" (12). In other words, the "letter" represents the social code that restricts women by narrowly categorizing their behavior.

Like the feminist reviews of *Tess,* Montefiore's review acknowledges the role cultural conditions play in shaping a woman's life and the tension between representing these conditions and showing how women resist such conditions. Though Montefiore questions Hardy's decision to have

Sue return to Phillotson, since it seems unlikely that a woman who had
been described by Jude as one "whose intellect was to mine like a star to a
benzoline lamp" would hardly "take such an entirely debasing course"
(12–13), she ends the review on a positive note. If one looks at Jude and
Sue up close, "as we would look at the microbes in a drop of water under
a powerful magnifying lens," Montefiore says, they do look flawed. But if
one looks at them from a wider perspective, "in relation to Humanity and
its solidarity of real . . . interests and aspirations," we see them in a different light. "[W]e begin to see beneath the fret and jar, the ironies and
apparent failures, and to recognise the story of their lives as the perfectly
told history of an infinitesimal part of a great whole" (13). In other words,
if we judge Hardy's characters according to their specific actions only, we
might take Oliphant's view of the novel, but once we widen our view of
realism to include more than characters' actions, it is easier to see clearly
Hardy's remarkable achievement with *Jude*.

The reviews of Hardy's work in *Shafts* and *The Woman's Herald* show
that the feminist realist aesthetic remained flexible enough to acknowledge
both representations of women asserting agency and representations of
their failure to assert agency due to cultural conditions. Hardy was far
from perfect in his representations of women, but *Shafts* and *The Woman's
Herald* recognized that he had engaged the aesthetic, and they praised him
for it. Whether Hardy actually read the reviews in the feminist periodicals
cannot be determined, but it appears that he was influenced by his female
readership. After the publication of *Tess*, Hardy knew that women were
reading and admiring his novel; he states in a letter to Edmund Gosse that
he received numerous letters from women about the book. "[T]he sex
[has] caught on with enthusiasm," he writes, "as I gather from numerous
communications from mothers (who tell me they are putting 'Tess' into
their daughters' hands to safeguard their future) and from other women of
society who say that my courage has done the whole sex a service (!)"
(*Collected Letters* 1:255). While the first half of this statement suggests a
certain degree of conservatism among women readers (since they believe
they must "safeguard" their daughters), the second half of this statement,
punctuated by Hardy himself by the inclusion of the exclamation point,
suggests that it was not just women, but politically aware women, who
were reading the novel.

Further, Hardy received letters from some well-known women who
identified themselves as feminist, and this suggests that even as Hardy felt
pressure to appeal to the traditionalists such as Oliphant by including
descriptions of rural scenes in his work, he also was aware of the opinions
of his feminist readership. Among those who read the book were Millicent
Fawcett, the suffragist leader, who wrote to praise *Tess* (1:263–64), and

George Egerton, author of strongly consciousness-focused *Keynotes* (1893), who wrote to express her approval of *Jude*. Sue Bridehead, Egerton thought, was "a marvellously true psychological study of a temperament less rare than the ordinary male observer supposes" (2:102). Hardy responded to Egerton's compliment, first by praising *Keynotes* ("I need hardly say what my reply was: and how much I felt the verisimilitude of the stories, and how you seemed to make us breathe the atmosphere of the scenes") and then by revealing that his own feelings about Sue matched up with Egerton's: "I have been intending for years to draw Sue, and it is extraordinary that a type of woman, comparatively common and getting commoner, should have escaped fiction so long" (2:102). What is interesting here is that Hardy, who had remarked to Florence Henniker only two years earlier that he was "not greatly curious" about Egerton as a writer (2:47), is remarkably admiring of her now. More significantly, he shifts his definition of realism to accommodate Egerton's more feminist take on fiction, one in which the psychological aspects of a woman's character rather than just the tragic aspects are emphasized. Such a shift in Hardy's definition, at least for this particular letter, suggests that he was aware of his feminist audience and had an appreciation for the principles, including raised consciousness, of the feminist realist aesthetic. Even if Hardy did not fulfill the feminist aesthetic as fully as Grand did, he clearly was aware of the aesthetic and incorporated it into his work.

Chapter 2

"What the Girl Says": Spoken Word as Political Tool

For *Shafts* and *The Woman's Herald,* expression of agency through spoken word was as important as expression through consciousness, though such expression often occurred as a result of increased consciousness. From its first issue *The Woman's Herald* set as its aim to "speak" for those women who had thoughts but could not express them. As part of the introduction written to readers in the first issue, the periodical promises to leave behind the "conservative" and "mechanical" treatment of women's issues seen in other papers and to "speak the truth without fear of consequences" as well as "reflect the thoughts of the best women upon all the subjects that occupy their minds" (Anonymous, "Our Policy" 1).

Likewise, *Shafts* chronicles the rise of women's voices via increased consciousness in its first issue in a column titled "What the Girl Says," which promises to publish the "thoughts of the girl on any point" about which she wished to speak. The hypothetical girl, according to the columnist, has been thinking for some time but has not been given the encouragement needed to voice her thoughts, since all the encouragement has gone to the boy, who speaks his thoughts "loudly" while the girl sits by and listens to him (Anonymous, "What the Girl" 5). Still, with encouragement, girls will begin to express their thoughts, including: "The Girl says, she always thought God was a man, because everything written in the Bible thinks of men first"; "The Girl says, girls and women have had to fight their way step by step, they have suffered and grown strong; soon this will make such a change in the world"; and "The Girl says, she wonders why the names of singers and actors always come last when the singers and actors are women? Also, why do they give women parts to act that mean nothing, make them represent such silly women—such women as are never seen in real life?" (5). This last thought suggests that once girls start expressing their thoughts, *representations* of women will play a key role in the movement for political and social equality. This attention to the relationship between representations of women and political change is significant given the space *Shafts* and *The Woman's Herald* devoted to reviews of literature.

For some authors negotiating feminist realism, spoken word became the dominant method for representing woman's agency. George Gissing, whose 1893 novel *The Odd Women* directly engages feminist discourse through the intentionally single Rhoda Nunn, was praised by feminist periodicals for his use of dialogue in representations of woman's agency. Mona Caird, whose *Daughters of Danaus* (1894) features extensive philosophical debates about the rights of women, was also admired for her attention to the dialogue of her female characters. In this chapter I examine how these two authors employed dialogue in order to represent assertions of agency via spoken word. Feminist periodicals, I argue, were correct to emphasize Gissing's use of dialogue rather than his use of internal perspective, since his attempts to represent assertions of agency through internal perspective—especially in *In the Year of the Jubilee* (1894)—fall short of the feminist ideal. This failure can be traced to Gissing's early ideals about literary representation: that dialogue was the key narrative strategy for building character. Caird achieves a better balance of increased consciousness and spoken word in *Daughters of Danaus,* and *Shafts* and *The Woman's Herald* recognized Caird as the more successful author: they ran numerous articles about her work and only an occasional article about Gissing's work. Still, both Caird and Gissing create characters who struggle to translate resistance through spoken word into resistance through action, so their heroines often do not fulfill the feminist ideal as well as they might. Nevertheless, both authors were given credit for their attempts to represent woman's agency, showing that the feminist aesthetic remained flexible and inclusive.

Gissing's work was not reviewed by *Shafts,* but it was discussed by *The Woman's Herald,* whose anonymous reviewer believed *The Odd Women* to be at least as realist as Grand's *The Heavenly Twins.* As Gissing himself recognized, this was the supreme compliment considering the regularity with which *The Woman's Herald* wrote about and praised Grand's novel (Gissing, *Collected Letters* 120). In addition, the reviewer praises Gissing's tendency to build character through dialogue rather than through action, indicating that Gissing had fulfilled the feminist realist aesthetic to at least some degree: "The action proceeds in the slow, seemingly inevitable manner which marks the movement of nature itself. The characters have not to subordinate themselves to the necessities of the plot, but work out their destinies in a manner perfectly compatible with their circumstances and their individualities" (Anonymous, "Study in Average" 281). Then, describing the details of the story—the struggle of the Madden sisters to find alternatives to marriage and the assistance of their feminist friend Rhoda Nunn in this endeavor—the reviewer emphasizes Gissing's use of dialogue, especially as a means for women to discuss the conditions of their lives.

First, the reviewer cites a conversation between two of the sisters, Virginia and Alice Madden, who worry over how to live on the meager inheritance they have from their father, who taught them never to work but to rely on the men in their lives for financial support. Then the reviewer turns to Rhoda Nunn, who not only talks about the desperate conditions of women's lives but tries to do something to change these conditions. Writes the reviewer, "This Miss Nunn is the most striking character in the book—one of the most striking characters in recent fiction. . . . A keen opponent of marriage, she was never tired of preaching the personal completeness of every woman; and the conversations in which she shares are as suggestive and stimulating as anything upon the subject of woman's position that has lately appeared" (281). The reviewer iterates the importance of dialogue when summing up the novel, stating that it is the "conversations"—which "although almost entirely polemical, seem, nevertheless, for some reason, never to overstep the limits of the novelist's art"—that are the most important aspect of the book (282). Although this particular review does not articulate the *three-part* feminist definition for successful representation of woman's agency, the attention given in this review to dialogue illustrates the importance of particular narrative strategies to the realist approach advocated by feminist critics.

In addition to receiving a review from *The Woman's Herald*, *The Odd Women* was reviewed by Clementina Black in *The Illustrated London News*, and this review also highlights Gissing's ability to represent women expressing agency through spoken word. Black not only addresses Gissing's use of dialogue to promote a feminist message to readers but also connects his use of dialogue to other methods of expressing agency, including increased consciousness and physical actions. Black opens her review with the statement that *The Odd Women* is "a distinct advance upon anything which [Gissing] has done yet" (222), in part because he covers such a wide array of women, some of whom have unhappy lives but others who "make the bright spot in a gloomy picture" because they are able to work together and support themselves (223). Black then draws attention to Gissing's use of dialogue, especially between these successful women, as one of the real achievements of the novel. She writes:

In the conversations of these women is contained the argumentative kernel of the book; and Mr. Gissing has succeeded in the feat, so often attempted in the modern novel, but so seldom achieved, of giving to discussions of social problems the twofold interest attaching to them in real life—an interest, namely, in the thing said, for its own sake, and an interest in it as a display of character on the part of the person saying it. (223)

In other words, dialogue becomes a way of building character, though, as Black points out, it also retains its own worth—in this case, the ability to express a feminist message.

Despite her praise of Gissing's use of dialogue, Black takes issue with his characterization of Rhoda Nunn's actions as the novel progresses. While the conversations between Rhoda and her unconventional love-interest Everard Barfoot, who favors a free union over traditional marriage, illustrate Gissing's ability to bring the "twofold interest" to readers, Black is disappointed in Gissing's failure to bring these two characters together in what she believes would be a "real marriage—that is to say, an equal union, in which each would respect the freedom and individuality of the other, and in which each would find the completest development" (223). Gissing's description of Rhoda's actions, especially her immature attitude when she learns that Everard has engaged in suspect behavior with another woman in the past, is "gravely out of character" (223). Further, in making Rhoda a woman who cannot bring herself to admit her immaturity to Everard and to accept his love, Gissing depicts Rhoda as "an ungenerous, a selfish, and especially an undisciplined woman, and it is out of keeping with all the previous history of Rhoda Nunn" (223).

While Black thinks that the better ending to the novel would be for Rhoda and Everard to marry, she believes Gissing's "hatred" of the "happy ending" prevents him from writing such a conclusion. "It would almost seem as if hatred of the conventional 'happy ending' had led Mr. Gissing to that same sacrifice of truthful portraiture into which so many of his predecessors have been betrayed by their love of it" (224). In questioning Gissing's depiction of Rhoda's actions, Black, though unmindful of the way in which Rhoda consistently values work over a personal relationship with a man, does draw attention to the connection between consciousness, spoken word, and physical actions in expressions of woman's agency. It is Rhoda's intellect, Black suggests, that Gissing forgets in the course of writing the novel, and it is the connection between spoken word and action, which enables women to create new definitions of already existing institutions such as marriage, that Gissing fails to achieve in *The Odd Women*.

Both Black's review of *The Odd Women* and the review in *The Woman's Herald*, then, thoroughly acknowledge Gissing's effective use of dialogue to represent woman's agency, an approach tied to Gissing's more general ideal about building all characters through dialogue. Gissing's letters to his brother Algernon, also a novelist, show that he valued dialogue over other narrative strategies, especially narratorial comment. In one letter, Gissing advises Algernon to avoid direct narratorial comment, stating, "[T]he secret of art in fiction is the *indirect*. Nothing must be told too plumply" (*Collected Letters* 2:178). He also tells Algernon exactly how he can achieve this style in his own work. Instead of beginning his story with long descriptions of characters told by the narrator, he should allow dialogue between two characters to start the story: "Let it [the first chapter of the story] be the first day after Lucy's arrival . . . and let Miss F. be describing the *associations* of the scene to her . . . This will help to give her character. . . . I would in short let this first conversation contain only *hints* of the personal circumstances of each. . . . Now, only in the *next* chapter I would describe Lucy and her circumstances in detail" (178). More generally, Gissing advised Algernon: "[U]nless you have some very extraordinary character, it's better not to give a set description of face, etc., but to let hints come out now and then" (178). This feedback from Gissing illustrates his commitment to limiting narratorial comment and allowing characters to develop through dialogue with each other instead.

Gissing's ideal about realistic depiction of characters was not far from the feminist ideal, at least one aspect of it, since both valued the use of dialogue. Still, one important point about the feminist realist aesthetic is that dialogue alone cannot adequately represent expression of woman's agency; instead, the dialogue of women is intimately tied to increased consciousness and description of characters' actions to create social change. Nevertheless, when reviewing *The Odd Women*, *The Woman's Herald* perhaps is not as faithful to its own ideal as it might be. The reviewer could say more about the other narrative strategies, including internal perspective, employed by Gissing, for, as my analysis below shows, he does achieve a fairly strong balance of internal perspective, dialogue, and description of characters' actions in the novel. Further, Clementina Black's review could, by looking more closely at the ways in which specific narrative strategies work, uncover a more sympathetic reading of Gissing's characterization of Rhoda's actions, since Rhoda's commitment to her work over a personal relationship with Everard can be admired by readers.

If we turn to analysis of *The Odd Women*, we can see how these feminist reviews might have been more complete in their discussions of the novel. *The Odd Women* is remarkable, from a feminist perspective, for its depiction of a range of issues important to late-Victorian progressive women: the issue of the superfluous woman, who could not marry even if she wanted to due to the unbalanced ratio between women and men; the problem of finding work for women who could not marry but also the rise of new professional opportunities for women, such as secretarial work; and, perhaps most importantly, the emphasis on organizing women in order to expand the opportunities open to them. Central to the exploration of these issues, of course, are the primary characters in the novel: the Madden sisters, their long-time friend Rhoda Nunn, and her mentor Miss Barfoot. The Madden sisters, who have been raised by a father who believes that they should not work but must be supported by men, face both personal and social struggles after the death of their father, since most of them are unlikely to receive marriage proposals. While the youngest daughter, Monica, does have the opportunity to marry, the older sisters, Virginia and Alice, are left with only a small inheritance on which they must scrape by. Fortunately, their friend Rhoda Nunn, who even as a child resisted cultural norms that support the subordination of women and who has started a training school for middle-class women with Miss Barfoot, offers assistance. Still, Rhoda has obstacles of her own to conquer. Faced with the opportunity to fall in love with Miss Barfoot's cousin, Everard, she is caught between her attraction to Everard and her feminist ideals, which tell her that to fall in love with Everard is to betray her commitment to living in the world on her own, as an odd woman.

With these dilemmas at its core, *The Odd Women* serves as a fine example of the successful combination of narrative strategies to represent assertion of woman's agency, at least through Rhoda if not the other female characters in the book. Gissing employs an especially tight rhetorical style in this novel, one that is not present in many of his other novels concerned with woman's agency: *The Unclassed* (1884), *The Nether World* (1889), and *In the Year of the Jubilee* (1894). While the connections between the various methods of asserting agency and their corresponding narrative strategies tend to be loose in these novels, in *The Odd Women* Gissing's use of Rhoda's internal perspective is consistently and effectively tied to resistance through spoken word and physical actions.

To understand how Gissing achieves the feminist aesthetic, we need to look more closely at the way in which he constructed the novel, using the various methods of expressing agency. Initially, Gissing's use of Rhoda's internal perspective is sparse, but this makes sense given that Rhoda is presented as a woman of action, already confident in her feminist beliefs and focused on implementing these beliefs in a practical manner through her work at Miss Barfoot's school. Even as a child Rhoda shows her tendency to resist cultural norms that support the subordination of women by resisting Mr. Madden's discourse that women should be financially supported by men and not play a role in public life (3–4). When the Madden sisters meet Rhoda again as an adult, it is clear that her strong beliefs about women's independence remain. When Rhoda suggests that the sisters use their inheritance to open a school, Virginia recognizes Rhoda's commitment to women's independence by saying that her conversation with Rhoda is "the first time in her life that she had spoken with a woman daring enough to think and act for herself" (26). Virginia's assessment of Rhoda as a woman who thinks and acts indicates that representation of Rhoda's thoughts through internal perspective is not necessary at this point in the novel: her increased consciousness is implied through her suggestion that the women open a school.

Though there are brief instances of Rhoda's internal perspective in the scene between her and Virginia, and also when Rhoda and Miss Barfoot argue over the "character" of Bella Royston, a pupil who has left the school and become a "kept" woman (61–68), Gissing waits until Rhoda questions her own feminist beliefs to bring in her internal perspective in a sustained manner. Further, most of the early scenes focusing on their relationship are told through Everard's internal perspective, and it is only after Rhoda's relationship with Everard has progressed significantly and Rhoda has developed a "plan" to convince Everard to ask for traditional marriage rather than a free union that Gissing begins to use Rhoda's internal perspective on a regular basis.

In chapter 14, appropriately titled "Motives Meeting" because it highlights Rhoda's and Everard's motives in pursuing a relationship, Gissing shifts from developing Rhoda's character through speech and action to focusing on her internal perspective. In this chapter Rhoda finally decides that she will let Everard pursue her but only because she wants to reject him and strengthen her own belief in living the life of the odd woman. At the beginning of the first sustained section of narration through Rhoda's internal perspective, she reflects, "No man had ever made love to her; no man, to her knowledge, had ever been tempted to do so. In certain moods she derived satisfaction from this thought, using it to strengthen her life's purpose" (166). After a long monologue about her "complex" feelings for Everard, in which she recognizes that she at least "regard[s] him with sexual curiosity," Rhoda again reflects, thinking she can make Everard ask her to marry him in the traditional manner rather than in the free union he prefers:

> [I]f he loved her, these theories would sooner or later be swept aside; he would plead with her to become his legal wife. To that point she desired to bring him. Offer what he might, she would not accept it. . . . To reject a lover in so many respects desirable, whom so many women might envy her, would fortify her self-esteem, and enable her to go forward in the chosen path with firmer tread. (168)

This sustained moment of internal perspective makes clear the plan Rhoda has in mind, and from this moment Gissing effectively couples internal perspective with direct speech and action, as Rhoda resists cultural norms that support the subordination of women through her relationship with Everard. For example, when Everard confesses his love to Rhoda in chapter 17, titled "The Triumph," she firmly rejects him, politely saying, "It is usual, I think—if one may trust the novels—for a woman to return thanks when an offer of this kind has been made to her. So—thank you very much, Mr. Barfoot" (207). When Barfoot refuses to accept her polite rejection, begging her to speak to him in "plain, honest words" (207) and claiming that it is her "womanly resistance" that appeals to him (209), she declares that she "never shall [marry]," for "[i]t would interfere hopelessly with the best part of my life," her life at the school (209). These moments of spoken resistance, as well as her act of standing up so Everard will leave (210), are coupled with Rhoda's internal perspective, which explains to readers her thoughts after Everard has left. "She had gained her wish, had enjoyed her triumph. A raising of the finger and Everard Barfoot would marry her. Assured of that, she felt a new contentment in life" (213). In this scene, Gissing effectively combines all three narrative strategies in order to represent a woman who is thinking about her cultural status and whose speech and actions follow from this awareness.

This effective combination of narrative strategies appears at other times in the novel, as in chapter 21, "Towards the Decisive," in which Rhoda's internal perspective reveals that she suspects Monica Madden of having an affair with Everard (when she is actually having an affair with another man, Bevis) and prompts Rhoda to take action by going to confront Monica (249). It also appears in chapter 25, "The Fate of the Ideal," in which Rhoda's internal perspective reveals her decision to spend time with Everard, despite her continued suspicion he is having an affair with Monica, in order to convince him to propose to her (291). These instances of dialogue and/or description of actions coupled with internal perspective serve to iterate the first sustained instance of Rhoda's internal perspective, in which her plan to control Everard becomes central to her thoughts. Even if Rhoda's plan makes her an unsympathetic character, as Clementina Black's review suggests, I believe that it is possible to admire Rhoda for her commitment to her feminist principles. Further, Black's criticism of Gissing's decision to make Rhoda inflexible needs to be contextualized; at the end of the novel, Rhoda seems to have adopted the position of the purity feminist, and that may help explain why Rhoda acts as she does.

Ultimately, I believe that Gissing is more effective than the reviews in *The Woman's Herald* and *The Illustrated London News* give him credit for, but, because Gissing did not achieve such an effective combination of narrative strategies in earlier novels, it is understandable that the feminist reviewers might not give him as much praise as he perhaps deserved. In fact, *The Odd Women* is the only Gissing novel reviewed by the feminist press, and the reviewer for *The Woman's Herald* believed that the novel would "greatly enhance" Gissing's reputation (281), suggesting that the reviewer did not consider Gissing's previous novels to have met even one aspect of the feminist aesthetic. Still, despite ignoring other ways in which Gissing fulfilled the feminist aesthetic, the feminist press did praise Gissing more than did the mainstream press, which generally characterized the novel as journalistic rather than artistic and as more of a "polemic" than the critics cared for.[1]

After *The Odd Women* Gissing's representation of women according to the feminist ideal is less impressive, and an examination of his technique in *In the Year of the Jubilee,* the novel written immediately after *The Odd Women,* shows why *The Odd Women* is the most successful of his novels in terms of the feminist aesthetic. Characterized by Gissing as a novel which was a "reversion" to his "old style" of writing and in which he wanted to avoid the "Woman Question" (*Collected Letters* 5:114, 229), *Jubilee* points out the problems, from the feminist perspective, of relying *too* heavily on dialogue and ignoring the link between spoken word and increased consciousness. As we know from our analysis of Grand and Hardy, if a female character does not possess increased consciousness in general, she is less likely to have the feminist consciousness needed to use spoken word to resist cultural norms that support the subordination of women. While the main female character in *Jubilee,* Nancy Lord, initially exhibits some degree of increased consciousness, by the end of the novel Gissing's commitment to building characters primarily through dialogue seems to overpower any interest in Nancy's consciousness, and the result is a novel in which the female character cannot assert agency effectively.

In the Year of the Jubilee is not unlike *The Odd Women* in that it features a female character, Nancy, who must decide whether she is willing to participate in a free union rather than a traditional marriage with the primary male character, in this case a man named Lionel Tarrant. The difference between Nancy and Rhoda, however, is that while Rhoda has already firmly established her own views on women's rights when the novel begins, Nancy is less sure of her views. She does know that her current life—that of a typical middle-class young woman whose father believes that her education is irrelevant and her future depends on a good marriage—is dissatisfying. Toward the beginning of the novel the narrator paints a picture of Nancy as "a well-grown girl of three and twenty, with the complexion and the mould of form which indicate, whatever else, habitual nourishment on good and plenteous food" (12). From the narrator's point of view, Nancy's life seems to be just fine, but once the perspective shifts from the narrator to Nancy herself, a somewhat different picture of her life in Camberwell emerges: "Nancy hated it. She would have preferred to live even in a poor and grimy street which neighboured the main track of business and pleasure. Here she had spent as much of her life as she remembered,—from the end of her third year" (14). Much of Nancy's dissatisfaction can be traced to her father's expectations for her, and as he imposes his plan that she will be supported by him until she marries his business partner, Samuel Barmby, Nancy realizes that this way of living is unacceptable to her. While she is unsure about how to live her life as an independent woman, she does know one thing: "All she knew was, that she wished to live, and not merely to vegetate" (14).

Given this early focus on Nancy's awareness of the conditions of her life and Gissing's use of Nancy's internal perspective at the beginning of the novel, one expects that Nancy might assert agency as strongly as Rhoda does in *The Odd Women*. Furthermore, since Nancy's internal perspective introduces the relationship between her and Lionel, in contrast to the relationship between Everard and Rhoda in *The Odd Women* where Everard's internal perspective introduces the relationship, it is possible for readers to believe that *Jubilee* will be even more feminist than Gissing's previous work. Still, as soon as Lionel proposes marriage (he will later suggest the free union to Nancy), his internal perspective begins to dominate. This shift in internal perspective validates the charge by some literary critics— such as Robert Selig, John Sloan, and Barbara Harman—that Gissing allows a male character to usurp the power of his female protagonist, and from this point to the end of the novel the struggle between Nancy and Lionel (and their perspectives on marriage) intensifies and is played out primarily through combative dialogue.[2] Likewise, the link between Nancy's internal perspective and her use of spoken word to resist cultural norms that support the subordination of women breaks down at this point in the novel. Early on, Nancy attempts to resist cultural norms via a clear link between increased consciousness and spoken word (17–18, 27–29), but once she becomes involved with Lionel, her resistance is strictly through spoken word rather than through a combination of more than one method.

Nancy's spoken resistance is best divided into two parts: her resistance occurring before Lionel goes to the Bahamas and "abandons" her, and that occurring after Lionel's return to England when the couple attempts to negotiate a nontraditional marriage. Before Lionel's departure Nancy's resistance is fairly muted, in part because she is falling in love with Lionel and finds his nontraditional perspectives about marriage charming. Also, despite Lionel's objections to traditional marriage, he acts as though he will marry, making it unnecessary for Nancy to resist too much at this point. Still, the occasional moments of resistance by Nancy early in their relationship are important because these moments establish the dynamic that will characterize their relationship once they attempt to negotiate a nontraditional marriage later in the story. For example, when Lionel visits Nancy while she is on holiday at Teignmouth, they argue over their perspectives on education, an issue directly connected to women's independence (120–26). Although Nancy ultimately submits to Lionel's opinion about education, as well as many other opinions expressed by him as he courts her, her resistance becomes much stronger when she learns that he is going to leave England for the Bahamas shortly after marrying her, even though she is pregnant. She pleads with Lionel to stay in England, even if it means that she must come clean about her marriage to him and lose the money her father has bequeathed her on the condition she not marry before age twenty-six (195–96).

The conflict set up between Lionel and Nancy, especially in terms of their differing views about relationships, carries over to the resistance Nancy exerts after Lionel finally returns to England, a year after he has left and long after she has decided that he has abandoned her. Nancy's patience with Lionel's unconventional views of marriage vanishes after one of Nancy's neighbors learns of Nancy's pregnancy and confronts her about it. In a moment of self-reflection, expressed in one of the few sections in which Nancy's internal perspective dominates, Nancy comes to the conclusion that she has never been Lionel's wife but only his mistress. "[S]he looked back in the stern spirit of a woman judging another's frailty. . . . Tarrant never respected her, never thought of her as a woman whom he could seriously woo and wed. She had a certain power over his emotions . . . but his love would not endure the test of absence. . . . One night about this time she said to herself: 'I was his mistress, never his wife'" (290). Nancy recognizes that the "angel/whore" binary has been applied to her, since she can be either Lionel's "angel" (wife) or his "whore" (mistress). Following this realization, Nancy's resistance to Lionel after he has returned is not just resistance to the cultural norm that women should be subordinate to their husbands, the "angel in the house" trap, but resistance also to the idea that there are only two kinds of women: "angels" and "whores."

Aware of the deeper implications of Lionel's unconventional attitudes toward marriage, Nancy adopts a new strategy for resisting Lionel's ideal. When Lionel insists on separate living quarters, Nancy counters his ideal with practical solutions—first, that they live together because it will be less expensive than if they live apart (408), and, second, that they purchase a larger house so that Lionel will not feel as though his freedom has been taken away (409). But in each case Lionel rejects Nancy's suggestions and characterizes them as impractical, the result of idealizing marriage and of an unhealthy attachment to social convention. It is arguable that Nancy has developed an unhealthy attachment to social convention, for she wants a traditional marriage, but it is also arguable that she has not given up the ideal of individual freedom over social convention but has altered her definition of freedom as the result of having a child. In fact, Nancy believes the freedom Lionel wants is impossible for a woman with a child. In a conversation that takes place shortly before her argument with Lionel, Nancy says to Mary Woodruff, their long-time housekeeper and now Mr. Lord's companion, "It comes to this. Nature doesn't intend a married woman to be anything *but* a married woman. . . . [S]he must either be the slave of husband and children, or defy her duty. She can have no time to herself, no thoughts for herself. . . . I should like to revolt against it, yet I feel revolt to be silly. One might as well revolt against being born a woman instead of a man" (404).

Despite Nancy's frustration, she does make one concrete attempt to speak out publicly about the conditions of her life and also create some change in her own material conditions by writing a novel about her experience. Were she to become the successful woman writer she imagines she might become (298), Nancy would be on her way to solid independence, which might allow her to support herself and her child without Lionel's involvement. Although Nancy presents her decision to write the novel as one aimed at helping *Lionel* rather than herself and her child, it is clear that she understands the financial opportunities possible through professional authorship. Not surprisingly, Lionel feels threatened by such opportunities. Not only does he return to Nancy's lodgings after only four days (instead of the usual ten they take between visits) to discuss her novel, but his rationale for not publishing it is not that it is poorly written but that it is a "private," "domestic" story not meant for public consumption (427–28). Lionel's reaction suggests that he is worried both about the world hearing his wife's story and about the chance Nancy will be published and establish her independence.

Nancy resists Lionel's suppression of the novel, arguing that the qualities that make Lionel want to suppress the book from the public are precisely the qualities he admires in published books. After he says that the novel "isn't literature, but a little bit of Nancy's mind and heart," Nancy states, "Lionel, if it is a bit of my mind and heart, it must be a good book. You have often praised books to me just on that account—because they were genuine" (428). In addition, when Lionel suggests to Nancy that she should be focusing on their child instead of writing books, since bearing children is the proper method of creation for women, Nancy again resists, and her reaction reveals her awareness of the power of authorship for women. When Lionel suggests that Nancy simply relax and spend her time reading instead of writing, Nancy says indignantly, "I wanted to *do* something. . . . I have read enough" (429). Nevertheless, Lionel has the last word and succeeds in convincing Nancy to "seal up" her novel and save it for her elderly years, when the two of them will look over it again and "drop a tear from our old dim eyes" (430).

Though Nancy obviously is aware of the conditions of her life and has tried to make changes, eventually she finds that defying Lionel is simply not worth the effort. Their arguments about the possibility of living together, her desire to publish her novel, and other subjects routinely end with Nancy acquiescing to Lionel's "better" judgment. Still, despite Nancy's tendency to resist and then acquiesce, the novel ends in the midst of yet another argument about living together, an ending that is significant precisely for its narrative neutrality. Having received half of her brother's money after he dies of consumption, Nancy once again suggests that she and Lionel purchase a house together. Although Lionel refuses to move in, he does agree to make the appearance of living with Nancy. When she asks, "Will it be known to everybody that we don't live together?" Lionel replies, "Well, by way of example, I should rather like it to be known; but as I know *you* wouldn't like it, let the appearances be as ordinary as you please" (442). Though Nancy wishes that she could push Lionel further, she knows she already has reached a new point with Lionel, one that brings him closer to her ideal for their life together, and the novel ends with this compromise.

Ultimately, Nancy falls short of asserting agency with tangible results, though the end of the novel suggests that she may continue to try to achieve the life she wants rather than always adhering to Lionel's standards. There is a sense that the conflict between them about living together is not over, and, as they continue to debate the issue, there will be small sacrifices by each. While critics such as Selig, Sloan, and Harman are correct to see Nancy's perspective usurped by Lionel's at particular points in the story, and while Constance Harsh is correct to point out those places where the narrator seems to accept Nancy's perspective over Lionel's (see note 2), it is significant that the ending of the novel seems relatively even-handed, weighted toward neither Nancy's nor Lionel's internal perspective. Instead, Gissing uses only dialogue and the briefest description of characters' actions to indicate that Nancy and Lionel will continue to express their differing opinions: "I think we ought to take a house," says Nancy, to which Lionel replies, "You know my view of that matter" (442). While Nancy and Lionel argue, both believe that they have matured as individuals and as a couple, and neither seems ready to give up their method of quarrel and compromise. Still, the presence of Nancy's sustained internal perspective early in the novel—and its disappearance later in the novel—perhaps remains on the minds of some readers as they encounter the conclusion of the novel. Certainly, in abandoning Nancy's internal perspective and relying heavily on dialogue, Gissing takes the middle ground in terms of representing woman's agency in *Jubilee*, especially when one compares the novel to *The Odd Women*. In comparison to *The Odd Women*, the novel by Gissing most thoroughly acknowledged by the feminist periodicals, *Jubilee* had to have been somewhat of a disappointment, so it is not surprising that *Shafts* and *The Woman's Herald* chose not to review it.

๛

Like Gissing's novels, Mona Caird's *The Daughters of Danaus* advocates spoken word as *the* site for expression of agency, and highly philosophical debates about women's rights play an important role in the female protagonist's development. Hadria Fullerton's story centers on her desire to become a musical composer, her disastrous marriage to Hubert Temperley, and her struggle to find ways to balance her need for individual liberty with the expectation she will fulfill marriage and family duties. While Hadria possesses feminist consciousness and resists cultural norms that support the subordination of women, this resistance is expressed primarily through spoken word rather than the ideal combination of increased consciousness, spoken word, and action. Nevertheless, while dialogue is privileged over other narrative strategies in this novel, Caird does balance resistance through dialogue with at least some attention to Hadria's internal perspective and with some acts of resistance, which results in a slightly more balanced representation of woman's agency than we see in Gissing's *Jubilee*.

My reading of *Daughters of Danaus* is informed by the work of the various critics who have explored the views espoused in Caird's nonfiction essays as well as in the philosophical conversations between characters in her novels.[3] It also is informed by the work of Angelique Richardson, who, in "'People Talk a Lot of Nonsense about Heredity': Mona Caird and Anti-Eugenic Feminism," perhaps best articulates the central tension in Caird's nonfictional work, as well as the central tension expressed by Hadria in her conversations with other characters: individual liberty versus submission to circumstance, especially circumstance created by societal expectations regarding gender. As Richardson explains, for Caird, more so than for the social purity feminists such as Sarah Grand, individual liberty was key to the advancement of society, and this clarifies why the marriage contract should remain a private matter rather than a contract controlled by the state. In addition, Richardson cites J. S. Mill, a champion of individual liberty, as a significant influence on Caird, and this influence is confirmed by Caird's acknowledgment of Mill in her interview with *The Woman's Herald,* where she states that he was "the first to help me to bring these thoughts and feelings [about equality for women] into form by his writings" (Anonymous, "Interview: Caird" 421). While there are times when Richardson pushes her reading of Caird's commitment to liberty too far (as when she argues that Caird advocates realistic representation in her own fiction because of this foundational belief), understanding the importance of individual liberty to Caird's philosophy enhances our reading of *Daughters of Danaus,* since many of the conversations Hadria has with others center on the tension between liberty and submission to circumstance (or duty, as Hadria often refers to it).

My reading of the novel is also informed by the fact that Caird herself understood the power of spoken word to resist cultural norms that support the subordination of women, since she often was put in the position of defending her views to the wider public. By looking at how Caird embraced public debate and used spoken word to defend her position on women's rights, one can clearly see that Caird understood the power of dialogue, both verbal and written, to resist cultural norms. Caird is perhaps best known for her role in the "Is Marriage a Failure?" debate, started by the *The Daily Telegraph* in August 1888 in response to Caird's article "Marriage" which had been published in *The Westminster Review* the same month. In "Marriage," Caird argues that modern marriage dates back only as far as the Reformation and is a result of historical forces, especially the rise of the bourgeoisie. She shows how modern marriage, which she believes to be a complete failure, destroys any chance for individual liberty; when women marry, they simply replace a world in which their liberty has already been denied for an equally restrictive world. Ultimately, Caird advocates a new form of marriage, one that is based on a free contract between the two people involved and one that takes into account each person's needs and desires. In describing this new form of marriage, Caird emphasizes that it will be possible only when women have economic independence and when both women and men have become more thoroughly educated about sexual matters.

After *The Daily Telegraph* responded to Caird's article by asking, "Is Marriage a Failure?," 27,000 people wrote in to give their opinions on the subject, and it was only after the *The Daily Telegraph* called for an end to the letter writing that the responses ceased (Quilter 2–3).[4] Though Caird herself felt that most readers had not addressed the *real* issue—"marriage as an institution historically and philosophically considered" (Quilter 40)—and perhaps had not even read her article, the article and subsequent debate did open up discussion of marriage issues within the general public, and Caird continued to debate this subject and others related to women's rights throughout the *fin de siècle*. For example, Caird played an important role in the "Wild Women" debate of 1891 and 1892, which originated with a series of articles in *The Nineteenth Century* by Eliza Lynn Linton, in which she criticized the modern woman. In May 1892 Caird published "A Defence of the So-Called Wild Women," in which she stated that the personal attacks Linton had made against the modern woman were generalizations unworthy of response. Caird preferred to focus on the ways women could achieve individual liberty, especially through economic opportunity and stability.

Though Caird's "dialogue" with the public regarding "Marriage" and "Wild Women" was staged in writing, Caird herself seems to have treated these written dialogues in much the same way she would treat verbal debate, and it is clear that she had certain expectations about how debate in the public sphere should operate. In response to the letters written to *The Daily Telegraph* as part of the "Is Marriage a Failure?" discussion, Caird notes in her solicited reply to the letters that she had assumed the "candid and intelligent" reader when she published "Marriage" but now realized that perhaps this type of reader is a "mythical personage" (Quilter 39). Further, when she responded to Linton's "Wild Women" articles, she refused to discuss the personal attacks Linton had made against modern women because she believed that to do so would reduce the debate to a "simple school-room form of discussion, consisting in flat contradiction, persistently repeated until the energies give out" ("Defence" 811).

Caird's expectation—that debate in the public eye would be intelligent and informed—can be traced, I believe, to her involvement in club life of the late-Victorian period, where written and verbal dialogue were intertwined and where club meetings often centered on debates about specific social concerns. Caird was active in more than one suffrage society: she belonged to and served on the central councils of the Women's Franchise League and the Women's Emancipation Union.[5] These societies advocated the use of both spoken and written word to resist cultural norms, and Caird herself adopted both methods. She wrote two articles about suffrage (both titled "Mrs. Mona Caird on Women's Suffrage") for *The Woman's Herald,* and she articulated her support for suffrage in verbal dialogue with reporters. Among the questions asked of her during an interview with *The Woman's Herald* in 1890: "Do you support women's suffrage?" To which she responded, "Of course I am ardently in favour of the vote for all women, irrespective of condition and circumstance. . . . Men and women should have equal rights in every respect, and the same laws should apply equally to both" (Anonymous, "Interview: Caird" 421).

Caird also was a member of the Pioneer Club, which held debates on a variety of topics, including the rights of women, once a week. The club, founded by Emily Massingbred in 1892, had a number of prominent literary women in its membership, including Sarah Grand and Henrietta Stannard. Margaret Sibthorp also was a member, and Lady Henry Somerset was one of the speakers at a debate over suffrage in 1893 (Crawford 126–27; Anonymous, "Pioneer Club Records" 251; Anonymous, "Pioneer Club" Mar. 1893, 12). The debates held by the club featured a combination of written and verbal dialogue, with a speaker opening the debate by reading a paper on the subject and a verbal debate following the paper. Interestingly, the club sometimes took action on the item discussed by holding a vote at the end of the evening to see where the membership stood on a particular issue. Like the suffrage societies, the Pioneer Club advocated a combination of written and verbal dialogue that seems to have shaped Caird's expectations about debate in the public sphere.[6]

Finally, Caird was loosely associated with the Men and Women's Club, started by the socialist and eventually eugenicist Karl Pearson in 1885 to facilitate serious discussion about the relations of the sexes. As Lucy Bland, in *Banishing the Beast: English Feminism and Sexual Morality, 1885–1914* (1995), indicates, the club was made up of a select group of men and women and had very strict guidelines about how to approach the topics under discussion. Most importantly, the club insisted on "objective" rather than emotional debate, and topics had to be considered from a "historical and scientific" perspective and not from a "theological" perspective (4–5).[7] This characterization resonates with Caird's comment in her solicited reply to the letters in *The Daily Telegraph* that her aim in "Marriage" had been to consider marriage as an institution "historically and philosophically," rather than emotionally as many of the letter writers had. To highlight the difference between emotional and intelligent debate, Caird cites people who talked about some specific aspect of their home life as an example of not engaging the subject matter seriously:

> Perhaps it is through a natural bias that I fail to detect the arguments intended to be conveyed by the many interesting details of family life which this controversy has brought to light, by picturesque and charming descriptions of English homes, or even by the communications from affectionate parents about the colour of Tommy's eyes and Tommy's thoroughly excusable predilection for jam. One feels powerfully drawn towards Tommy, who, I am sure, is a delicious child (this in genuine good faith); only when one tries to rise from the contemplation of Tommy to the subject of marriage as an insti-

tution, historically and philosophically considered, the connection
between the two subjects becomes annoyingly obscure. (Quilter
39–40)

Caird's point seems to be that an emotional response is understandable but
does not have a place in public debate.

Though Caird was not an official member of the Men and Women's
Club, she was "seriously considered" for membership in the first year the
club met but was not asked to join because Olive Schreiner (the author of
The Story of an African Farm and a member of the club) considered her too
narrow-minded and prejudiced against men to be a part of the group
(Bland 126). Still, Caird attended the May 1887 meeting of the club, during which birth control was the topic of discussion (126), so she experienced the typical method of debate used by the club. Further, members of
the club recognized Caird's reliance on the group's ideas in her own writing: Maria Sharpe, one of the female members of the club, believed that
Caird, when writing "Marriage," had drawn on Pearson's *The Ethic of
Freethought* which included the essay on the Woman Question given by
him at the club's first meeting (127).[8]

Given this atmosphere of written and verbal debate in the late-
Victorian period, it is not surprising that Caird's novels devote significant
time to the debate of social issues. Still, since Caird's nonfictional essays
tend to focus on social issues rather than literary approach, it is difficult to
know how Caird herself thought about the connection between her participation in public debates and the role of debate in her novels. Nevertheless,
it is clear that she believes in some connection between social change and
literary representation, since she occasionally discusses literary works in her
essays about social issues and uses them as examples for real-life situations.
For example, in "The Ideal Marriage," which was published in *The
Westminster Review* in 1888, Caird cites Grand's *Ideala,* which had been
used by others to try to refute some of Caird's claims about marriage.
Though Caird agrees that the "general drift" of the novel "cannot be said
to be favourable" to her view of marriage, she recounts the scene in which
Ideala discusses with the Bishop the hypothetical case of a woman signing
a marriage contract, only to learn later that she was kept "in ignorance of
the most important clause in it" (620). Caird argues that Ideala is justifi-
ably enraged that such a thing might occur: "Surely no one will seriously
deny that Ideala's principle is perfectly right, and that to substitute a legal
form for the sentiment that possesses the real binding force between two
persons, is to found our kingdom upon sand, to base our social world
upon a mockery and a sham" (621).

Lyn Pykett rightly warns against equating Caird's nonfiction essays and her fictional work because Caird's nonfiction essays tend to present one voice on social issues whereas the fictional work tends to be more multi-vocal, allowing for disagreement on social issues between characters (Pykett, "Cause" 140). Still, Caird's use of Grand's novel to defend her own position in this nonfiction essay illustrates her belief that the two genres do influence each other, and the connection between social change and literary representation is also seen in Caird's essay "Phases of Human Development" in which she discusses Henrik Ibsen's *A Doll's House* as an example of the ways in which society marginalizes women who resist the traditional ideal. Of Nora, Caird writes:

> It is true that under present conditions complete resistance to aggression is not really possible to a woman. There are methods of compulsion which scarcely admit of defiance. She can be placed, if her resistance grows desperate, between the devil and the deep sea: between the alternatives of submission in marriage to whatever may be required of her,—injuries and insults if need be,—or the surrender of her children, perhaps into hands that she regards, as of all others, the most unfit to train them. This is the weapon by which many a wife has been forced to obedience, as by the application of the thumbscrew. The feeling that was aroused in the public mind by the character of Ibsen's "Nora," shows what a mother would have to contend with, in popular sentiment, who dared the terrors of the social torture-chamber, and thus threatened the efficacy of this venerable instrument of government. (210)

Clearly, Caird is using Nora as an example of what some real-life women encountered in their struggles to balance motherhood with the impulse for freedom and nonsubordination. When she writes, "This is the weapon by which many a wife has been forced to obedience," she makes the connection between Nora's experience and those of real-life Victorian women.

Further, the connection between social change and literary representation is seen in Caird's "The Duel of the Sexes," which was published in *The Fortnightly Review* in 1905. Here, Caird argues that women who have benefited from the women's movement often criticize or betray it through what they write and say about the relations of the sexes. As examples Caird cites Pearl Craigie ("John Oliver Hobbes"), Mary Harrison ("Lucas Malet"), and even Elizabeth Robins, who would become the first president of the Women Writers' Suffrage League in 1908. Caird believes that Robins betrays the movement through her novel *A Dark Lantern* (1905), which depicts the "old order of sex-relationship in its most brutal, least decorative form," since it features a heroine who "rejects the love of dozens of men, more or less true and chivalrous, to lavish hers upon a man who gratuitously insults her every time he opens his mouth" (109–10). Caird's criticism of Robins's novel suggests that Caird connected representations of women to social conditions endured by real-life women and believed that authors had a responsibility to portray the relations of the sexes in a particular light. She claims that Robins "betrays sympathy with the submission of the heroine" to her cruel husband and that "no 'emancipated' writer would have dared to paint it [the relationship between the heroine and her husband] in such colours!" (110).

Still, Caird herself recognized, at least early in her career, the problems of associating too closely the ideas expressed in her nonfiction essays with literary representations. In the preface to her novel *The Wing of Azrael*, published in 1889 shortly after *The Daily Telegraph* debate, Caird is careful to separate the two genres. She begins the preface by stating, "Much has been said for and against the writing of 'novels with a purpose,'" and she distinguishes the novel with a purpose, the "work of fiction whose motive is not the faithful rendering of an impression from without, but the illustration of a thesis," from the novel that does not have a decided purpose but depicts an impression of the world (vii). The writer who produces the novel with a purpose, Caird argues, has "adopted the form of a novel for the purposes of an essay, and has no real right to the name" of novel. Still, Caird believes that "[s]o long as there is true consistency in the actions and the thoughts of the characters, so long as they act and think because circumstances and innate impulse leave them no alternative, they cannot be fitted into exact correspondence with any view or made into the advocates of any cause" (vii). In defining the novel without a purpose so specifically—as one that has consistency of character but acknowledges that characters react to the circumstances of life in a variety of different ways—Caird creates the room for her work to be accepted on artistic terms rather than labeled as too polemic.

In fact, in the preface Caird goes on to describe the process of writing novels as one in which the writer must be selective to at least some degree (rather than producing an exact photograph of life), yet this selective process should not be confused for a "purpose." It is possible to be selective yet also avoid letting a polemic overpower the artistic. Further, at the end of the preface Caird directly states that she has described "the art of fiction in order to show as convincingly as possible that however much this book may be thought to deal with the question so recently discussed, there is no intention on the writer's part to make it serve a polemical 'purpose' or to advocate a cause" (ix). Caird likely was aware that readers of her novel would still have the question posed in the *The Daily Telegraph* on their minds, and she wanted to discourage them from attaching the label "novel with a purpose" based on the controversy over her "Marriage" article. While Angelique Richardson believes that Caird's preface reflects her personal commitment to individual liberty (196–97), I believe that Caird is displaying a certain degree of market savvy. Like other writers of the late-Victorian period, including Sarah Grand (who made similar claims in the preface to her collection of short stories *Our Manifold Nature*), Caird seems to have realized how easily critics could dismiss novels as inartistic and written to serve a purpose. Her separation of the two genres of novel and essay is an attempt to defuse this criticism but not an attempt to separate the two genres so thoroughly as to undermine the power of literature to transform society.

With this context in mind, we can now turn to discussion of *Daughters of Danaus*, which highlights spoken word as a method for asserting agency. Like Rhoda Nunn in *The Odd Women*, Hadria Fullerton possesses an acute awareness of the problem faced by women in the latter part of the nineteenth century: the need for individual liberty set against the expectation that a woman will be dutiful to her family and society, an expectation which may not place much value on her liberty. And, as is the case with Rhoda in *The Odd Women*, Hadria's feminist consciousness is already established when the novel begins, so representation of increased consciousness through internal perspective is not necessary early in the novel. Instead, dialogue can be employed immediately to depict resistance to cultural norms, especially the assumption that men have individual liberty while women sacrifice freedom for the "good" of the community. When Hadria presents a speech to the members of the Preposterous Society, a group that meets in the garret of the family house to discuss philosophical topics, she refutes Emerson's theory that individual will can always overcome circumstances. Pointing out that Emerson does not account for the circumstances faced by girls, Algitha, Hadria's older sister, says, "[T]he conditions of a girl's life of our own class are pleasant enough, but they are stifling, absolutely *stifling;* and not all the Emersons in the world will convince me to the contrary. Emerson never was a girl!" (14). While Hadria is even more doubtful about the ability of girls to overcome these circumstances, she agrees with Algitha's assessment that circumstances, especially the opinions of other people, prevent girls from claiming liberty. She states: "[W]hat a frightful piece of circumstance *that* is to encounter, . . . to have to buy the mere right to one's liberty by cutting through prejudices that are twined in with the very heart-strings of those one loves! Ah! *That* particular obstacle has held many a woman helpless and suffering, like some wretched insect pinned alive to a board throughout a miserable life-time!" (15).

Though Hadria clearly possesses feminist consciousness and the ability to articulate her opposition to cultural norms, the first woman to move from speech to action is not Hadria but Algitha, who shortly after the meeting makes the decision to leave her family to live in London and work with the poor. Algitha's resistance comes first through dialogue with her mother (which is relayed only after the fact) and then through action when she leaves for London by train (42). After Algitha's departure, Hadria's frustration with her own life becomes more palpable (46–47), since she now feels the tension between liberty and duty more keenly, especially when Algitha writes to say that she loves her new life and no longer feels entrapped (48). From this point on, Hadria's conversations with others become a method for working through her frustration and figuring out whether she can overcome the circumstances that prevent her happiness. She asks Valeria Du Prel, a woman writer who has come to the country to relax, her opinion about the tension between individual liberty and sub-mission to circumstances, and Valeria initially encourages Hadria to assert herself, even though she believes that liberty sometimes comes too late to be fully appreciated (62). In addition, Hadria has many conversations with Professor Fortescue, a family friend who also encourages Hadria at least to sustain her individual liberty while doing her duty to her family, even if she cannot resist her duties. Interestingly, once Professor Fortescue enters the debate over liberty versus duty, Valeria takes a more traditional line, even arguing that Hadria should marry Hubert Temperley (with whom she shares an interest in music but who is thoroughly traditional when it comes to gender relations) in order to avoid the isolation Valeria has expe-rienced as a result of asserting agency too often (111).

Still, despite some encouragement from friends, Hadria is unable to assert agency fully. Though she does resist the cultural norms that support her subordination, mainly through dialogue with her mother (109–10), she continues to try to balance individual liberty with her sense of duty to her family. Still, the narration makes it clear that Hadria suffers as the result of this juggling act: "The incessant rising and quelling of her impulse and her courage—like the ebb and flow of tides—represented a vast amount of force not merely wasted, but expended in producing a danger-ous wear and tear upon the system" (109). Hadria also resists cultural norms in her conversations with Temperley about her possible marriage to him (142–43), but eventually the stress of these conversations leads Hadria to accept Temperley's proposal, which he makes at a dance with Hadria's brothers and sister in attendance. The power of Temperley's speech in swaying Hadria to accept this proposal is highlighted by Algitha, who is aware of "Hadria's emotional susceptibility . . . Temperley's convincing faculty, and also Hadria's uneasy feeling that she had done wrong in allowing the practices [playing music with Temperley] to be resumed" (143). Further, it is evident that Hadria's own ability to speak is diminished when she agrees to marry Temperley and returns to the dance "flushed and silent," unable to speak when her brother Fred tries to engage her in conversation (143–44).

Once married, Hadria becomes more and more unhappy, her frustration evident in her conversations with the few people sympathetic to her feelings. For example, in her conversations with Valeria Du Prel, it is evident to Valeria that "Hadria had indeed changed greatly since her marriage, but not in the manner that might have been expected. On the contrary, a closer intimacy with popular social ideals had fired her with a more angry spirit of rebellion" (170). Hadria speaks of the "insult" to women, which began as early as the ancient Greeks when Aristotle wrote that "a wife ought to shew herself even more obedient to the rein than if she entered the house as a purchased slave" and when a woman who "blazed up in anger at the well-meant speech [of Aristotle] . . . would have astonished and grieved her contemporaries" (170–71). Interestingly, though Valeria tries to defuse Hadria's rebellion in this scene, the narration reveals that Valeria has used Hadria's rebellious attitude as inspiration in her own writing (170). Caterina, the heroine of Valeria's latest book, expresses many of the same feelings Hadria has, and Caterina becomes the centerpiece of a conversation among Valeria, Hadria, and others about whether or not the method of rebellion employed by Caterina, who leaves her family to live independently, is appropriate (182).

Eventually, Hadria's unhappiness leads her to make the same decision Caterina does, but not before she makes the equally radical decision to adopt the child of a fallen woman, Ellen Jervis, who has died and left the child in the care of a neighbor. Shocked by Hadria's decision, Valeria claims that Caterina would have never made a similar choice and Hadria is "inconsistent" since she often has complained about the burden of mothering her own children (190). Arguing that her own children are part of society's method of "bringing women into line with tradition" but an illegitimate child symbolizes the opportunity to "avenge" the socially imposed death of Ellen (187–89), Hadria takes the child, Martha, to Paris, where they live on their own and Hadria pursues a musical career. Though Hadria's flight to Paris clearly is an *act* of resistance, it is worth noting that this act is prefaced by Hadria's articulation of her plan to go to Paris: she tells everyone exactly what she is going to do before she does it, showing that her *act* of resistance follows from her articulation of this resistance.

Still, when Hadria is forced to return home to England because of her mother's illness, she falls back on resistance to cultural norms through spoken word, since she has been told that *acts* of resistance will ensure her mother's death, and throughout the rest of the novel spoken word remains the primary method for Hadria to assert agency. For example, when Valeria continues to insist that it is better for a woman to accept conventionality than endure the loneliness she has suffered as a result of her unconventional views, Hadria straightforwardly rejects Valeria's advice. To Valeria's insistence that "I believe I should have been happier, if I had married some commonplace worthy in early life, and been the mother of ten children," Hadria replies: "By this time, you or the ten children would have come to some tragic end. . . . [T]hink, Valeria, of ten particular constitutions to grapple with, ten sets of garments to provide, ten series of ailments to combat" (424). Further, when Hadria decides to break with Theobald (the man with whom she has an affair after she returns from Paris) after realizing that she is being untrue to herself by getting involved with him, Theobald assumes that Hadria is a fallen woman. In response, Hadria looks at him with a "cold, miserable smile" and states, "That is really amusing! . . . I should not hold myself responsible to you, for my past, in any case" (434), indicating that his assumption of her fallenness is yet another insult to her.

While dialogue is privileged over other narrative strategies for much of the novel, Caird does balance this dialogue with at least some attention to Hadria's internal perspective, and this ensures that readers have a clearer sense of the motivation behind Hadria's resistance than perhaps they have for Nancy's resistance in *Jubilee*. Hadria's internal perspective first becomes evident in chapter 2 when, the evening following her refutation of Emerson at the meeting of the Preposterous Society, Hadria goes out into the Scottish landscape and reflects more fully on the dilemma of liberty versus duty. Until this point the narrator's internal perspective has been controlling the narrative, but suddenly the narration shifts to Hadria's internal perspective: "In spite of the view that Hadria had expounded in her capacity as lecturer, she *had an inner sense* [my emphasis] that somehow, after all, the will *can* [Caird's emphasis] perform astonishing feats in Fate's despite. Her intellect, rather than her heart, had opposed the philosophy of Emerson" (17). Yet, as the narration continues, it is clear that Hadria must satisfy her intellect as well as her heart, and she wonders: "If the best in human nature were always to be hunted down and extinguished, if the efforts to rise in the scale of being, to bring gifts instead of merely absorbing benefits, were only by a rare combination of chances to escape the doom of annihilation, where was one to turn to for hope, or for a motive for effort?" (17). Hadria seems to find inspiration in the beautiful vision of distant lands which she, her sister, and her brother create through building a bonfire, but, as the material conditions of her life are explained in the novel, rebelling against cultural norms that support the subordination of women seems more difficult than simply recognizing the existence of these cultural conditions.

Hadria's internal perspective emerges more fully after Algitha leaves for London, and Hadria struggles to maintain her individual liberty even as she tries to fulfill her family duties. After her brothers return to school and Valeria and Fortescue end their vacations in the country and return to London, Hadria's isolation increases with their departures, and her internal perspective increases once again. Though Valeria and Fortescue write to Hadria, each giving her the opposite advice about how to maintain her peace of mind, Hadria feels as though it is her responsibility to figure out not only how to maintain the balance between liberty and duty but also how to absorb her misery. In chapter 12, which contains more emphasis on Hadria's internal perspective than earlier chapters in the book, the narration reads: "Hadria did not keep up an active correspondence with Miss Du Prel or with the Professor. She had no idea of adding to the burden of their busy lives, by wails for sympathy. It seemed to her feeble, and contemptible, to ask to be dragged up by their strength, instead of exerting her own. If that were insufficient, why then let her go down, as thousands had gone down before her" (113). These thoughts lead Hadria to consider abandoning music by throwing her scores into a fire, but she talks herself out of succumbing to defeat by recognizing her own strength of will: "You know perfectly well that you are *not* going to give in," she tells herself, and, at the end of this pep-talk, she has convinced herself to fight on, with a "shaft of light" guiding her way (114).

Hadria's internal perspective further increases once her marriage worsens. She makes the decision to adopt Martha, and she leaves Temperley and goes to Paris, the first substantial *act* of resistance she takes. For instance, Caird uses internal perspective when Hadria arrives in Paris and finds herself enjoying her freedom, albeit with some struggle to reconcile this new freedom with her previous mode of living.

> Having been, from childhood, more or less at issue with her surroundings, Hadria had never fully realized their power upon her personality. But now daily a fresh recognition of her continued imprisonment, baffled her attempt to look at things with clear eyes. She struggled to get round and beyond that past-fashioned self. . . . It was sweet to stretch one's cramped wings to the sun, to ruffle and spread them, as a released bird will, but it was startling to find already little stiff habits arisen . . . that made flight in the high air not quite effortless and serene. (307)

Further, Caird uses Hadria's internal perspective to show how she concludes that her affair with Theobald is wrong and that she should *act* to
resist it by ending the relationship with him. After Professor Fortescue,
who has been in Italy trying to regain his health, returns to Craddock to
die among friends, his presence makes Hadria realize that she has made a
mistake in flirting with Theobald. At the end of the day, she sits alone,
thinking about the contrast between the two men.

> The picture of those two men came back to her, in spite of every
> effort to banish it. Professor Fortescue had affected her as if he had
> brought with him a new atmosphere, and disastrous was the result. It
> seemed as if Professor Theobald had suddenly become a stranger to
> her, whom she criticized, whose commonness of fibre, ah me! whose
> coarseness, she saw as she might have seen it in some casual acquain-
> tance. . . . Why, for the first time in her life, did she feel ashamed to
> meet Professor Fortescue? Obviously, it was not because she thought
> he would disapprove of her breaking the social law. It was because she
> had fallen below her own standard, because she had been hypocriti-
> cal with herself, played herself false, and acted contemptibly, hateful-
> ly! (418–19)

Though others, especially Algitha, have expressed the same sentiment to
Hadria (389–90, 395–96), it is only after Fortescue returns that Hadria
recognizes the contrast.

In addition to developing Hadria's internal perspective more thoroughly than Gissing does Nancy's internal perspective in *Jubilee,* Caird also pays
more attention to Hadria's actions than Gissing does to Nancy's. Not only
does she detail Hadria's act of adopting Martha and going to Paris, but she
also elaborates on Hadria's act of *returning* Martha to Theobold because
she refuses to serve as his "deputy." This scene is particularly effective, since
Hadria combines resistance through speech with the act of forcing
Theobald to take Martha immediately rather than keeping her for a month
while Theobold makes arrangements for her care. Initially, Hadria is
stunned by Theobald's threat to take Martha away from her, but she
attempts to resist his action first by threatening to prove that he is not the
father and then by claiming a legal right to the child through Martha's
mother. "I am acting for her mother," says Hadria, "and her mother, not
having made herself into your legal property, *has* some legal right to her
own child. I don't believe you can make me give her up" (439). But when
Theobald tells Hadria he believes that the law, which "has infinite respect
for a father's holiest feelings" (440), is in his favor, she turns to action to
resist Theobald's assumptions about his dominance over women. When

Theobald sends Lady Engleton to inform Hadria that Martha must come to his house in a month, Hadria replies, "Really? It has not struck him that perhaps I may not keep her for a month. Now that it is once established that Martha is to be regarded as under *his* guardianship and authority, and that my jurisdiction ceases, he must take her at once. I will certainly not act for *him* in that manner. . . . Does he really think I am going to act as his deputy?" (444). With that, Hadria sends Martha to Theobald immediately.

Still, while Caird does emphasize Hadria's increased consciousness and even her occasional actions more than Gissing emphasizes Nancy's use of the same methods in *Jubilee,* both novels fall back on resistance through spoken word as the stories progress, and this gives readers the sense that complete assertion of agency remains limited for both women, since Nancy and Hadria struggle to translate awareness of their life conditions and articulation of these conditions into action. At the end of *Daughters of Danaus* the focus is not on Hadria's resistance but on the death of Professor Fortescue, who is ill for much of the latter part of the novel. While Fortescue does give Hadria one last talk of encouragement before dying, his ultimate advice to her is *not* to take action but to find a way to live that keeps her body healthy and her mind peaceful (454). Interestingly, it is Valeria who argues for resistance by Hadria at the end, telling her: "[I]f women won't repudiate, in practice, the claims that they hold to be unjust, in theory, how can they hope to escape? We may talk to all eternity, if we don't act" (448). But even Valeria agrees that Hadria should not ignore the doctor's orders and take actions ensuring the death of her mother, and the novel ends where it begins—with a conversation about the basic tension between individual liberty and the power of circumstances to limit liberty.

Both *Daughters of Danaus* and *In the Year of the Jubilee* close with the message that life goes on much in the same way it has in the past, and what has been a struggle in the past most likely will continue to be a struggle in the future. Still, perhaps there is slightly more hope for Hadria than for Nancy. Hadria is inspired by a robin that appears after Fortescue's death and that seems to represent his spirit. From the robin she gathers the strength she needs to go on, even if the circumstances of her life are less than ideal. Further, there seems to be more hope for Hadria than for Nancy because Hadria has a stronger circle of friends to support her than Nancy does. Still, Hadria seems not to have the advantages of Rhoda Nunn in *The Odd Women:* free from the constraint of duty to family and with the organized support of other women through Miss Barfoot's school, Rhoda is much more capable of using individual will to overcome circumstance. Ultimately, Caird's novel is more effective in fulfilling the feminist realist aesthetic than Gissing's *Jubilee* is but perhaps less effective than *The Odd Women*.

The woman's press seemed to recognize the ways in which *Daughters of Danaus* fulfilled the feminist aesthetic, even if it did not fulfill it completely. *Shafts's* review of *Daughters of Danaus,* which spanned four issues and discussed specific scenes from the novel in great detail, is particularly striking, since Margaret Sibthorp addresses the strong contrast between the mainstream press's extremely negative perception of Caird's novel with the feminist press's more positive perception of her novel. For members of the mainstream press, *Daughters of Danaus* contained *too much* spoken word, and Sibthorp details the various derogatory ways the press articulated this complaint. One mainstream reviewer complained that Caird's novel, with "its array of hollow masks, and its voluminous arguments," would cause people to dismiss new ideas about marriage completely, while another characterizes the stuff of the novel as "nonsense so liberally dispersed" (Sibthorp, "Reviews" 5). But for Sibthorp it does not matter how much spoken word is included because those words found in Caird's novel are the "truth" and will help change the cultural status of women (5). Sibthorp speaks of the novel in glowing terms:

> *The Daughters of Danaus* will be acknowledged by the wise and far-seeing, by those who think ahead of their times, to be one of those great developments of human thought, which every now and then stir up from the still waters of life, and waken the under currents into strong moving power: a book whose utterances will arouse those that have slept. . . . To the gifted author of this book, the world of women owes a deep debt of glad and grateful thanks; the work which she espouses so nobly will be consummated only, by the complete and world-wide emancipation of woman from every shadow of thraldom. (6)

Here, it is *Caird's* speech that is praised for its contribution to social change, but once Sibthorp begins to articulate the details of the book, she emphasizes the role of the *characters'* speech in the novel. Pointing out a "readerly wish" for interesting female characters, Sibthorp writes that the reader immediately recognizes that Hadria, "the girl with the pale, mysterious face," is "meant to be the character of the book," in part because of the "earnest discussion" among Hadria's siblings about Hadria's ability to dance a reel like no other person (6). Sibthorp sees their "earnest discussion" as an effective manner of building character, since readers "gain a glimpse of the character of these young people, and a gleam of their probable future" through it (6). Further, the conversation helps Hadria and her sister to see "the difference in the life conditions of the sexes as created by society, and the greater difficulties arising therefrom for the woman," which indicates the sisters' growing awareness of the restrictions on their freedom (6). Finally, Sibthorp argues that Caird uses speech to indicate the thoughts of the characters early in the novel, making it clear that the link between consciousness and spoken word is present in the novel. Sibthorp writes that readers are "well acquainted with the young Fullertons, and especially with the heroine. . . . [Caird] gives her readers every opportunity of studying them and their characters, wandering with them in the quiet walks, listening to *their expressions of interest,* of rapture, of youthful, onward imaginings, of *deep and earnest thought*" (my emphasis 7). All this, states Sibthorp, prepares readers to judge the characters, especially Hadria, once she is "launched into the great whirlpool" and the "tragedy of her life" occurs.

In the other three installments of this review, Sibthorp continues to stress the role of speech in the novel. In the second installment she details the sisters' and brothers' discussion of a girl's lot in life, and she points out that the "conflict of words" found in their conversations may lead to social change in the future. "[I]n this conflict of words among her young characters Mrs. Mona Caird leads us, with wise suggestiveness, to the central purpose of her book: to the beginning of that wonderful and profound revolt, the revolt of women against the existing conditions of their lives, especially those imposed upon them through marriage" (23). In the third installment, Sibthorp draws attention to yet other conversations suggesting women's revolt—those between Hadria and Valeria Du Prel. As Caird puts it, these conversations lead to a new way of thinking and living: the "New Dispensation" which "thoughtful women demand" (41). Also in this installment Caird emphasizes that the conversations found in the novel are "essays in themselves, on woman's subordination, and consequent suffering, showing between the lines, and breathing from the speaker's lips, how dire has been the loss to the world which has come through the cruel and ceaseless fight to suppress and silence its highest creature" (41), and in the third and final installments she encourages readers to read these conversations with the care they deserve. To "those who desire to learn" and "those who see evils in society and heartily desire to remedy them," Sibthorp states in the last installment, "we recommend it [the book], to be not only read, but studied slowly and carefully, every paragraph on every page. There hath not yet appeared such a book as this, nor one which will so powerfully sway the future of women" (56). Ultimately, Caird's *Daughters of Danaus* provides a learning tool for readers, in part because of the role of spoken word in the novel.

In the review Sibthorp does pay attention to Caird's use of increased consciousness and actions in the novel, though she might have done more to discuss some of the concrete actions Hadria takes. She describes Algitha and Hadria as thinking women (23), and she discusses Algitha's revolt (40); but she discusses neither Hadria's flight to Paris nor her decision to adopt Martha as acts of resistance. Further, Sibthorp could bring more attention to the narrative strategies employed by Caird. When she refers to Caird's technique, it is in more general terms and in relation to the type of social change Sibthorp expects to see as a product of Caird's writing rather than in the specific terms needed to show the *direct* relation between narrative technique and the methods by which fictional characters assert agency. Still, this review of the novel is similar to those we already have seen from the woman's press at the *fin de siècle*. It emphasizes how the author meets the feminist aesthetic, and it ignores the ways in which the author fails to fulfill the ideal.

While *The Woman's Herald* did not review *Daughters of Danaus*, it did review *The Wing of Azrael*, the slightly more sensationalist novel published by Caird in 1888, in which the heroine Viola Sedley stabs her husband after he threatens to keep her under lock and key in order to control her. Refusing to be "saved" by her true love Harry Lancaster, Viola runs to the sea, presumably to throw herself off a cliff in order to avoid punishment for her actions. Interestingly, despite the sensational aspects of the novel, the reviewer applies the feminist realist aesthetic to this novel by describing the female characters in particular as drawn with a "sympathetic touch" that makes them "stand out as in real life" (Anonymous, "Reviews: *Wing*" 10). The reviewer also asserts that the strength of the novel is "the elaborate tracing of Viola's mental development," which suggests that the reviewer values increased consciousness. This comment is especially interesting given that the reviewer addresses the issue of whether Caird's novel is similar to or different from her nonfiction essays. Noting that the topic of the novel is one "on which Mrs. Caird has already written with so much boldness," the reviewer states that "from the artistic standpoint, the novel is a little bit spoilt by the obviousness of the moral lessons it conveys" (10). Still, since so few women embrace the idea that "freedom for individual development is the highest good," Caird "deserves the grateful thanks of her sex" for writing a novel that helps to do this (10). Ultimately, the reviewer also thinks that other women writers can learn something from Caird's style, so the reviewer finally seems to want to uphold Caird's work as realistic, even if the reviewer is unwilling to separate Caird's literary work from her nonfiction.

The Woman's Herald also reviewed *The Morality of Marriage*, the collection of Caird's essays published in 1897, as did *Shafts*, but the two periodicals differ in their opinions of the book. *Shafts* characterizes it as a work of "profound, experienced and cultured thought" which "gives light enough to guide many wayfaring steps" (Anonymous, "Thoughts" 25) and argues that it offers the "same lessons as . . . have been set forth by the author in *The Daughters of Danaus*, one of the best books the century has produced" (24). On the other hand, *The Woman's Herald*, now under the editorship of Florence Fenwick Miller, believes that while Caird points out the "serious flaws in our present day customs and opinions," she rarely offers solutions to these problems (Anonymous, "A Book" 116). Further, *The Woman's Herald* objects to the fact that Caird had not condensed the essays published in the book, had not removed repetition between essays, and did not make more of an effort to present opposing views in the essays (115). The difference in opinion between the two reviews speaks, I believe, not only to differences in the editorship of the two periodicals but also to the plurality of the women's movement in the 1890s. Despite their shared literary aesthetic, *Shafts* was edited by Sibthorp for its entire run and was written primarily by her too, so it more consistently reflects her own perspective. *The Woman's Herald*, on the other hand, seems to reflect a wider range of opinions at any one given time. Further, as the 1890s waned and frustration with slow progress of the women's movement grew, *The Woman's Herald* seems to reflect a certain amount of weariness with women's issues. This weariness is not unique to *The Woman's Herald*—it is seen to a much greater degree in the mainstream press—but it may help explain why the paper was more critical of progressive writers as the decade came to a close.

Ultimately, the periodicals that comprised the 1890s woman's press did not agree on every aspect of the movement for social change, but the reviews of Caird's and Gissing's novels reveal that *Shafts* and *The Woman's Herald* did appreciate strong literary representations of woman's agency. Likewise, they recognized that even when authors did not fulfill the feminist aesthetic completely, it still was worthwhile to praise their efforts. Though Caird and Gissing weighted their representations toward assertion of agency through spoken word, to the degree that their female characters often could not move from spoken word to action, both authors clearly created novels that contributed to the feminist cause. In *Shafts*'s review of Caird's *The Morality of Marriage*, the reviewer iterates the sentiment expressed by Sibthorp three years earlier in her extensive review of *The Daughters of Danaus*. "*The Daughters of Danaus* is worth reading many times, it deserves close, serious study, and the day is not far distant when it will be welcomed and valued as the forerunner of a great reform.

Such books as these should be in the libraries of Women's clubs, in women's home libraries; and might with immense profit to the present and future generations, be used as the basis of reformed life on more than one point" (24–25). For feminists, there was a deep connection between literary representation and social change, and the woman's press wanted to highlight this connection, even if it meant overlooking certain flaws in the literature of the period. Teaching girls to speak up for themselves, as had the hypothetical girl in the first issue of "What the Girl Says," was a vital part of women's emancipation, and novels such as *The Daughters of Danaus, The Odd Women,* and, to a lesser degree, *In the Year of the Jubilee* were important contributions to this effort.

CHAPTER 3

Women at Work, at War, and on the Go: Feminist Action

According to the feminist realist ideal, expressions of woman's agency were not complete without concrete action, and in *Shafts* and *The Woman's Herald* the commitment to action is most evident in articles about women and work, which focused on the everyday activities of women. From the first issue, *Shafts* published a regular column, "Influential Lives," featuring important women and their work. Interestingly, these women, often middle class, are characterized as "labourers," a term distinctly associated with the rural and working classes. For example, Matilda Sharpe, the daughter of a biblical scholar, is praised for opening a series of schools with the help of her sisters. *Shafts* writes of the sisters:

> They always *do the next thing*, so have been saved from vague specu-
> lation and waiting for opportunities—the rock on which so many fall
> to pieces, while all around them lie, fields waiting for the labourer to
> enter in, with plough, or seed, or sickle. Wherever these ladies have
> seen a chance of pushing forward the cause of higher education, there
> they have gone to work, and their reward has been with them.
> (Anonymous, "Influential" 3)

Here the sisters are identified with performing manual labor, suggesting that women in the movement might draw on rural and working-class concepts as they took action to create change.

Further, in the same issue *Shafts* highlights the need to combine new work opportunities with education for working women, a suggestion assuming the connection between action and thought. In "Typewriting as an Employment for Women," the author emphasizes that typewriting is not simply a "mechanical art which can easily be acquired" but a profession requiring a "good general education" and "quick intelligence," since the typist must understand the ideas in the manuscript (Anonymous, "Typewriting" 11). While the article discourages uneducated women from pursuing typewriting as a career, on the same page of the paper a letter from a working-class woman suggests that women of her class can be intelligent, though the writer is distressed by the number who refuse to engage in intellectual activity. Still, this woman recognizes that connecting thought and action is vital to enacting social change: "I know that women in my position are not supposed by many to have any ideas, and should they happen to have thoughts, as is sometimes the case, if they wish to earn an honest living and preserve their characters, they find it more profitable to treasure their opinions in their hearts" (11). Here the commentary about the need for working women to be educated highlights feminism's belief in *meaningful* work rather than simply doing for the sake of doing.

Just as *Shafts* placed strong emphasis on the actions of women to create social change, *The Woman's Herald* ran articles encouraging women to participate in a much wider range of activities than previously allowed so that they could change their cultural status. *The Woman's Herald* front page featured interviews with prominent women, and these interviews often highlighted the value of work in women's lives. For example, Frances Willard's interview with Clementina Black, "Questions of the Day," focuses on the efforts of women in the textile industry to organize and create better working conditions for themselves, including the reduction of work hours per week so that work could become more meaningful. Of these women Black states: "The women in these trades are about the best organised of women workers, and are in the same unions as the men. . . . These women, who are an intelligent and competent body of people, a great deal more likely than any of us middle-class women to know what is really for their advantage, appear to be practically unanimous in desiring further legal restriction of hours" (Willard 129). Again, the suggestion is that middle-class women can learn from working-class women and that the connection between thought and action to create social change is key to the feminist ideal.[1]

The Woman's Herald also makes the connection between the work ethic of working-class women and what women writers can do to enact change. While the staff of the paper believes that some women writers were contributing to the cause, it also believes that some could do more to advance the movement, as indicated in the article "Present-Day Women Novelists":

> [W]hile they show us fair pictures of what our best women desire to be in relation to the trinity of marriage, religion, and society, they have, as yet, turned to us little more than blank canvas, when we ask

that their word-painting include the attractive figure of a politically
emancipated woman. . . . Present-day novelists are wanted to use
their pens in the direction of a very possible heroine, who will readily enlist the interest, and sympathy of ordinary work-a-day readers.
(Anonymous, "Present-Day" 4)

The overarching sentiment is that women can and must do important
work to create social change, and novelists could act as role models in this
endeavor.

While *The Woman's Herald* sometimes admonishes women writers for
not doing enough to advance the women's movement in articles, they also
praise novelists who write about the modern woman, as the two previous
chapters of this book have shown. Especially admired for his belief women
could *do anything* was George Meredith, author of *Diana of the Crossways*
(1885) and *The Amazing Marriage* (1895). In these novels, women refuse
to be controlled by the men in their lives and hence take up meaningful
work: Diana Merion becomes a novelist, whereas Carinthia Kirby nurses
soldiers during the Carlist War. Meredith's commitment to showing
women at work, at war, and on the go is so strong that *Shafts* presents his
work as a model for other authors, male and female, to follow. Meredith
shares an interest in action-oriented women with Ménie Dowie, whose *A
Girl in the Karpathians* (1891) and *Women Adventurers* (1893) also express
the view that women are capable of any activity, including traveling the
world and going to war. *A Girl in the Karpathians* follows the actions of a
young woman traveling through Eastern Europe on her own, while
Women Adventurers features the activities of four real-life women who pose
as soldiers in order to travel the world and make a living. Though Dowie
received less coverage by the feminist press than did Meredith, she was recognized for her work and was seen as an important contributor to the
advancement of women.

In this chapter I examine the characters in Meredith's and Dowie's novels who act as well as think and speak and who therefore illustrate the
attention to action advocated by the feminist realist aesthetic. Ironically,
though Meredith often was criticized by mainstream reviewers for his
inability to write novels with sufficient plot, feminist reviewers recognized
that Meredith's use of plot was more extensive than one might expect, in
part because plot was the site for description of women's actions. Yet, while
feminist reviewers mentioned Dowie's work from the early 1890s, they did
not review *Gallia* (1895), even though it is the best-remembered of her
works now and does feature significant actions by the primary female
character. The reviewers' satirization of the novel at one point can be
attributed in part to the actions taken by Gallia, who rejects a free union

with one man and marries another for reproductive purposes only. Such actions pushed the limits of what was acceptable content to feminists, and the result was a less enthusiastic reception of Dowie's work overall. In ignoring Dowie's work but presenting Meredith as a model for the feminist aesthetic, the woman's press indicated that it did not always favor women writers over male authors and there were limitations to the flexibility of the feminist realist aesthetic.

The making of plot—and, by extension, the description of characters' actions—has been a central issue in discussions of Meredith's novels for over a century. Readers of Meredith still complain that his stories have "no plot," echoing the sentiments of late-nineteenth-century critics who claim that Meredith's dense and difficult style often interfered with readers' basic understanding of the storylines in his works. By 1895, with the publication of Meredith's last novel, *The Amazing Marriage,* complaints about his style had reached a pinnacle. Edmund Gosse, in the *St. James's Gazette,* wrote that "the Alexandrian extravagance of Mr. Meredith's style has now reached such a pitch that it is difficult to enjoy and sometimes impossible to understand what he writes" (429). Likewise, the anonymous reviewer for *The Pall Mall Gazette* states: "That which on the whole is most to be regretted is an increasing tendency to shirk the crucial scenes and episodes of the story, and to vouchsafe but the vaguest of allusions and sketchiest of accounts, introduced into the casual talk or letters of outsiders" (Anonymous, "Unsigned" 442).

The criticism leveled at Meredith for *The Amazing Marriage* was not unique; it simply built on criticism of his earlier works, many of which were found to have the same faults. In her review of *Harry Richmond* (1871) in 1872, Margaret Oliphant complains about the "thicket" of events in the latter part of the book, which she thought were told in a less-than-straightforward style (166). The result, Oliphant states, is what happens when "the luxuriance of unrestrained imagination runs riot. . . . [I]t is very difficult to trace out the meaning of the latter part [of the novel], or not to believe that all the personages [in the novel] have gone mad together" (166). Likewise, when Oliphant reviews *The Egoist* (1879) in 1880, her comments are similar. The novel becomes "an appalling ordeal . . . three huge volumes made up of a thousand conversations, torrents of words in half lines, continued, and continued, and continued, till every sentiment contained in them is beaten to death in extremest extenuation, and the reader's head aches, and his very bones are weary" (236–37).

Despite the complaints of mainstream critics, Meredith received something of a respite from feminist critics, who, because of their invest-ment in changing the definition of realism to better connect it to the accurate representation of women in literary texts, often found ways to explain away Meredith's stylistic idiosyncrasies and even praise his use of plot. For example, Arabella Shore, in "An Early Appreciation" (1879), one of the first feminist assessments of Meredith's work, asserts that the "indirect" expressions frustrating to other critics were only "occasional" and "always worth making out," so much so that readers "love the work the more for the trouble it has given us" (192–93). Further, in com-menting on the primary female character in *Emilia in England,* Shore writes, "The object of *Emilia in England* is to paint a being accidentally evolved and developed, under no conventional constraint, of absolute naturalness, and with the addition of one splendid faculty. . . . [Emilia] is at once vividly real, and singularly difficult to define. We feel only a strong and constant attraction, as if we were always watching some object of curious study" (194–95). Finally, Shore includes a detailed dis-cussion of Meredith's focus on "that most fruitful of subjects—the social relations of the sexes" in her evaluation of *Beauchamp's Career* (199). While she faults Meredith for letting one of the female characters in the novel "retrograde into what the hero and we imagine the author would regard as the prejudices of more commonplace women," she is happy to see another female character experience significant "intellectual growth" (200). While Shore does not agree with every action taken by every char-acter created by Meredith, she is able to see the overarching commit-ment from him to represent women realistically.

Similarly, an anonymous writer for *The Woman's Herald,* commenting on a lecture about Meredith's novels by Miss Alice Wood in December 1893, depicts Meredith as especially skilled in terms of realistic represen-tation of women and not to be faulted for the complexity of his charac-ters, especially the complexity of their actions. Miss Wood, states the writer, has "reverence and admiration for the master hand that has drawn women with such truth to nature; they stand before us as absolute reali-ties; women to be studied closely and faithfully if we would gain any clue to their actions, strange and unexpected as these often are" (Anonymous, "Woman's View" 710). The writer continues to say that there are "[n]o milk-and-water heroines of romance, no airy, ideal creations of the brain" in Meredith's work, but instead "women of the nineteenth century, bear-ing its sins, sharing in its advantages, living its life through and through" (710). In highlighting the unexplainable aspects of Meredith's characters, the writer for *The Woman's Herald* suggests that it is precisely the complex-ity of these characters that should be admired. Further, the writer empha-sizes Miss Wood's sense of Meredith's heroines as "women at war, in the very thick of life's battlefield" (710), a characterization highlighting actions rather than other methods of asserting agency.

Finally, John Stanley Little, in "George Meredith's Heroines," which appeared in the March 1893 issue of *The Woman's Herald,* states that in only ten years Meredith had been transformed from being "practically unknown, certainly unread" to one of the "foremost, if not the foremost" author in the literary scene, in part because "the distinguishing characteristic of his writings lies in his treatment of his heroines and in the ideal of womanhood thereby displayed" (34). In fact, Meredith's idea that women should be given the freedom to develop their own personalities becomes the plot of many of his novels. Writing of *The Egoist,* Little explains, "The plot is slender enough. It is rather the swift, incisive utterance of the needs of a woman's soul and the defects in a man's way of meeting them that create the main interest of the story, and give Meredith a claim to be the historian of the struggle between the old Adam and the new Eve" (34). Further, this emphasis on the new Eve carries across Meredith's novels, including *Diana of the Crossways.* Speaking of Meredith's heroines, including Diana, Little writes, "Nor does Clara Middleton stand alone among Meredith's heroines, for are there not Diana, Vittoria, Rhoda Fleming, each in their way claiming the same right 'to be themselves'?" (34). In depicting Meredith as an author who has become popular precisely because he presents a new ideal for womanhood and because he is willing to explore the complexity of women's characters, Little recognizes that realism can be defined more broadly than external description of character and linear plot. Further, like Shore, Little mitigates Meredith's faults, especially those concerning his use of plot.

Diana of the Crossways deserves special attention because both contemporary and current critics have questioned two of Diana's actions—to sell Dacier's political secrets and to marry Redworth—and have used these actions as evidence Meredith did not know how to construct or control plot. The novel centers on Diana Merion, who rejects men who try to control her and who uses physical movement as a method of resistance as she tries to find a partner who will accept her as she is. Discouraged by a series of negative experiences with men, including the advances of her best friend's husband, Diana makes a marriage of convenience with Augustus Warwick, who later divorces her based on rumors she has had an affair with a political figure, Lord Dannisburgh. Frustrated by the false accusation, Diana at first isolates herself from public life by fleeing England but later becomes a well-known figure, in part through the publication of social satire novels. Meanwhile, two men, Dacier and Redworth, express interest in Diana; initially, Diana agrees to elope with Dacier, but after she sells his political secrets, the possibility of romance between them ends. In the end Diana agrees to marry Redworth, who has always loved her but has acted primarily as her friend through difficult times.

As previously mentioned, mainstream critics of the late nineteenth century found Meredith's work particularly difficult to comprehend, and when reviewing *Diana* they often questioned Diana's actions. For example, the reviewer for *The Pall Mall Gazette* opens his or her review of the novel by stating, "In reading Mr. George Meredith one is perpetually divided between admiration for his genius and irritation at his perversity. The genius was always there, but the perversity increases" (Anonymous, "Unsigned Review" 265). The reviewer then continues to discuss Meredith's theory of style, which is to ignore the public's "banal preference for intelligibility" (265), and argues that Diana's motive in selling Dacier's secret is "inadequate to explain the fateful act" (266). Likewise, F. V. Dickins, writing for *The Spectator,* believes that a woman as intelligent as Diana has "no need to come to hasty resolutions" (271), and Dickins believes that Diana's selling of the secret can be regarded only "as a blot in the story. [Diana's] excuse that she did not know the secret was a secret at all, or, at any rate, an important one, is an absurdity" (273). Even those reviewers who liked the novel, such as William Cosmo Monkhouse of *The Saturday Review,* question Diana's decision to sell Dacier's secret: "[I]t seems incredible that Diana should do so; and it is still more improbable that this woman, so full of knowledge of the political world should plead that she 'had not a suspicion of mischief' in doing so" (263).

While mainstream critics clearly had a difficult time comprehending Meredith's construction of plot in *Diana,* Gertrude Kapteyn, whose review of *Diana* ran in *Shafts* in two parts in November and December 1895 and was almost six pages in length, shows the degree to which feminist reviewers were able to appreciate Meredith's construction of plot and his focus on women's actions. In this review Kapteyn argues that *Diana* deserves a "front place in the fiction devoted to the modern woman's cause" (109), and she believes that Meredith should be admired for his realistic approach in the novel. In a series of rhapsodic statements, she characterizes Meredith as one who can depict realistically the modern woman as few others can. "Diana! The very name is suggestive! suggestive of a keen, rich temperament, of a wide awake soaring spirit. . . . But Diana was not [just] the hunting goddess of placid Greece. Diana was a human being, not only a woman, but essentially a *modern* woman. . . . How G. Meredith loves the type, how he realises it, how he understands it, how subtly he analyses it!" (109). Then, as Kapteyn summarizes and analyzes large portions of the novel, she discusses directly the three narrative strategies important to feminist realism.

Referring to the presence of Diana's internal perspective, Kapteyn describes a scene in which Diana mourns her girlhood yet realizes she has freed herself from the memories of the past.

> Listen to Meredith's splendid understanding of that feeling of the loss of girlhood, so tragic in every married woman's existence. . . . I know hardly any page in the other novels of Meredith which surpasses or even equals this page of descriptive psychology with its poetic vision of the human soul. . . . [I]n none do we find a more striking testimony of that characteristic power of the author to show us the inward throbbing life. (111)

In other words, Meredith does "descriptive psychology," or internal perspective, well, and Kapteyn feels the same about his use of dialogue, the second of the three narrative strategies valued by the feminist aesthetic. Especially striking to Kapteyn is Meredith's use of Diana's "own words" in chapter 1 of the novel, where, having shown what others say about Diana, he turns to her own perceptions about life, which include: "When I fail to cherish it in every fibre, the fires within are waiting" and "If I can assure myself of doing service, I have my home within" (109). Kapteyn stresses the importance of Meredith's use of Diana's speech, saying, "Thus quoting from her own words, written diaries and notes, Meredith gives his readers at once the true glimpse of the soul, whose history is his theme" (109). Here Kapteyn suggests it is through a woman's own words that we best understand her "soul," or her inner life.

While Kapteyn does not possess the critical jargon we have today, which might replace the word "soul" with "subjectivity," she clearly is aware that certain qualities result in a female character who seems true-to-life to readers, and this true-to-life impression is what constitutes accurate representation for feminist critics of the period. In addition to recognizing Meredith's use of consciousness and spoken word as methods of asserting agency, Kapteyn indicates that Meredith also uses the third narrative strategy needed for realistic representation of woman's agency: description of a character's actions as she works to change her own cultural status. Not only does Kapteyn describe Diana as a contrast to her friend Emma Dunstane because of her "action," which is a "tonic" that must be "tempered" by her friend's "reflection" and "contemplation" (109), but she also focuses on the implications of Diana's actions, especially her selling of Dacier's secret and her marrying Redworth. Unlike other critics, Kapteyn easily reconciles Diana's actions. When she describes the selling of Dacier's secret, there is no indication in her summary that this action was problematic, and when she describes Diana's marriage to Redworth, she explicitly states, "We can feel reconciled to her marriage because: 'Redworth believed in the soul of

Diana. For him it burned, and it was a celestial radiance about her, unquenched by her shifting fortunes, her wilfulness, and, it might be, error'" (126). In other words, Redworth's support of Diana, which makes him different from the other men in her life, is all we need to accept Diana's decision to marry him.

Like Kapteyn, late-twentieth-century feminist critics have argued for a more sympathetic reading of Diana's actions. Gillian Beer, in "*Diana of the Crossways:* The Novelist in the Novel" (1970), and Judith Wilt, in "The Meredithian Subplot" (1975), both examine how Diana's actions reflect her psychological development over the course of the novel. Beer, in particular, argues that Meredith explores issues of selfhood and the artist's responsibility to society by making Diana a novelist, asserting that Meredith abandons the notion of "congruous character" and adopts a theory that allows characters to act in contradictory ways. Adopting this theory flies in the face of traditional Victorian ideas about why people act as they do, but it allows Meredith to develop more complex characters and to show the degree to which people's actions are determined by societal conventions. While Beer believes Meredith's realism is limited by his love for Diana, once one understands that Meredith is working with a different theory of character, it is easier to accept Diana's actions. Likewise, Wilt provides a more sympathetic reading of Diana, arguing that Meredith assumes a "civilized" reader who identifies with Diana and can understand her actions. As long as the reader sees Diana's decision to marry Redworth as a *personal* one, her character is not inconsistent.

I want to extend the idea that Diana's character can be understood through her supposed "inconsistencies" by addressing the issue of how we might define "feminist action." To some degree the feminist ideal assumes that when women take action, they will be doing something to change cultural conditions that support the subordination of women. This ideal often assumes actions based on "presence" rather than "absence"; that is, an action based on presence, such as going somewhere and gaining access to better opportunities, is better than an action based on absence, such as leaving a place and losing access to particular opportunities. Yet, Meredith's novels show that while an action should have an end result that is feminist, actions based on presence are not necessarily better than those based on absence. In Meredith's novels there usually is a range of possible actions (a woman can go somewhere, stay where she already is, flee, escape, stand by and wait, and so on), and any of these actions can be effective in resisting cultural norms that support the subordination of women.

In *Diana* and *The Amazing Marriage*, "fleeing" is key to acts of resistance. When Diana first learns she is to be divorced from her husband, she considers fleeing England in order to escape the embarrassment of facing the public, and from that moment fleeing becomes a way for Diana to deal with the difficult circumstances she faces. In *Diana,* to flee—to be absent—is not always an act of cowardliness; nor is staying—remaining present—always proof of assertion of agency. In *The Amazing Marriage* fleeing becomes an even more overt act of resistance: while the female protagonist Carinthia adopts actions associated with both presence and absence as she resists her husband's attempts to control her, ultimately she finds actions associated with absence to be the more effective strategy. By emphasizing absence, Meredith expands the range of actions available to women for resistance to cultural norms, indicating that the range of options is broader than even feminist critics might expect.

Fleeing first becomes significant for Diana in chapter 8 of the novel, when she escapes to her family home, The Crossways, in the Sussex Downs. Having received the notice her husband is filing for divorce, Diana goes there to prepare for her departure from England, but Emma sends Redworth to retrieve her. Redworth, who sees Diana as a "warhorse . . . beset by battle" (88–89) rather than someone avoiding contact with the world, tries to convince Diana to remain in the country by initiating a conversation in which the various options for action are explored. During this conversation Diana feels torn between staying, which Emma and Redworth believe is the best decision because "the one thing to do is to make a stand" (93), and fleeing, which Diana believes is the "wisest course" for her (94). While readers understand that remaining in England might be the "braver" decision, they also are aware of other factors at work in Diana's mind as she considers what to do. Redworth and Emma do not know, for example, that Emma's husband once tried to seduce Diana and his attempt at seduction is in part responsible for Diana's quick marriage to Warwick. Though this memory from the past should have no bearing on the divorce proceedings, Diana's past justifies her fear of the future, and fleeing appears as legitimate an option to the current situation as remaining in England.

Even if readers do not immediately accept Diana's reasoning, in the next chapter her perspective is clarified as she thinks through her decision:

> The unfriendliness of the friends who sought to retain her recurred. For look—to fly could not be interpreted as a flight. It was a stepping aside, a disdain of defending herself, and a wrapping herself in her dignity. Women would be with her. She called on the noblest of them to justify the course she chose, and they did, in an almost audible murmur. And O the rich reward. A black archway-gate swung open to the glittering fields of freedom. (95–96)

For Diana, to flee means to gain freedom, while to stay in England means to be chained not only to her husband's control over their relationship through the divorce proceedings but also to the wishes of her friends, who are thinking about their own desires, even if they are presenting their case as one concerned with Diana's needs. When Diana thinks about staying in England, her skin actually burns: "It was the beginning of tortures if she stayed in England. By staying to defend herself she forfeited her attitude of dignity and lost all chance at her reward" (96). To Diana, to flee means keeping her dignity intact, whereas to remain in England suggests exactly the opposite.

Still, Diana ultimately decides to stay in England, choosing her friends' definition of dignity over her own, but she expresses regret over her decision, saying to Emma, who wonders how Diana could even consider leaving her husband's charge of adultery unanswered, "What does it matter? I should have left the flies and wasps to worry a corpse. . . . [P]erhaps once on foreign soil, in a different air, I might—might have looked back, and seen my whole self, not shattered, as I feel it now, and come home again compassionate to the poor persecuted animal to defend her" (109). Fleeing might have given Diana the perspective needed to separate her sense of herself from the person her husband's charge of adultery has created, and having this perspective might have made a significant difference in the way she would approach defending herself in the public sphere.

Still, once Diana decides to stay in England, she wholeheartedly embraces different types of action, including those associated with both presence and absence, and this indicates that Diana is learning to use all available actions to their fullest extent. When Emma suggests that Diana stay at Copsley, in Surrey, rather than return to London, Diana refuses, saying, "If I am to fight my battle, I must be seen; I must go about—wherever I am received. So my field must be London" (112–13). Further, at the beginning of chapter 14, as Diana prepares for her divorce trial, she is described one who does battle, as though she is a soldier. "She fancied she had put on proof-armour, unconscious that it was the turning of the inward flutterer to steel which supplied her cuirass and shield. The necessity to brave society, in the character of honest Defendant, caused but a momentary twitch of the nerves. Her heart beat regularly, like a serviceable clock; none of her faculties abandoned . . . and none belied her" (123). After the trial Diana continues to use a variety of actions to fight her battle, by remaining present in the minds of the English public but in a more subtle way—by writing novels. As an author, Diana can be physically absent but mentally present to the public, and she uses her novels to comment on the conditions of her life. In *The Princess Egeria*, she critiques aristocratic society and uses "stinging epigrams" aimed at "discernible personages" (164), which shows Diana's refusal to back down from the people who condemn her; in *The Young Minister of the State* she shocks English society by writing about Dacier (200).

Perhaps the best symbol for Diana's combination of presence and absence becomes the mask, first mentioned in chapter 11, when Diana claims she will not wear the facade of virtue women must wear when they marry.

> "Let me be myself, whatever the martyrdom!" she cried, in that phase
> of young sensation when, to the blooming woman, the putting on of
> a mask appears to wither her and reduce her to the show she parades.
> . . . That she had never worn it consentingly, was the plea for now
> casting it off altogether, showing herself as she was, accepting martyr-
> dom, becoming the first martyr of the modern woman's cause—a
> grand position! (99)

Later, in chapter 14, when the narrator describes Diana's life in London in the days of the trial, he acknowledges that Diana has put the mask back on, but he explains that the mask is a necessary device for women in the position of defending themselves to the world. "She discovered the social uses of cheap wit; she laid ambushes for anecdotes. . . . These were Diana's weapons. She was perforce the actress of her part. . . . It is a terrible decree, that all must act who would prevail; and the more extended the audience, the greater need for the mask and buskin" (124–25). Through the mask, Diana manages to be present yet absent, as circumstances require.

As the novel progresses, Diana seems to balance actions associated with presence and those associated with absence with increasing ease, and the rest of the book displays the interplay between these two types of action. Among the highlights are Diana's insistence to be present at Lord Dannisburgh's deathbed, despite grumbling from the family (chapters 19–20); her refusal to reconcile with Warwick, an act of resistance which others believe cause Warwick to fall ill (chapter 23); her consideration to flee England with Dacier, an action that would ensure freedom from Warwick, who continues to pressure Diana to reconcile (chapter 25); and her decision to remain in England when Emma must undergo surgery, an action confirming Diana's commitment to her female friend and her refusal to let even Dacier control her movements (chapter 26). In the end Diana chooses permanent presence in England through her marriage to Redworth, but Redworth promises many trips to Ireland, a symbol for Diana's desire for complete independence. At the end of the novel, to flee is to go to a place she loves, Ireland, with a husband who understands her.

Diana's use of both types of action confirms Meredith's complex understanding of the methods of expressing agency, and this understanding carries over to *The Amazing Marriage,* the novel that distressed mainstream critics so much. *The Amazing Marriage* tells the story of Carinthia Kirby, who, even more than Diana Merion, struggles to find acceptance from a male partner. Living in the shadow of her parents' romantic elopement, Carinthia initially believes she is better suited for work than for marriage, but when her brother and his wife pressure her to marry, she accepts the proposal of Lord Fleetwood. Fleetwood turns out to be a scoundrel: he shows little interest in Carinthia after the wedding and spends most of his time cavorting with friends. While Carinthia initially accepts Fleetwood's neglect, she eventually decides to leave him, only to have him pursue her once he learns they have a child together. Possessing the power to make her own choices now, Carinthia refuses to allow Fleetwood into her life, and she adopts resistance through absence rather than presence. Eventually Fleetwood comes to respect Carinthia for her resistance, but he is never able to win her back. He joins a monastery and dies, while Carinthia travels to Spain to nurse injured soldiers, work to which she has always aspired. Upon her return from Spain, she marries a man named Owain Wythan, who is much more understanding than Fleetwood.

As discussed previously, late-nineteenth-century mainstream critics took an extremely negative view of *The Amazing Marriage,* and feminist critics of the 1890s did not review the novel, a decision that will be explained later in this chapter. The limited late-twentieth-century criticism on the novel is mixed in its opinion, both on the issue of Carinthia's ability to assert agency and on the issue of her marriage to Wythan. Beer, in "*The Amazing Marriage:* A Study in Contraries" (1970), traces the shifts in internal perspective across the novel and takes the view that as the amount of internal perspective granted Lord Fleetwood over the course of the novel increases, it becomes more and more difficult to sympathize with Carinthia (170). According to Beer, while we know not to align ourselves entirely with Fleetwood because we receive some of Carinthia's internal perspective early in the novel, maintaining a balance of sympathy between the two characters becomes impossible in the end. When Carinthia refuses to reconcile with Fleetwood after he realizes he has wronged her, readers are disappointed by Carinthia's rejection of his repentance (172).

While Beer's analysis traces well the developments in internal perspective across the course of the novel, her analysis is not as complete as it might be, since she ignores other methods of asserting agency. Further, Beer claims that Carinthia is "uncivilized" and "instinctive," and this seems overstated. Barbara Hardy, in "*Lord Ormont and His Aminta* and *The Amazing Marriage*" (1971), picks up on this distorted characterization of Carinthia and argues for a more positive view of her. Hardy asserts that Carinthia should be respected for her refusal to reconcile with Fleetwood, particularly through her refusal to let him sleep in her bed, and she highlights the pivotal speech by Carinthia to Fleetwood, in which she states, "I guard my rooms" (307–8). Unlike Beer, who is limited by her focus on internal perspective, Hardy seems to understand that assertions of woman's agency come in multiple forms. By touching on Carinthia's resistance through speech and action, Hardy sees the complexity of Meredith's representation of woman's agency. Still, Hardy acknowledges that Meredith backs off from making Carinthia a fully developed subject at the end of the novel. Carinthia's "capacity to endure," writes Hardy, is in the end "limited," and a novel that begins with "really creative and strongly affined people" ends with the same people "just giv[ing] up" (311).

I agree that *The Amazing Marriage* is less feminist than *Diana,* but close examination of the novel shows why, like feminists of the 1890s who accepted Diana's marriage to Redworth, it is possible for us to accept at least *some* of Carinthia's actions at the end of the novel. It is, in fact, relatively easy to accept Carinthia's decision to become a nurse in the Carlist War in Spain, once one acknowledges the way in which the narrative anticipates such a decision. While it is more difficult to accept her decision to marry Wythan after her return from Spain, by looking at Meredith's use of actions associated with presence and absence in the novel, a strategy not addressed explicitly by Beer or Hardy, we can see why it is more difficult to accept Carinthia's marriage to Wythan than it is to accept Diana's marriage to Redworth.

Unlike *Diana,* in which the internal perspective of the female protagonist plays a minimal role, *The Amazing Marriage* puts more emphasis on the "problem" of a young woman's independence, and we see Carinthia thinking through this problem in a way Diana does not. Though it takes three chapters for the narrator, Dame Gossip, to sort through the story of Carinthia's parents, as soon as Carinthia comes into the story, her internal perspective is foregrounded. As Carinthia reflects on her brother Chillon's decision that they will leave Austria and go to England, where Chillon's bride-to-be waits for him, her perspective is one of reluctance, in part because she believes she is unlikely to find a man in England, or elsewhere, who will accept her. "But who would marry me! . . . Her father had doted on her face; but . . . a plain girl should think of work, to earn her independence" (1:55–56).

These early thoughts about marriage from Carinthia perhaps help explain the difference in Meredith's use of internal perspective in *Diana* and *The Amazing Marriage.* Women like Carinthia, because of their lack of beauty, tend to think through the issues of marriage in a way women like Diana, who possess the beauty needed to ensure marriage, need not. Still, as Carinthia's story progresses, the amount of internal perspective granted her does decrease dramatically as the amount granted to Fleetwood increases (1:170). In fact, from the end of chapter 7, in which Carinthia reads a letter from Chillon's bride concerning the social happenings in England, until the middle of chapter 9, when Carinthia and Fleetwood meet for the first time, Carinthia is entirely absent from the story. At this point her absence can be attributed to the development of other characters in the novel, but later Carinthia's absence becomes an important strategy for asserting agency. Meanwhile, until Carinthia decides to employ this strategy, readers are left wondering why, despite Carinthia's revived presence in the story beginning with chapter 9, her thought processes are absent at certain key points, such as her engagement to Fleetwood, which is related to readers through a letter from Chillon's bride (chapter 12), and her marriage, which is told to readers by Dame Gossip and the wedding guests (chapter 13).

Married, Carinthia finds herself the victim of Fleetwood's absence, which he justifies by presenting his estrangement from Carinthia as being her "choice." "You have chosen," he says to her when she claims she would rather see a fight between two lightweight champions with him than be alone (1:176), and "You choose it," he says when she refuses his offer to have someone take her home in the midst of the fight (1:179). In adopting this rhetoric, Fleetwood assigns Carinthia more agency than she has, in retaliation for other displays of power by Carinthia immediately following their marriage: her refusal of Fleetwood's hand when stepping into their carriage (1:158) and her refusal of his offer to hire a maid for her (1:170). Carinthia's resistance thoroughly irritates Fleetwood, and his response is to shut her down, refusing to let her express her opinions anymore. Angered by Fleetwood's attitude, Carinthia's first significant act of resistance—one that takes advantage of actions associated with absence—comes swiftly and decisively after the birth of their child, the conception of whom was logically impossible until Meredith made revisions to the novel after the publication of the first edition (Wilt, "Survival" 225). When Fleetwood wants to see the child, Carinthia allows him to do so, but she absents herself while he visits (2:63).

Until this moment, Carinthia has worked under the assumption that actions associated with presence will be most effective: she has demanded a meeting with Fleetwood in an attempt to convince him to fulfill his marital duties, and she has refused to leave Wales without a significant amount of money from her husband (2:47). Once Carinthia is in Wales, however, her strategy for resisting Fleetwood begins to shift from actions associated with presence to those associated with absence, just as Fleetwood begins to see that presence rather than absence will be to his advantage. Readers learn of Fleetwood's shift in strategy at the end of chapter 27, when he realizes "a man must fly, or stand assailed by the most intolerable of vulgar forces" from the public if he remains separate from his wife (2:34), as well as at the end of chapter 28, when he realizes that Carinthia is challenging him by fleeing to Wales (2:52). Suddenly, Fleetwood seems much more concerned about Carinthia's whereabouts, and he seems ready to change the frequency and quality of his interactions with her. Yet in the following chapter readers learn that Carinthia, too, has had a change of heart about how to interact with her husband. "The conviction that her husband hated her had sunk into her nature. . . . The time for the weaning of the babe approached, and had as prospect beyond it her dull fear that her husband would say the mother's work was done, and seize the pretext to separate them" (2:52–55). Worried about losing her baby, Carinthia refuses to see Fleetwood, an act that enrages him (2:79–80), particularly since he has gone out of his way to be in the same place as Carinthia.

Over the course of the next two chapters, Carinthia's use of absence to resist Fleetwood becomes stronger, and it is important to note Meredith's description of characters' actions as the primary narrative strategy for representing Carinthia's resistance. When Fleetwood tires of waiting for Carinthia to return to the castle where she is staying and prepares to leave Wales altogether, Meredith constructs the scene so that Carinthia's actions appear to mean one thing when they actually mean another. Fleetwood, on the verge of leaving, sees Carinthia and her entourage approach from afar. Given Fleetwood's earlier reference to the possibility Carinthia might appear—"She might choose to come or choose to keep away" (87)—the appearance of Carinthia at the top of the hill suggests she has come to reconcile with her husband (and perhaps even to go away with him), yet Carinthia has come only to wish him goodbye (2:90). While Meredith is often criticized for skipping over, or drastically summarizing, key events in the story and playing up seemingly less important events, his writing of this scene shows the effectiveness of extending what initially appears to be an unimportant plot point. After a page or two of discussion between Carinthia and Fleetwood about the baby, we learn that Carinthia has no plans to go with her husband but only wants to know if he will agree to give her money—about £2000 per year!—before leaving Wales (2:93). Meredith's strategy of revealing the motives behind Carinthia's actions only after they have occurred (as opposed to giving us her internal perspective or even narratorial commentary on her motives previous to the actions seen here) heightens the tension between Fleetwood and Carinthia and emphasizes the ways in which actions associated with presence and absence play off each other as multiple options for expressing agency. Now, even when Carinthia is present, she is equally absent, withholding what Fleetwood wants (her subordination to him) and prioritizing her own needs (supporting her child).

The battle between Fleetwood and Carinthia continues through the rest of the novel, and actions associated with presence and absence remain important strategies for Carinthia. Eventually, Carinthia does return to England and resides with her baby and her maid at Fleetwood's estate, but she does not allow Fleetwood to live with her, and when he comes to the house to do business, she is conveniently absent (2:133, 2:181). Ideally, Carinthia wants to live with her brother rather than at Fleetwood's estate (2:149), but she stays on, in part because one of Fleetwood's friends commits suicide and Carinthia thinks it inappropriate for her to leave after such a tragic event. Still, though Carinthia is more lenient with Fleetwood after his friend's suicide (she even agrees to let Fleetwood stay overnight, though in separate quarters [2:188]), she makes it clear she still controls the degree of contact between the two of them. In the famous "I guard my rooms" scene, Carinthia tells Fleetwood that should he enter the house, something to which he is entitled as owner, she will "guard [her] rooms" (2:150), implying that she views him as a sexual threat. This statement of resistance from Carinthia becomes a refrain that stays with Fleetwood, angering him whenever he thinks of it (2:189).

Carinthia's statement about guarding her rooms also signals the beginning of yet another strategy to resist Fleetwood's attempts to subordinate her: emotional absence. That is, Carinthia learns to use absence in such a way that she can be in the same house as Fleetwood and still be emotionally, if not physically, absent. After Fleetwood reestablishes his own rooms at the estate, a step Carinthia believes he takes in order to "feel her presence in her absence" (2:189), he is immediately aware of a "fixed" distance between them. "She was Arctic," he thinks, "and Antarctic he had to be, perforce of the distance she had put between them" (2:188). Further, when Carinthia goes to Croridge to help her brother, whose enemies are causing problems for him, a brief return to the estate to view the week's bills shows Carinthia's skill at using emotional absence with Fleetwood. When Fleetwood insists on walking Carinthia back to Croridge, she agrees, with the narrator noting a physical action—"Her head assented"— and then Fleetwood's reaction: "There was nothing to complain of, but he had not gained a step" (2:203). Although Carinthia's physical action, nodding her head, suggests she will be present during the walk, it is clear from Fleetwood's reaction that he has not moved any closer to Carinthia than before; she is only physically, and not emotionally, present as they walk.

Although Fleetwood goes to great lengths to open new lines of communication, Carinthia refuses to change her mind, and toward the end of the novel she flees to Spain to work as a nurse with her brother and other men fighting in the Carlist War (2:220). Carinthia's decision to go to Spain might be seen as an act of subordination to men, for Carinthia's brother Chillon seems to exert as much control over Carinthia's life as Fleetwood, but Carinthia's decision to be a nurse cannot be questioned by feminist critics, given the way in which Meredith presents this type of work earlier in the novel. When Carinthia initially tells her brother of her dream of nursing men at war, such work is painted as unconventional: Carinthia's brother is surprised by her interest in such work and jokes about her possibly recruiting other women to do the same (1:56). Similarly, when Fleetwood goes to see Lady Arpington about Carinthia's decision to stay in Whitechapel with her maid, Carinthia's work with the poor there is characterized by Lady Arpington as unconventional as well (1:242). Finally, in a scene in which a child is bitten by a dog and Carinthia takes control of the situation (2:94–95), nursing is presented as a profession that brings Carinthia the feeling of independence she cannot find through marriage.

Unlike Carinthia's decision to become a nurse, which is supported by earlier characterizations of this profession, Carinthia's decision to marry Wythan is not explicated well through internal perspective, dialogue, or description of characters' actions. Further, as Judith Wilt points out in "The Survival of Romance" (1975), Carinthia's marriage to Wythan is told through the perspective of Dame Gossip (the less reliable of the two narrators in the novel) rather than the Modern Novelist narrator (who is more analytical and battles with Dame Gossip to retain control of the narrative). This helps explain why it can be difficult to accept Carinthia's decision to marry. Referring to the sudden shift in narration in the last chapter of the novel (2:278) Wilt writes:

> The Modern Novelist ends his task with the cessation of mental change in his characters, the setting of attitudes. The Dame wants to follow the action to its end. The trouble is that with the Modern Novelist withdrawn the Dame is free to do her worst to the story, and she does. . . . Carinthia went to Spain, returned with her brother, and married her dog-like Welsh squire after Fleetwood's death, but what were her deeds in Spain and her thoughts on second marriage we know better from our assessment of her character than from the thrilled enthusiasm of the Dame. (239)

I believe that Wilt is correct in her interpretation of the effect of the end of the novel on readers: we do not understand why Carinthia chooses Wythan because Dame Gossip rushes through the action without explaining Carinthia's motives.

This lack of explanation might be contrasted to the more thorough explanation of Diana's decision to marry Redworth at the end of *Diana of the Crossways*. Part of the reason feminists were, and are, able to accept Diana's actions is that her thinking on the matter is more fully developed than Carinthia's is. Wilt's suggestion that we should be able to make some assessment of Carinthia's decision to marry on the basis of "what we know" about her character raises problems for readers. What we know about Carinthia is that she has matured dramatically over the course of the novel, developing her analytical skills to the degree that she successfully resists Fleetwood's attempts to pull her back into a marriage in which she would be subordinate. Yet we also know that Carinthia is the sort of woman who seems dependent on male companionship, whether it is by relying on a husband, a brother, or a male friend. With this knowledge we can imagine that Carinthia marries *either* because she has a more equal relationship with Wythan *or* for emotional comfort rather than love.

Ultimately, our own feelings about the end of the novel probably should be ambiguous, and it is impossible to discern exactly how late-nineteenth-century feminists felt about it, since neither *The Woman's Herald* nor *Shafts* reviewed the novel.[2] Still, it is clear that reviewers for the feminist periodicals did not go out of their way to fault Meredith for his representation of woman's agency in this novel. While the end of the novel might have raised some of the same questions it raises for feminists today, the reviewers for *Shafts* and *The Woman's Herald* were satisfied with focusing on the decidedly positive work Meredith had already produced, and the lack of space given to *The Amazing Marriage* in *Shafts* and *The Woman's Herald* is mitigated by the ample space given to *Diana* in the mid-1890s, a good decade after its publication. As I already have discussed in this chapter, *Shafts* and *The Woman's Herald* saw *Diana* as a model text in relation to the feminist realistic aesthetic and spent ample time discussing it. Rather than criticize Meredith for *The Amazing Marriage,* the woman's press opted to focus on a novel about which they knew they could speak positively.

Feminist critics of the period seem to have taken a similar approach to the work of Ménie Dowie, whose books *A Girl in the Karpathians* and *Women Adventurers* were mentioned in *The Woman's Herald* but whose novel *Gallia* was not discussed in either *The Woman's Herald* or *Shafts*, except in satirical form. *Gallia,* which tells the story of one woman's decision to marry for the practical purpose of reproduction rather than for love, was not as feminist as Dowie's earlier works because it pushed the limits of what was acceptable to late-nineteenth-century feminists in terms of gender relations, so it is likely that reviewers for *Shafts* and *The Woman's Herald* chose to ignore this novel rather than review it negatively. Instead, reviewers focused on work by Dowie that better fit the feminist realist ideal, especially *A Girl in the Karpathians*. Still, they did not respond to Dowie's earlier work with the overwhelming praise given to Meredith's earlier work, and this likely shaped the degree to which Dowie was remembered beyond the 1890s.

Like Meredith's heroines, Dowie's can be characterized as particularly action oriented. The primary female character in *A Girl in the Karpathians* travels through East Galicia, a province of Russia, an action that would have been perceived as unusual for a girl of the period. The girl does travel with local guides but not with the Western chaperone whom women would have typically employed for such a trip; as a result, it seems that the girl takes particular actions in order to make her travel easier, such as disguising herself as a man. At the beginning of her journey she says she takes off the "trappings of an average woman" and puts on the clothes of a man for the sake of "comfort" and to "equalise our chances of escape in case of tumbles" (17). But it also seems that her disguise will bring her a certain degree of authority, since she cites as her model other women who have worn men's clothing in order to combat "masculine vanity" (17), which she perhaps expects to encounter on the trip.

The issue of whether Dowie's female characters are intentional in their resistance to traditional gender roles is important, and I will discuss this issue in more detail later; for now, it is enough to say that it is not entirely clear that the girl goes far enough with her disguise to fool everyone she meets. After the girl leaves Kolomyja, the beginning point for her journey, and heads for Mikuliczyn, it becomes apparent that most of the women the girl encounters recognize her as a woman, while the men are less sure of her gender. "I took notes of the handsome faces only vaguely, saw the shy, coquettish, sidelong glances of the women, and the bold surprise of the even more shy men. The women, of course, though I was so strange to them, knew I was only a woman after all, and could not take time and courage to smile at my cloth cap or what not; the men thought there might be something more about me, and were not so sure" (32–33). While the girl seems to benefit at least somewhat from disguising herself, it seems more important to her to disguise her nationality, though it is unclear why she feels she must do so. Nevertheless, near the beginning of the trip the girl speaks German rather than English so that people will think she is German (8), and later on she dispels the myth she is English by lighting a cigarette from a case with a coronet on it, which makes the girl's driver assume she is a Russian princess (19). In fact, the girl is Scottish, and she feels her Scottish patriotism coming out when the scenery resembles the Highlands (57).

The lack of explanation about why the girl wants to disguise her nationality points to two important aspects of the personality of the female adventurer, which Dowie clearly draws on in *A Girl in the Karpathians* as well as in her other works. I discuss this character type in more detail when I analyze *Women Adventurers,* but already it is evident that from Dowie's perspective the female adventurer truly is action oriented rather than thought oriented. Since the female adventurer is defined primarily by her actions and not by her thoughts, explanations about why she thinks certain things are scarce. Second, the female adventurer is not necessarily a figure to whom we should attach important symbolism. That is, she is a light character, not necessarily meant to be seen as a precursor to the modern woman, so it is not important for the female adventurer to use thought, speech, and action to resist cultural norms that support the subordination of women, and it is less important for any assertions of agency to be explained, as would those of the modern woman.

Still, as the girl moves from one place to another, she finds that she learns things about her own culture, especially its treatment of women, from observing Eastern European culture. For example, when she stops at a family farm in Mukuliczyn, she is initially shocked by the killing of chickens, but she recognizes the benefits of observing this event. The killing of chickens brings her "face to face with things which civilisation saves its women the need of looking at," and she believes that being exposed to such events might change the way Western European women think about themselves. It may "do much to hasten the extinction of the fussy and mouse-screeching woman, a type of which the world is at least a little weary" (68). While the girl may not be intentionally resisting cultural norms that support the subordination of women, the experiences she has (and which other women might have if they become female adventurers) might contribute to social change by increasing her (and other women's) awareness about cultural expectations of women.

Several other scenes suggest that the girl does have some interest in shaping cultural expectations of women, since she observes other customs that highlight the Western tendency to confine women. For example, when the girl observes Eastern European women drinking as much alcohol as the men do and asks the locals how they feel about this, they say it is fine for women to drink. This makes the girl realize that Western Europe has a double standard for women and men: "I began to wonder why we express so much more horror at the sight of an intoxicated woman than an intoxicated man. Is it because we have been taught, with an amusing lack of reason, that a woman's standards ought to be higher, and that we have a right to expect a greater purity, a finer decency, in her than in him? I am afraid it is" (102). Then, when the village schoolmaster brings the girl a French collection of stories to read, one of them makes her aware of the bias Western society has against women living alone. "It is very good for a man or woman to live alone, calmly and quietly," she thinks, yet she realizes that the "public resents fiercely the conclusion that a woman, a fairly light-hearted young woman more especially, is happy alone and from choice. A preference of Nature to human nature, of green trees to people, and of her own reflections to their witless comments, is an oddity" (108–9). Both examples support the idea that while the girl prefers action, sometimes the actions taken by others cause her to think seriously about the cultural expectations for women. The connection made between action and thought here seems to be in line with the feminist ideal that the two cannot be separated—nor can they be separated from the third method of asserting agency, spoken word.

Still, it seems that the girl does privilege action over thought and speech, and as the trip progresses, she reveals she is influenced by the action-oriented adventure tradition. At one point the girl is ascending a mountain when she encounters a man attending a herd of oxen and trying to protect them from bears. When the man reveals he has run out of slugs for his gun, the girl suggests loading it with small stones so that he can shoot out the bears' eyes and escape from them. This trick she learned from reading *The War-Trail*, a book so influential in her life that it belongs in the "Books Which Influenced Me" category (172). The girl's enthusiasm for action also is evident in the fact that she becomes frustrated anytime there is a *lack* of adventure on the trip. Although she seems to learn something while staying at the farm where the chickens are killed, she realizes she is bored there and decides to leave. Yet her guide, Jasio, is afraid to travel through the woods, a confession that prompts the girl to refer to Jasio as a "cowardly wretch" (132). When the girl finally convinces Jasio to follow her, he thinks he hears a bear and is frightened, but the girl thinks the whole event "preposterous" and fires her gun to show Jasio that no bear is present (140). Soon the girl settles at a priest's house in Kosmacz, but she again is bored by the lack of adventure in this place. Even the "accidents" she encounters, such as losing her watch and spending endless hours looking for it, are boring.

> One gets to know the sort of accident which occurs to one. I know mine perfectly. Nothing serious ever comes of it. I emerge from the most threatening circumstances cheerful and unharmed in the smallest particular. Hair breadth 'scapes are unknown to me, likewise moving accidents by flood and field. This is very disappointing, and would always stand in my light did I aspire to be a traveller. (168)

Despite the lack of adventure, the girl does feel regret when her trip comes
to an end because returning to Western Europe means putting on the
restrictive feminine clothes she hates so much. She describes the shoes and
stockings she must put on as "a terrible discomfort. . . . [E]ven the nicest
silk stockings, and the lightest, prettiest French shoes, are dreadful after
the postoli and rough socks that had been my portion" (284). Further, she
hates the act of having to "*pin* a hat on to your head and keep it there,
however inclined you might be to pluck it off and ram it in your pocket
in order to let the noonday sun simmer and shimmer in your hair" (285).
Still, she makes the adjustments, putting aside her comfortable masculine
garb for a dress and fixing her hair in the upswept style typical for a
nineteenth-century woman.

While *A Girl in the Karpathians* seems to focus on what "every girl"
might do if she had the chance to become a female adventurer, *Women
Adventurers,* published two years later by T. Fisher Unwin as part of its
"Adventure Series," emphasizes what real-life women *did* do as female
adventurers, especially female soldiers. The book details the adventures of
four women from the late seventeenth century to the mid-nineteenth century: Madame Velazquez, Hannah Snell, Mary Anne Talbott, and Mrs.
Christian Davies, all of whom followed their husbands into the military
and wore men's clothing in order to disguise their identities. The chapter
on Velazquez, a Mexican woman who fights for the Confederate Army in
order to be near her American husband, not only includes pictures of
Velazquez in her everyday womanly dress as well as her lieutenant's uniform, but at the end of the chapter the commentary about Velazquez
paints her as a woman who took action rather than just thinking about
what she might do. Velazquez "lived her life; she did not dream it, think
it, hope for it, or regret her inability to experience it. She had the gift of
actualising her ambitions" (51).

The chapter about Snell, who entered the military in order to find the
husband who had abandoned her, emphasizes Snell's ability to withstand
difficult conditions, including a series of bad voyages and difficult battles.
According to the commentary at the end of the chapter, she is "a grand
pattern of patience and perseverance under the worth of afflictions," and
she should serve as a model for others about how "we may learn to bear
our misfortunes whenever they befall us" (130). Talbott, too, survives
harsh conditions as she works her way up the hierarchy after her partner,
a captain, takes her to sea as a footboy (144). Eventually, her secret is discovered, and she is discharged and must make her way doing a variety of
different jobs. She continues to dress as a man when necessary, since she
finds it easier to cope with her difficulties in men's dress (172), yet she
maintains the "sensibility of her sex" (196). Finally, Mrs. Christian Davies,

who is described as a "tomboy" from her earliest years, perhaps has the most adventurous tale of the four women. She falls in love with her family's servant, Richard, and follows him into the military after he gets drunk and enlists without realizing what he is doing (219). Davies has a tumultuous relationship with Richard: once, when he cheats on her with another woman, Davies cuts off the woman's nose to keep Richard from straying again (283). After Richard's death, as well as the death of her second husband, Davies manipulates others in order to support herself, and she lives to be 108 years old (288).

The commentary about Talbott's ability to maintain her womanly sensibility despite cross-dressing parallels Dowie's discussion in the introduction to the book about why the female adventurer wears men's clothing and whether this habit makes the female adventurer a precursor to the modern woman, the type of woman feminist periodicals of the 1890s were so interested in. The ideas in the introduction separate Dowie, who states she does not see the actions of the female adventurer to be relevant to the modern woman, from Meredith, who does see this link. Dowie opens the introduction by describing the issue of women's independence as an age-old question, like so many other questions that surface again and again (vii–viii). While Dowie wants to avoid the question of suffrage, claiming she has not been "summoned to give evidence" regarding this specific issue (viii), she is willing to write about some of the other specific questions related to women's independence: "Should women smoke?"; "Should women propose?"; and "Should women go to war?" All of these questions Dowie answers simply and straightforwardly: yes, if women feel so inclined. In fact, from Dowie's perspective the answer does not matter all that much, since women who want to defy social conventions always have (ix–x).

Still, while the female soldier/adventurer is courageous, she is not a precursor to the modern woman. Of female adventurers Dowie writes that "their day is done, their histories forgotten, their devotion dead, and they have left us no genuine descendants. The socialist woman, the lecturing woman, the journalising woman—none of these must call them ancestress. All these are too serious, too severe. Their high, stern code leaves no room for the qualities of 'the female soldier'"(x–xi). Further, the female soldier, who wears masculine dress in order to make her way in the world, no longer needs to exist, in part because women have much more freedom of movement than they once did. "Allowed now to understand the world in which they live, and the conditions of its and of their own being, there is no longer any need for them to put on the garb of men in order to live, to work, to achieve, to breathe the outer air. Woman was never freer" (xx–xxi). In fact, Dowie believes that it would be wrong for women to take on the persona of the female adventurer, especially her use of masculine dress, to fight the battles of the modern world.

> An observation of women's success in public matters leads me to be certain that, for the moment, advantage lies with women as opposed to men. They do well to keep to their own clothes. An air of masculinity, however slight, goes against the woman who would be successful in the eye of the public and on platforms. Her frills and her laces are, in the meantime, a weapon, or if not a weapon to fight with, at least an implement to work with. . . . I look forward to the day when no howl of amazement, no blare of delight, will rise up whenever a woman chances to have evinced the bravery, the intelligence, or the foresight which is expected of men. . . . Then no undue notice will be taken of the fact that the human being who accomplishes something worthy or reasonable is dressed in skirts or trousers. (xxii–xxiii)

Here, Dowie separates herself from certain factions of the feminist movement, such as Rational Dress advocates, when she suggests that women should stick to more feminine clothing.

The woman's press recognized that Dowie was departing from some feminists on the issue of dress, and it responded to her statement. In discussing *Women Adventurers,* the reviewer for *The Woman's Herald* quotes the same section of the introduction about the problem with modern women wearing masculine dress and states: "One would hardly have thought that Miss Dowie found the jaunty cap and masculine knickerbockers—not to mention cigarette—against her" (Anonymous, "Extinct" 297). This comment, which is accompanied by an illustration from *A Girl in the Karpathians* in which the narrator wears a cap and knickerbockers, exposes Dowie's hypocrisy, though the reviewer later characterizes Dowie and her work in a more positive light: "Every friend of woman's progress and advancement will, however, welcome her prophecy of the time, when the woman of the future shall have succeeded in blotting out the general impression of foolishness, cowardice, and imbecility of the woman of the past with her own very different stamp" (297). In closing the review on a positive note, the writer for *The Woman's Herald* seems to recognize that Dowie was generally supportive of the women's movement, and in acknowledging this fact, the writer follows the trend of feminist reviewers to give credit to novelists for supporting the cause whenever possible, even if the writer's articulation of the cause was not ideal.

Still, *The Woman's Herald* did criticize Dowie more directly in a satirical article titled "Between the Lights" by "Aurora," which relayed the events of the 1895 Women Writers' Dinner, an annual dinner held at the Criterion Restaurant. The satire also featured a mock dinner menu, in which *A Girl in the Karpathians* is served up as the meat course, lamb with hot sauce, and *Gallia* as the dessert course, Bombe Glacée. In the article Dowie, who according to *Today's Woman* gave the keynote address while holding a cigarette in her hand (Anonymous, "Lady Journalists" 17), is satirized, primarily because she smoked while speaking.

> "But wasn't the 'Girl in the Karpathians' present?" asked the Ordinary Person.
>
> "The Girl who was there," said the Advanced Woman, stiffly, "was not in the Karpathians."
>
> "Where was she then?" demanded the Ordinary Person.
>
> "She was all at sea," answered the Advanced Woman. [. . .] "The girl in the Karpathians ignored the Past—perhaps she was wise."
>
> "I imagine the speeches were not so good as the dinner," said the Woman of No Importance. "The toast of the Future took up so much time there was none left for the Present."
>
> "And the worse of it was that the Future began with a puff and ended in smoke," said the Advanced Woman.
>
> "Cigarettes?" whispered the Society Dame, eagerly.
>
> "Hush!" said the Woman of No Importance. "Only the *debutantes* thought them manly." (Aurora, "Between" 384)

Interestingly, it is the *act* of smoking, controversial in the woman's press throughout the 1890s but accepted by Dowie in the introduction to *Women Adventurers,* that is the focus of the satire, and this act might be seen as pointing to the limits of the feminist periodicals' flexibility because smoking seemed to mark the feminist who had "gone too far" in her embrace of nontraditional gender roles.

By 1895 it seems that Dowie's person had become too extreme for some writers at *The Woman's Herald,* and this helps explain why *Gallia* did not receive a serious review from the paper. In addition, the content of *Gallia,* particularly its attention to eugenicist views of motherhood, may have played a role in feminist reception of the novel. *Gallia* tells the story of Gallia Hamesthwaite, a modern woman who was educated at Oxford as a nondegree student and who has "free movements" and "free mode of thought" but is, according to the narrator, "very unhappy" (39). Gallia is in love with "Dark" Essex, who is "vain" and "rude" but also "an interesting companion" in Gallia's eyes because he treats her "with the same want of deference he would have shown to a man" (41). However, when Gallia expresses her love for Essex, he rejects her, and she turns to Mark Gurdon, an ordinary, even dull, man but a better physical specimen than Essex. Gallia agrees to marry Mark in order to produce a healthy child and uses eugenicist ideas to justify her decision. Gallia's perspective on marriage and reproduction seems extreme, and praising her might have done more to promote the caricature of the New Woman as overly intellectual and emotionally cold, a description which some mainstream journalists promoted and which feminists were trying to avoid.[3]

Until *Gallia,* there were few direct references to eugenics in the New Woman novel, though an emphasis on the need for women to control reproduction for the sake of their health is suggested in literature published before *Gallia.* For example, in Grand's *Heavenly Twins,* when Edith contracts syphilis from her husband and gives birth to an infected baby before dying, there is the suggestion that women should choose as husbands men in good health or perhaps avoid marriage altogether until men stop being sexually promiscuous. Still, Grand presents a social-purity view of reproduction but not necessarily a eugenicist view.[4] While social purity was a precursor to eugenics, the distinction between the two is important: social purity advocates restraint from sexual intercourse to create a change in cultural attitudes toward women, while eugenics advocates reproduction in order to advance a particular "breed" of people. Thus social purity does not have quite the same potential for racist perspectives, a characteristic I discuss in more detail below, that eugenics does. Unless a novel made a direct statement about reproduction for the purpose of advancing the race, as *Gallia* does, the novel might well have been interpreted by the feminist press as advocating social purity but not necessarily eugenics.[5] What makes *Gallia* the marker for the introduction of eugenics into the New Woman novel, then, is Dowie's explicit statement that Gallia will marry a particular man for reproductive purposes only and chooses him over other men because of his physical features and good health.

By appearing to advocate eugenics, Dowie pushed the boundaries of what was acceptable to feminists, since eugenics relied on a hierarchical philosophy based on class and race. As Richardson indicates in *Love and Eugenics in the Late Nineteenth Century* (2003), attention to physical features when marrying for reproductive purposes in 1890s Britain was born primarily out of class prejudices, though it came to advocate racist views in the early twentieth century. "Born and bred among the competitive Victorian middle class," writes Richardson, "eugenics was a biologistic discourse on *class:* a class-based application of the evolutionary discourse which proliferated in the wake of Darwin" (3). Still, these class prejudices were discussed in racialized terms via the emphasis on physical features, so class prejudice cannot be separated from race prejudice entirely, even in the 1890s. Writing of the Victorian tendency to marginalize the poor via racialized characteristics, Richardson states:

> Racial language was readily used to distinguish groups of varying social as well as ethnic backgrounds, as exemplified in the study of the popular ethnologist John Beddoe, *The Races of Britain: A Contribution to the Anthropology of Western Europe* (1885). Galton's definition of eugenics as "the study of agencies under social control that may improve or impair the racial qualities of future generations, either physically or mentally" demonstrates this slippage between class and race, between the social and the natural. (25)

When Gallia chooses Mark Gurdon based on his physical features, then, she is choosing him on the basis of racialized characteristics, and the expression of this hierarchical philosophy based on class and race possibly put some reviewers for the feminist periodicals in an uncomfortable position with regard to Dowie's work.

Still, it is true that the woman's press was not necessarily antiracist either, and in ignoring and even satirizing Dowie, they may not have been resisting the racialized discourse of eugenics consciously. Certainly, the feminist press praised authors who expressed racial prejudices in their novels. For example, both *Shafts* and *The Woman's Herald* regularly wrote about Olive Schreiner, whose *Story of an African Farm* (1883) includes racial epithets. Still, *The Woman's Herald* actively rejected racialized discussions of intelligence, especially those claiming that European men were more intelligent than other groups of people. In "Weight in Sex," *The Woman's Herald* bemoans the "annual interest" in the size of men's brains, most recently reported by a German professor, Waldeyer, who points out that the average European man's brain is 141 grams heavier than the average European woman's brain. To this *The Woman's Herald* sarcastically replies: "It must be a source of unmitigated chagrin to the professors that the average brain weight of Chinese coolies is 1,430g. The average coolie, then, by force of argument must be a more intellectual person than the average man" (131). The use of the term "coolie" here suggests that feminists had not unlearned all of their race and class prejudices, but it does seem that their goal to disrupt traditional hierarchies did extend beyond England and beyond gender.

Although the feminist periodicals did not review *Gallia*, most likely because it pushed the limits of what was acceptable to feminists, Gallia does exhibit the three-step method of thought, speech, and action advocated by *Shafts* and *The Woman's Herald.* While the novel begins with much stronger emphasis on Gurdon's character and his internal perspective, with the first five chapters of the book focusing on his holiday in Paris, Gallia soon becomes the center of attention in the story. When she enters the story in chapter 6, it is evident she fits the description of the unconventional modern woman. She immediately wants to see the day's papers, and when she comes across a story about the repeal campaign against the Contagious Diseases Act, she and her aunt argue about whether she even should read about the subject. Mrs. Leighton thinks it "a waste of time" since Gallia cannot do anything to settle the matter, an allusion to the fact women did not have the vote and therefore could not influence government policy (34). To this Gallia replies: "I can't make the State do this or that—I couldn't even cause father to support a Bill—but I, in my own person, must read and think about it, because it is a question that only girls can settle ultimately" (34).

Clearly, Gallia is prepared to resist cultural norms that support the subordination of women through spoken word, and readers do receive some indication why Gallia resists such norms, through information provided by the narrator, who details how Gallia was educated in the natural sciences and foreign languages rather than music, the more popular subject for girls (38). The narrator also explains that Gallia did not participate in the same activities most girls do at a young age. "As a child," states the narrator, "Gallia had never had a doll; had never played at keeping house, teaching school, having callers, as most other girl-children do. If there was a baby about, she had shivered and left the room. Nothing terrified her like the society of young married women" (39). Furthermore, readers get an indication of Gallia's unconventional views about gender relations when the story focuses on her love for Essex. While the narrator points out that Gallia's interest in Essex is in vain, since men like Essex inevitably marry the "pretty foolish kitten style of person" (42), readers learn that Gallia approaches Essex about her love rather than waiting for him to come to her, and, after she confesses her love, the narrator tells us, "She stood back from him, her arms at her sides, waiting, as though for a sentence, for his reply" (57). When Essex does not accept her love, she boldly engages him in discussion about the "typical" expectations men and women have regarding love and then moves on, telling herself, "That is the end of that. . . . If I had foreseen his coming at all, I should have foreseen his going too. It is no worse and no better than I imagined it" (60).

Gallia's highly rational response to Essex's rejection shows she will not succumb to cultural norms that would have her feel distraught over the rejection, and the story moves on to the details of Gurdon's courting of Essex's sister and to the three months Gallia spends in Algiers with her dying mother. These scenes function as the interval during which Gallia's eugenicist ideas supposedly develop, though readers are given no indica-

tion of her beliefs until after her return from Algiers. Gallia's earliest articulation of her beliefs comes in chapter 18, when she, Essex's sister, and
another acquaintance, Miss Janion, sit down for tea and end up discussing
the advantages and disadvantages of "eugenic love," as Richardson refers to
romantic relations for the purposes of producing a "better race." Gallia
begins mildly enough, simply stating she thinks there are two ways of looking at men, in terms of their place in society and in terms of their relationships to women, and, for the latter, men must be "well-grown and healthy
and sound—in wind, limb, and temper" (112). The other two women
accept this opinion, but Gallia shocks them when she suggests that some
men and women are better suited for bearing children and this suitability
is based on strictly physical qualities. When Gallia says it would be better
to bring in a healthy surrogate mother than to have an unsuitable woman
bear a weak child, the other women cannot believe her words. "A moment's
silence fell upon the three. Their brains were a little burdened, and no
wonder, by this astounding piece of social reform" (113).

As readers, we too may be surprised, since there has been no previous
indication Gallia holds eugenicist ideals. Likewise, when Gallia focuses on
Gurdon as a potential mate, her thoughts develop abruptly, with little set-
up from the narrator. While Gallia initially feels no attraction to Gurdon,
she becomes aware of his potential as a mate during a visit to her aunt's
house, at which he is present. She first is drawn to Gurdon's voice, but his
other physical features quickly become attractive to her as well:

> She listened, and admired his speaking voice, it was so much lower
> and rounder than the usual modern man's. . . . His voice was not the
> only good thing about Mark to strike a girl's fancy; there was a firm-
> ness and a faint pinkness about his face which did not suggest a
> London life in any way, and yet would have been too delicate for a
> countryman. His eyes were bright and clear—those curious ringed
> eyes of grey and hazel; his teeth were perfect; not too small, and very
> white. Gallia saw all these things rather as a dealer might notice the
> points in a horse than as a lady might perceive a young man's claims
> to handsomeness. (121)

In this passage there is no indication that Gallia has in mind marrying
Gurdon for purely reproductive reasons, but in the following chapter,
when Essex returns and asks Gallia whether she will ever be the sort of
woman to "be happy, and look pretty, and marry, and love, and bring up
children" (126), she expresses a desire to have children: "I certainly hope
to bring up a child. I think it is all I do want" (126).

This sentiment seems to work against all we have been told about

Gallia's character by the narrator, but Gallia explains why she wants to have children, especially after Essex claims that Gallia and all other modern women are "a complete waste of material" and have "no use" in society (127). Gallia says motherhood is one purpose she can fulfill, since she agrees she is unfit to provide the kind of "romantic love" (i.e., emotional support of man) most men want. Gallia tells Essex:

> One should be beautifully made and beautiful to be a mother. . . . [P]erhaps there is a bigger object in my appearance than the satisfaction of any man's senses. . . . If I were to fall in love again, it might be with someone quite unsuitable to be the father of my child—someone who would not be fine and strong and healthy, and of a healthy stock. As it is, when I marry—I talk of it quite as a certainty because it is a certainty to me, being rich and good-looking, and the only child of my father—I shall marry solely with a view to the child I am going to live for. (128–29)

By the end of this chapter Gallia's reason for embracing eugenic love is clear, and her response to Gurdon's proposal in chapter 28 signifies her ability to act upon, as well as think and speak about, her view that women are constrained by certain cultural expectations, especially the idea they will marry for romantic love.

Gallia continues to express unconventional ideas when Gurdon proposes marriage. She immediately asks why he wants to marry her, subverting the traditional proposal scene in which a woman would not question a man's motives. Gurdon's response to her question, which is to detail his past romantic history, plays into another stereotype about proposal scenes: that the man must confess his sinful past before declaring his love for his current romantic interest. Gallia again subverts the typical proposal by refusing to let Gurdon go into the details of his past. "You shan't suffer the unfairness of the average proposal scene," she says to him. "A man has to say all the humble, uncomfortable things—in the sweat of his brow—and a girl listens calmly and allows smiles to dawn at intervals. We won't do that. We'll try and be more honest" (185). At this point Gallia accepts Gurdon's proposal and quickly gets to the reason she has accepted it: "I must tell you. I am not marrying you because I love you. . . . I do not love you. . . . But I admire you; you fill out my idea of what a man should be, not only in looks, but in qualities. . . . I have wanted the father of my child to be a fine, strong, manly man, full of health and strength" (191–92). With this statement Gallia's belief in eugenic love is put into action, and the novel ends with the anticipation of their marriage, set against the news that Essex has a hereditary heart condition, confirming that, from a eugenicist point of view, he indeed would have been the wrong man to marry.

The novel, then, is in keeping with the feminist realist ideal articulated by *Shafts* and *The Woman's Herald,* since it depicts a strong woman resisting cultural norms through thought, speech, and action, but it is problematic in terms of this ideal because of the content of Gallia's actions. Ultimately, the lack of attention paid to Dowie's *Gallia,* especially when compared to the attention given to Meredith's novels, serves as a good example of the limits of the feminist realist ideal, since it illustrates that all authors, regardless of gender, had to meet feminist expectations about the content of a woman's actions in order to receive praise. Since *Gallia* pushed the boundaries of the feminist realist aesthetic too far, the woman's press chose not to praise Dowie as much as it did Meredith. Instead, it focused on those works by Dowie that better articulated the feminist realist ideal. In 1896 Mary Krout, who had written the seminal "Women in Fiction" article for *The Woman's Herald* in 1893, was still focusing on Dowie as the author of *A Girl in the Karpathians* rather than the author of *Gallia.* In an article "Women's Clubs," which was reprinted in Krout's *A Looker-On in London* (1899), Krout covers a speech about scientific dairying given by Dowie at the Sesame Club, and she characterizes Dowie as speaking with the same "wit and originality" seen in *A Girl in the Karpathians* (95).

Similarly, in the late 1890s feminist periodicals were still focusing on Meredith as the author of *Diana of the Crossways* rather than the author of *The Amazing Marriage.* In fact, criticism of *Diana* experiences a significant resurgence in the mid- and late 1890s, and it seems that at least some portion of Meredith's literary reputation in the twentieth century should be attributed to this resurgence because it extended beyond the woman's press and into the mainstream press. Maurice Forman's extensive bibliography of Meredith's works, *Meredithiana* (1924), reveals that in 1896 and 1897 alone ten articles were published with titles specifically about Meredith's women characters, and many of these appeared in mainstream periodicals. Garnet Smith's "The Women of George Meredith," which appeared in *The Fortnightly Review* in May 1896, paints Diana as "the most virile of Meredithian women," made to "bear . . . the traces of the tyrannous Turkish training imposed, it would seem, by men upon them" (783), and W. L. Courtney's "George Meredith's Heroines," which appeared in the *Daily Telegraph* in July 1897, contrasts the "new type" of woman found in Meredith's novels to the early-Victorian angelic type and claims that Meredith's heroine is "wholly different" and "essentially modern . . . the woman in revolt" (12). Courtney says that this modern woman is one to "demand freedom of thought and action," and he claims that he hardly needs to cite examples of this type of woman in Meredith's work, though he includes "Janet Ilchester; Rhoda Fleming; to some extent the Princess Ottilia" and "above all, perhaps, Diana Merion" (12).[6]

The resurgence of *Diana* criticism in the period 1896–97, which provides the first indicator Meredith's feminism had been accepted in the mainstream press, continued into the new century. *Meredithiana* lists thirteen articles written between 1898 and 1909, the year of Meredith's death, specifically referring to Meredith and women in the titles. Two highlights of the post-1900 attention to *Diana* are prize-winning essays published in *The Lady* in 1900 and Herbert Bedford's 1914 book, *The Heroines of George Meredith*. The prize-winning essays in *The Lady*, written by readers of the magazine, show the degree to which *Diana* had become a cultural icon, for *The Lady* was not a feminist magazine but one aimed at the middle-class, educated, even "genteel" woman reader (Riley 105).[7] Bedford's book also indicates the degree to which Meredith's feminism had been incorporated into print venues aimed at mainstream audiences. With its coffee-table-book appearance, and individual portraits with large-print commentaries about twenty of Meredith's heroines, it is clearly aimed at a general audience familiar with Meredith's popularized reputation rather than the more negative reputation expressed by mainstream critics of the late nineteenth century.[8]

The sustained attention to *Diana* and to Meredith's heroines in general in the 1890s and beyond suggests that Meredith's acceptance by feminists of the 1890s contributed to his overall popularity in a way not experienced by Dowie. As the satire of the Women Writers' dinner shows, Dowie represented an extreme form of feminism, a form the feminist periodicals were not eager to embrace, especially since they spent so much time trying to combat negative images of the New Woman. A mainstream but feminist-friendly review of *Gallia* in *The Saturday Review* points out the problem with embracing Dowie and her strong female characters:

> "Gallia" is not a fair representative of the advanced woman. Plainness of speech and pluck may be common to both; but there the resemblance ends. The advanced women of the best type hold, if we mistake not, that love is necessary to justify and sanctify marriage at least as much as marriage is necessary to sanctify love. And they would regard such a union as Gallia deliberately enters on with a man she does not love as a grave breach of chastity. (384)

Unlike other mainstream reviews, which saw *Gallia* as typical of the advanced woman (Oliphant, "Anti-Marriage" 142–43; Anonymous, "Novels" 510), this review recognized that the feminist movement favored actions with a certain result, namely, the advancement of freedom for all women, and would draw the line at actions such as Gallia's, since they did not achieve this result.

Meredith and Dowie were not the only authors whose literary reputations were influenced by the woman's press. The degree to which a particular author received "face time" in the woman's press seems to have contributed to their literary reputations beyond the *fin de siècle*. Sarah Grand, for example, was the female author most often featured in *Shafts* and *The Woman's Herald,* and she emerged as the most readily recognized woman writer of the period. On the other hand, women writers mentioned in passing in the two papers have not emerged as central figures in late-Victorian fiction. When Grant Richards wrote an article for *The Woman's Herald* highlighting important women writers of 1893, he noted seventeen who he thought deserved special attention. Of the women, only four—Pearl Craigie ("John Oliver Hobbes"), Mary Chomondeley, Alice Meynell, and Katherine Bradley and Edith Cooper ("Michael Field")—are read today, and primarily by critics working to recover forgotten women writers. Others—Beatrice Harradan, Cecily Ullmann Sidgwick ("Andrew Dean"), Emilie Isabel Wilson (Mrs. Russell Barrington), and Jane Barlow—are listed in John Sutherland's *The Stanford Companion to Victorian Fiction* (1989) but are not widely read, even among Victorianists, and the rest are forgotten entirely, not even listed in Sutherland's very extensive catalogue. In the following chapter I discuss in greater detail the issues surrounding the literary reputations of two authors writing at the *fin de siècle,* and I show how the woman's press and its feminist realist aesthetic played a role in this process.

CHAPTER 4

"The Realistic Method in Its Best Expression": Successful Representations of Woman's Agency and Literary Reputations

Ultimately, both *Shafts* and *The Woman's Herald* looked for novels that incorporated all three methods of expressing woman's agency, and they found this ideal fulfilled in George Moore's *Esther Waters* (1894), the story of an independent-minded female servant who becomes pregnant but overcomes the stigma of being a single mother and successfully raises her child alone. This novel, which was banned by the circulating libraries because of its "immorality" and became the center of a debate about how much control libraries should exert over the distribution of novels, was seen by the feminist periodicals as an important contribution to the struggle for women's advancement. In "Esther Waters and What It Suggests," *Shafts*'s reviewer Gertrude Kapteyn characterizes the novel as an example of "the realistic method in its best expression" (24), and Florence Fenwick Miller, writing for *The Woman's Herald*, describes it as a "powerful and remarkable novel" because it "makes an effort to look at life from the woman's standpoint" (Miller, "Books" 297).

Certainly, Moore was an unlikely candidate for acceptance by the feminist community, given his ambiguous relationship with it. As Adrian Frazier points out in his biography of Moore, Moore engaged the "Woman Question" with his 1886 novel *A Drama in Muslin*, but he also condemned feminists for adopting an antisex attitude (Frazier 127). Further, Moore railed against Mona Caird's views about marriage, though he also took issue with the views of her critics in an 1890 article titled "Pruriency" (202). Still, *Esther Waters* represents Moore's concerted effort to refashion himself in the early 1890s, in part because he wished to distance himself from his earlier naturalist work but also because he seemed to recognize the influence of feminist realism in the literary market. While he writes about the composition of the novel as an attempt to become more "human," a statement that does not necessarily suggest the influence of feminism, he also writes about it as the continuation of themes begun in *Drama in Muslin,* which I have already identified as taking up the "Woman Question." As such, *Esther Waters*—the book and the character—became Moore's late-century "female helpmate," no longer just the traditional domestic housewife and the guiding force for the man of the house but now a stronger, more independent woman who could guide the author through a literary market fascinated with the modern woman.

With *Esther Waters* as a female helpmate, Moore achieved success, making more money than he ever had before (Hone 212) but also finding more acceptance within the feminist community. Sarah Grand wrote a letter of admiration to *The Daily Chronicle* in favor of lifting the library ban on the novel ("Letter" 3), and the Women's Progressive Society used the battle with the lending libraries over the novel as reason to open their own library (Langenfeld 49). While Moore's reputation with the feminist community was not transformed entirely, he recognized he had found a good thing with *Esther Waters,* and he looked for ways to capitalize on his success. As he was planning *Evelyn Innes* (1898), another woman-centered novel, he claimed, "If I am lucky in my choice [of subject matter], I shall do better than *Esther Waters*" (Frazier 249), and when his subsequent novel did not outdo *Esther Waters,* he looked for ways to ensure his literary reputation beyond his own lifetime using *Esther Waters* instead. In 1920 Moore urged a "fine" edition of *Esther Waters,* and in 1932 he wrote a "woman-centered" preface for an American edition of the novel, steps reflecting not only his tendency to aestheticize women but also his recognition that the New Woman novel of the 1890s had improved his own career and might continue to enhance it after his death.

Henrietta Stannard, who made her reputation on her military tales and sentimental romances written under the pseudonyms "Violet Whyte" and "John Strange Winter," also had a female helpmate, the main character in *A Blameless Woman* (1894), Margaret North. This character might have guided Stannard to more acceptance within the feminist community just as *Esther Waters* had done for Moore—if Stannard had been able to break away from her typical literary style more fully and if her own views about women's issues had not influenced her literary representations as much as they did. Not the typical liberal feminist of the 1890s, Stannard opposed suffrage for women but made her mark in the feminist community when, in 1893, she established the Anti-Crinoline League, which was designed to stop the return of the crinoline into women's fashion. Still, Stannard's commitment to shaping fashion rather than public policy clearly marks her as "moderate," and, like Moore, she needed a female helpmate to substantiate her place in the *fin-de-siècle* literary community, where a nod to the New Woman could go a long way in helping an author's reputation, especially within the feminist community.

In *A Blameless Woman,* Margaret North resists the label of "fallen woman" after learning that her marriage is invalid because her husband is already married to another woman. This book, which certainly possesses some elements of the sentimental (and even sensational) romance, shows Stannard's attempt to engage the feminist realist aesthetic, but it did not earn the positive reviews *Esther Waters* received from *Shafts* and *The Woman's Herald.* While the lack of attention from the woman's press is somewhat surprising, since the staff of both *Shafts* and *The Woman's Herald* knew about Stannard's work and her involvement in at least some women's causes, it indicates that, like Dowie's *Gallia, A Blameless Woman* marks the limits of the feminist realist aesthetic. While the ways in which Margaret North asserts agency are not that different from the methods employed by Meredith's heroines, who used the more subtle form of absence as a method of resistance as well as the more overt method of presence, *A Blameless Woman* retains too many elements of the romance to be embraced by feminist periodicals. By looking at Moore's and Stannard's engagement with the feminist aesthetic—how their representations of woman's agency were received by feminist periodicals and how they responded to this reception—we can see the ways in which authors confronted the issue of literary reputation at the *fin de siècle* and beyond.

As Helmut Gerber points out in *George Moore on Parnassus,* the collection of letters from the last portion of Moore's life, Moore wrote a letter to Edouard Dujardin in 1912 celebrating the success of his autobiography *Hail and Farewell* and indicating that he was well on his way to acceptance in the literary canon. In this letter Moore envisions himself as nearing the height of his career, symbolized by Mount Parnassus. "I am a little nearer the summit of Parnassus," writes Moore, indicating that literary fame was something he sought out and hoped to achieve (22). In adopting the ascent of Parnassus as a symbol for the struggle authors face, Moore paints a picture of himself as one who had struggled to be recognized for his writing but was a step closer to achieving the status of a great artist. Further, in using this image, he links himself to a tradition of strong men, since this image of Moore ascending the summit recalls Apollo, warrior and poet, standing on Parnassus.[1]

Moore's use of the image of Parnassus suggests he saw himself as part of a tradition of male authorship that could be traced back to the ancients, but a shorter yet equally significant tradition of male authorship was also at work at the end of the nineteenth century. In the late-Victorian period, novelists were working within a tradition of *British* male authorship, approximately 150 years old and traceable to the early male novelists of the eighteenth century, especially Samuel Richardson, Henry Fielding, and Daniel Defoe. This tradition has been thoroughly analyzed by twentieth-century literary criticism, most notably in Ian Watt's *The Rise of the Novel* (1957), and it has been the subject of revision by a number of critics interested in the development of the novel.[2] While these critics have shown that the British novel can be traced back much further than the mid-eighteenth century, late-Victorian authors often saw their own work as growing out of the Richardson tradition. For example, Moore's autobiographical *Confessions of a Young Man* (1888) details his immersion in English literature upon his return to London from Paris in the early 1880s, and as his career matured, he became increasingly interested in the history of English literature. In "Some Characteristics of English Fiction" (1900) Moore lays out his own interpretation of the history of English literature, and in "An Imaginary Conversation: Gosse and Moore" (1918–19), Moore, with Edmund Gosse's assistance, tells the story of the development of the novel. Through these articles, Moore marks his alliance with the masculinist tradition.

Still, Moore's early career in the 1880s and 1890s reveals none of the markers of an author who would someday be accepted into the literary canon. His early novels—*A Modern Lover* (1883) and *A Mummer's Wife* (1885)—were distinctly naturalist and despised by English critics, who feared the influence of Emile Zola in particular. Although Moore refashioned himself in the late 1880s, by separating himself from Zola and by infusing his work with other influences, including Pater, Huysmans, and Flaubert, his novels continued to sell poorly, in part because they were still *perceived* as Zolaesque. *A Mere Accident* (1887), for example, had been written in the Huysmans tradition, but critics of the period, including George Bernard Shaw, believed Zola's influence was still present (Hone 130; Frazier 155). By the early 1890s Moore felt marginalized by these critics and the public, especially as they paid closer attention to the work of his arch nemesis Hardy.[3] Acutely aware of the necessity of fitting into the British masculinist tradition in order to ensure his reputation after death, Moore once again refashioned himself in the early 1890s in the hope of attracting a wider audience. With *Esther Waters,* Moore attempted an even softer version of realism, chosen specifically because he hoped to be more thoroughly accepted by the public. In 1889 Moore wrote to his friend Clara Lanza of his plan to do something radically different with this novel: "*My next book will be more human;* I *shall* bathe myself in the simplest and most naive emotions, and shall not leave them—the daily bread of humanity" (Hone 161; Frazier 194).

In addition, in Moore's plan to write a more "human" book, he also drew on the "woman-centered" approach he first had attempted in *Drama in Muslin,* the story of Alice Barton, an Anglo-Irish woman who does not fit into the traditional, marriage-centered culture in which she lives. Moore details his woman-centered approach in *Drama in Muslin* in an article, "Defensio Pro Scriptus Meis" (1887), in which he describes the process of developing the character of Alice by drawing on the qualities of real women in order to construct an imaginary one.[4] He confirms a similar approach to *Esther Waters* in a letter to his brother Maurice, in which he claims that "*Esther Waters* is Alice Barton in another form" (Hone 187), and in *A Communication to My Friends* (1933), the autobiography written in the last year of his life, in which he comments on his choice of subject for *Esther Waters.* Of his search for the ideal subject, Moore writes:

> I was asking myself whether the hero of my book should be a footman, or should I take a cook for a heroine, and before I reached the Law Courts I decided that it could be neither. A footman would not be a pleasing object in the love passages and it is hard to think of a good-tempered cook, though no doubt there are such beings. A cook is too old, but not a scullery-maid. Ah, there I have it! A scullery-maid, said I, she shall be. (65)

This comment suggests he adopted the woman-centered novel precisely because he understood the power of such an approach, and his statement about the suitability of a scullery-maid versus that of a cook is telling, since it shows that only particular types of women were appropriate for the protagonist position in a woman-centered novel. Since a cook is "too old" for such a position, we can infer that the woman-centered novel needs a younger woman in part because discussion of female sexuality is central to this type of novel. The cook, who would most likely be married or widowed (as is the cook in *Esther Waters*), cannot bear the weight of the issues expected in a woman-centered novel, but the young (and often virginal) scullery-maid can.

While the conditions of composing *Esther Waters* and the role of woman-centered material in that composition are important, what happened *after* Moore published *Esther Waters* is equally, if not more, important. Not only was there widespread praise of *Esther Waters* from the mainstream press (Langenfeld 43–52), but Moore also received praise from feminists. As already mentioned, Sarah Grand wrote a letter to *The Daily Chronicle* in favor of lifting the library ban on Moore's novel, arguing that the novel should be available in "every library in the kingdom" ("Letter" 3), and the Women's Progressive Society set up its own library, which included books banned from the larger lending libraries because of their "liberal nature" (Langenfeld 49). In addition to this support, positive reviews appeared in both *Shafts* and *The Woman's Herald*. *The Woman's Herald*'s review, written by Florence Fenwick Miller, claims that although Moore's writing is flawed by "crudity of expression" and a tendency to overdescribe scenes, *Esther Waters* is "a powerful and remarkable book. It is one in which a man makes an effort to look at life from the woman's stand-point" (296). While Moore's effort to "realise the woman's mind" cannot match the efforts of Shakespeare, Meredith, or Zola (interestingly, Fenwick Miller is more open to Zola than most feminist critics of the time), Fenwick Miller acknowledges that "Mr. Moore has earnestly endeavoured" to represent the world from a woman's perspective, and "that alone is much" (296).

Fenwick Miller does not discuss specific narrative strategies used by Moore, focusing instead on content details she judges according to her own ideas about the amount of suffering women have endured, but the review of *Esther Waters* in *Shafts* does address specific narrative strategies in some detail. *Shafts*'s review shows that according to feminist realism, Moore's novel was a remarkable achievement. Gertrude Kapteyn writes that *Esther Waters* is "the realistic method in its best expression," since it avoids the pitfalls of both naturalism and aestheticism, in which the "humanity" of characters is lost in overemphasis on either external realities (naturalism) or form and language (aestheticism) (24, 26). In addition, Kapteyn makes clear the effectiveness of particular narrative strategies employed by Moore, especially his use of internal perspective, dialogue, and description of characters' actions.

Of Moore's use of internal perspective, Kapteyn writes:

> With utmost delicacy the author indicates the downward slide which takes [Esther] quickly to her fall, and we can hardly conceive any-thing more impressive than the way in which is described Esther's first realization of the terrible consequences of her weakness. "She (Esther) sat on her wooden chair facing the wide kitchen window. The glow from the fire showed on her print dress. And it was in this death of active memory that something awoke within her. . . . The truth shone upon her like a star." (24)

Kapteyn chooses a passage from the novel so infused with the language of the narrator that one might consider the internal perspective here to belong to the narrator rather than Esther. However, Kapteyn's emphasis on this passage as being the one in which Esther's "first realization" of her situation occurs suggests that she believes Moore has effectively captured the consciousness of Esther. It is true that there is less of Esther's internal perspective than perhaps her resistance to cultural norms through spoken word and action begs for, but Kapteyn succinctly points out how Moore at least acknowledges the importance of depicting woman's consciousness, whether it is through internal perspective, the narrator's perspective, or thematic devices.

Kapteyn also points out Moore's use of dialogue as a strategy for representing assertion of agency, for she refers to the resistance Esther puts up to cultural norms that support the subordination of women in the scene in which Fred Parsons (the Brethren lay minister who tries to "save" Esther by marrying her) chastises Esther for returning to her "seducer," William Latch. Kapteyn writes:

> Touchingly, she herself expresses the main motive which keeps her afloat . . . when Fred reproaches her with having changed so much. "No, I've not changed, Fred, but things has turned out different; one doesn't do the good that one would like to in the world, one has to do the good that comes to one to do. I've my husband and my boy to look to. Them's my good. At least that's how I sees things." So says Esther, and how many of her sisters in suffering with her? (25)

In the last sentence of this passage, Kapteyn makes it clear that Esther is a successful heroine precisely because she speaks out in the same way real-life women, the "sisters in suffering," might speak out about the conditions of their lives.

Finally, Kapteyn suggests Moore's commendable skill at describing characters' actions. Commenting upon Moore's presentation of the story after Esther's "first realization" scene, Kapteyn writes:

> From this moment the author evolves his story in sober intense earnestness through all the sorrowful and tragical details which naturally must follow the pitiful act. First Esther's coming home . . . where the drunken father insults, then follows the hospital, where she shrinks from the cruel coldness with which they handle human beings . . . [t]he horrible experience in trying to find nursing for her child . . . and at last the oasis in the house of Miss Rice. . . . [T]he author is perfect in his picturing of the unfaltering perseverance and

self-denial, the love and passion characteristic of true motherhood.
(25)

Although Kapteyn might have discussed Moore's description of characters'
actions more specifically, since it sounds as though she is providing plot
summary rather than analysis of literary technique, her reference to
Moore's depiction of Esther's "unfaltering perseverance and self-denial"
toward the end of the passage, at the end of a series of plot points, suggests
she recognizes Moore's description of actions as an artistic element in his
work.

In addition to the points Kapteyn makes in her review, perhaps the
other striking element of Moore's presentation of Esther's story—which
Kapteyn refers to only briefly and with little analysis of its narrative
significance—is the opening of the novel. The opening emphasizes Esther's
internal perspective, and Moore repeats this emphasis in the third-to-last
chapter of the book, when Esther returns to the house where she worked
as a domestic servant and where the story of her "fall" began. "She stood
on the platform watching the receding train," reads the opening, told first
from the narrator's perspective and then, several paragraphs later, from
Esther's perspective. "She had been in service in such houses," reads the
narration as it shifts to Esther's perspective, "and knew that a general servant was kept in each. But the life in Woodview was a great dream, and she
could not imagine herself accomplishing all that would be required of her"
(2). From the second page of the novel, Esther's internal perspective is at
the forefront, and when Moore repeats this opening at the end of the
novel, with variation to it after the first paragraph, it is clear that Esther's
consciousness has matured. Shifting once again from the narrator's perspective to Esther's, as she looks out at the same landscape after eighteen
years, the story reads, "[S]he noticed that the line of little villas had not
increased; they were as she had left them eighteen years ago. . . . Eighteen
years had gone by, eighteen years of labour, suffering, disappointment. . . .
And now it all seemed like a dream. . . . [H]ow had she done it? How often
had she found herself within sight of the workhouse?" (376–77). Esther's
questions about her own struggle highlight her increased consciousness,
since she recognizes she has achieved something in the years that have
passed.

Also striking in the novel is how rarely the internal perspective of other
characters is used, especially the internal perspective of Esther's male partners and her female employers, people Esther comes into conflict with over
the choices she makes about raising her child and remaining a single mother for much of her life. Not only are the first two chapters of the novel
dominated by Esther's internal perspective, with supplementary descrip-

tion of the scene from a fairly unintrusive narrator, but when other characters' perspectives come into the scene, they are used sparingly. For example, when Esther tells William's mother, the cook of the house, that her
son looks handsome as he prepares to go to the races, the narration reads,
"Mrs. Latch moved about rapidly, and she opened and closed the oven;
then, seeing that the other women were still standing in the yard and safely out of hearing, she said . . ." (51), and when Mr. Leopold, the lead male
servant of the house, tells the story of what has happened at the races that
day, the narration reads, "Mr. Leopold looked round, and seeing every eye
fixed on him he considered how much remained of the story, and with
quickened speech continued . . ." (58). In neither case does Moore spend
significant time on the thoughts or feelings of Mrs. Latch or Mr. Leopold,
in contrast to the time he spends when the narration is through Esther's
perspective.

This sparse use of internal perspective also applies to the characters of
Esther's male partners, William and Fred, though one might expect Moore
to put more emphasis on their internal perspectives. Look, for example, at
the first love scene between Esther and William, which takes place on the
downs of Woodview, the house Esther and William serve. Unlike other
love scenes in late-Victorian novels, where the man's internal perspective
often introduces and controls the scene, here Esther's perspective is the
more dominant, and William's perspective enters only once. After telling
us that Esther is "weary" for a male companion, the narrator shifts to
Esther's perspective as she walks on the downs. "Margaret [one of the
other servants] had gone down to the Gardens with her young man,"
thinks Esther, "and one of these days a young man would come to take her
out. Now what would he be like? She laughed the thought away, for it did
not seem likely that any young man would bother about her. But at this
moment, she saw a man coming through the hunting gate. His height and
shoulder told her that he was William" (42). Even after William enters the
scene, Esther's internal perspective continues to be the more dominant,
with lines such as "She was glad of the chance to get a mouthful of fresh
air," when William suggests they walk out a bit from the house, and "For
something to say, and hoping to please, Esther asked him where the race-
course was," when they are out of the immediate vicinity of the house
(42–43). The only time William's perspective enters the narration is in the
line "Esther looked at William in silent admiration, and, *feeling that he
had secured an appreciative listener,* he continued his monologue regarding
the wealth and rank his family had formerly held" (44, my emphasis).

Given Esther's interest in William and her voluntary participation in
activities such as this walk and dancing and drinking with him at a ball, it
is difficult to see William as her seducer. When he first kisses her, she

seems a willing participant: "She listened just as if she understood, for it mattered to her little what he talked so long as he was talking to her. . . . William's allusions to the police . . . frightened her; but her fears died in the sensation of his arm about her waist, and the music that the striking of a match had put to flight began in her heart, and it rose to its height when his face bent over hers" (46–47). And when William and Esther consummate their relationship, her feelings for William seem to contribute to the act, even though Esther also feels she cannot control the situation: "[O]ne evening, putting his pipe aside, William threw his arm round her, whispering that she was his wife. The words were delicious in her fainting ears. She could not put him away, nor could she struggle with him, though she knew that her fate depended on her resistance, and swooning away she awakened in pain, powerless to free herself" (73). The dominance of Esther's internal perspective in these scenes suggests she makes more independent decisions about her sexual relationships than does the typical fallen woman in Victorian literature.

This pattern of sparse internal perspective is paralleled in scenes between Esther and Fred, the Brethren lay minister who wants to marry Esther. In the first chapter focusing on the relationship between the two, the internal perspective of both Esther and Fred is rare, with the fairly unintrusive narrator describing the scene and setting up the dialogue. Still, Esther's emotions do come across in the narration at least three times. First, when it is clear that Fred does not approve of the woman for whom Esther works, since she is a novelist, we learn that Esther "would have liked to tell him that her mistress was not one who would write anything that could do harm to anybody" (187). Second, when Esther realizes that Fred probably will disapprove of her child, we hear Esther's thoughts: "Sooner or later he would find out that she had a child, then she would see him no more. That child came between her and every chance of settling herself. It were better to break with Fred. But what excuse could she give?" (189–90). Finally, at the end of the chapter, after Esther has told Fred about her child and he still wants to marry her, we learn that "in that moment she felt that she almost loved him" (192).

In Esther's interactions with her male partners, then, her internal perspective is the more dominant one, and even in Esther's scenes with her female employers, many of whom hold traditional views about the role of working-class women in society, the perspective shifts to the female employer on only the rarest occasions. For example, when Esther confronts her first employer, Mrs. Rivers (who has hired Esther to nurse her child while Esther's baby is sent to nurse at a baby farm) about the conditions under which she must work, Mrs. Rivers responds by giving Esther an ultimatum: follow the house rules (which prohibit Esther from visiting her own child), or be put out into the street. In this scene, Mrs. Rivers's internal perspective appears, but only when it is necessary to show she realizes Esther is morally superior. Immediately after Esther reminds Mrs. Rivers that every time she hires a new wet-nurse, she is taking the life of another woman's baby, "[a] strange look passed over Mrs. Rivers's face. She knew, of course, that she stood well within the law [in throwing Esther out], that she was doing no more than a hundred other fashionable women were doing at the same moment; but this plain girl had a plain way of putting things, and she did not care for it to be publicly known that the life of her child had been bought with the lives of two poor children" (150). Here, while there is a shift from the narrator's perspective to Mrs. Rivers's perspective, this shift upholds Esther's opinion rather than validating Mrs. Rivers's beliefs.

Our sense, then, is that the novel is really *Esther's* story and not one belonging to someone else—Esther's male partners, her female employers, or any of the other characters in the novel—and this effect of the narrative can be connected directly to Moore's use of internal perspective. Still, while Esther's consciousness of her own situation matures and expands over the course of the novel, she is not a woman with overabundant interiority, and this may have something to do with her class standing. Still, Moore clearly has given Esther significantly more interiority than the typical Victorian servant, and one of the few moments of direct address in the novel—"Hers is a heroic adventure if one considers it . . ." (172)—highlights the individuality of Esther, despite her working-class status. Ultimately, Esther is a successful heroine in the context of the feminist realist aesthetic, since she thinks about her own situation and has a heightened awareness of the cultural conditions shaping her work and her life.

In addition to possessing at least some degree of increased consciousness, Esther also speaks out and acts to change cultural conditions that support the subordination of women. Esther's use of spoken word is especially effective as a means of resistance in the novel: she continually confronts people who believe she is no more than an animal. This especially is true in Esther's battles with her female employers, since Esther directs her resistance toward middle-class women, who themselves are subject to the cultural norms that subordinate women but who generally uphold the dominant Victorian perspective about gender roles. For example, Esther confronts Mrs. Rivers about her double standard that middle-class women should have access to their babies but working-class women should not, and Esther argues she should have the right to be with her baby, just as Mrs. Rivers does:

[O]ne afternoon, after having put baby to sleep, [Esther] said to Mrs.

Rivers, "I hope, ma'am, you'll be able to spare me for a couple of hours; baby won't want me before then. I'm very anxious about my little one."

"Oh, nurse, I couldn't possibly hear of it; such a thing is never allowed. You can write to the woman, if you like."

"I do not know how to write, ma'am."

"Then you can get someone to write for you. But your baby is no doubt all right."

"But, ma'am, you are uneasy about your baby; you are up in the nursery twenty times a day; it is only natural I should be uneasy about mine."

"But, nurse, I've no one to send with you."

"There is no reason why anybody should go with me, ma'am; I can take care of myself."

"What! let you go off all the way to—where did you say you had left it—Wandsworth?—by yourself! I really couldn't think of it. . . . [I]f you like I'll write myself to the woman who has charge of your baby. I cannot do more, and I hope you'll be satisfied." (145–46)

Immediately following this resistance through spoken word, readers hear Esther's thoughts through her internal perspective: "By what right, by what law, was she separated from her child? She was tired of hearing Mrs. Rivers speak of 'my child, my child, my child,' and of seeing this fine lady turn up her nose when she spoke of her own beautiful boy" (146). These words confirm that Esther is aware of her situation and is willing to speak up to change the circumstances, but she also is willing to take action. At the end of Esther's thoughts about the injustice of the situation, the narrator tells us that Esther "experienced the sensation of the captured animal, and scanned the doors and windows, thinking of some means of escape" (146). Further, after Mrs. Spires, the baby farmer, comes to tell Esther that her baby is ill, Esther leaves the house, despite the fact she will lose her job by doing so. Although Esther's actions will not get her what she wants—the right to see her baby while working for Mrs. Rivers—Esther's actions do indicate the potential for taking action that will result in social change. If other female servants follow Esther's lead and refuse to accept the unstated assumption that they will sacrifice their own babies for the babies of middle-class women, this assumption might be dismantled and changed to one more sympathetic to the needs of working-class women.

Moore's effective combination of internal perspective, dialogue, and description of actions is striking, as are certain rhetorical aspects of Esther's dialogue. Like Hardy's Tess, Esther confronts competing ideologies about the cultural status of women, and these ideologies are expressed in a variety of different languages (religious, legal, economics-oriented, sympathetic, etc.). What makes Esther different from Tess is that she more effectively adopts different types of language to resist the ideologies of those people who unfairly judge her. With Mrs. Rivers, she uses the language of motherhood, a language Mrs. Rivers is likely to find appealing. When Esther justifies her concern for her own child to Mrs. Rivers by saying, "But, ma'am, you are uneasy about your baby; you are up in the nursery twenty times a day; it is only *natural* that I should be uneasy about mine" (145, my emphasis), she implies that there are emotions which *all* mothers feel, regardless of their class status or the legitimacy of their children. Further, when Mrs. Rivers tells Esther that it would be "cruel" for Esther to leave Mrs. Rivers's baby without milk, Esther responds practically, saying, "Why couldn't you [nurse it], ma'am? You look fairly strong and healthy" (150), a response again suggesting that she and Mrs. Rivers share the experience of motherhood, even if they do not share the same class background. By using the language of mothers with Mrs. Rivers, Esther attempts to break down class distinctions that contribute to the strong judgments made about "fallen" women.

In addition to employing the language of mothers to create social change, Esther also employs the language of religion to do the same. While it might be argued that religious language must always support institutional power, Esther's use of it shows that there is a wide variety of opinions within religion and that religious language can be shaped to change perceived notions, including those about fallen women. Because religious language includes concepts such as "repentance" and "forgiveness," the use of it in discussing the issue of fallen women can create more sympathy for women who are labeled as such. Through the language of religion, then, Esther has a tool she can use when confronting people who judge her because of her fallen status. For example, when Esther tells Mrs. Barfield (the mistress of the house at Woodview and also a member of the Plymouth Brethren Church) about her pregnancy, Mrs. Barfield reacts in a radically different manner than the other female employers Esther encounters. Asking Esther why she has done something a "good girl" should not do and why she has deceived the household by concealing her pregnancy for seven months, Esther is immediately apologetic, saying that she "hated being deceitful" but that she could no longer "think of myself. There is another to think for now" (87–88). When Mrs. Barfield presses Esther in specifically religious language, saying, "But, Esther, do you feel your sin? Can you truly say honestly before God that you repent?" (91), Esther responds by stating, "Yes, ma'am, I think I can say all that," and she then kneels in prayer with Mrs. Barfield (91). While Esther's acceptance of her "sin" may seem somewhat conventional, Esther does not see herself as solely responsible for the sin. She believes that William is equally responsible and that he, too, should repent (77).

Just as Esther uses religious confession with Mrs. Barfield, she uses it with Fred Parsons, since it is their shared religious background that allows Fred to accept Esther despite her fallen status. After hearing Esther's confession, Fred says, "But you've repented, Esther?" (190), and receiving an affirmative answer from her, he speaks sympathetically, stating, "I know that a woman's path is more difficult to walk than ours. It may not be a woman's fault if she falls, but it is always a man's. He can always fly from temptation" (191). While today this attitude might be seen as condescending, it is more caring than the attitude that the woman is at fault, and by accepting Esther, Fred recognizes her power. With this power, Esther later is able to use religious discourse to resist Fred's conventional ideas. After Esther returns to William and marries him instead of Fred, Fred tries to use the language of religion to convince Esther she has "fallen" once again. When Fred, preaching against gambling in the Salvation Army tent at Derby Day, sees Esther at the races with William and their friends, he questions Esther's religious commitment, saying, "You haven't forgotten your religion, I hope?" (280). Esther defends her decision to return to William, despite his gambling habit, using the language of religion to do so: "I haven't forgotten God, but I must do my duty to my husband. . . . A wife that brings discord into the family is not a good wife, so I've often heard. . . . It would be wrong of me to set myself against my husband. . . . I do not forget Christ. He's always with me" (280).

While Esther's use of religious language is effective in her confrontation with Fred, use of this language does not guarantee acceptance by others for Esther. When Mrs. Trubner, one of Esther's female employers, learns that Esther has an illegitimate child, she is less than sympathetic upon hearing her story, even though she seems to understand and value religious language. Esther tries to explain that she is the "thoroughly religious girl" Mrs. Trubner thought she hired and has "suffered a great deal" because of her sin (169), but Mrs. Trubner refuses to hear out Esther and quickly dismisses her from service. Even when Esther asks Mrs. Trubner, "Then don't you think, ma'am, there is repentance and forgiveness? Our Lord said—" (169), Mrs. Trubner cuts Esther off, leaving her befuddled and mumbling under her breath, "It is a strange thing that religion should make some people so unfeeling" (171). Still, despite this one unsuccessful attempt at resistance through the use of religious language, Esther is fairly successful in her attempts to convince others that a fallen woman need not be doomed for life.

Moore's construction of Esther's dialogue, then, is quite effective, and his combination of it with description of Esther's actions strengthens our

sense that she successfully resists cultural norms that support the subordination of women. This pattern of resistance through spoken word followed by related physical actions is found not only in the scene in which
Esther resists Mrs. Rivers's orders to sacrifice her own baby in order to
remain in service and then leaves the house, but also in the following scene
when Esther goes to see her baby and resists the baby farmer's suggestion
that Esther give her £5 to take the baby "off her hands" (157). Caught in
an argument with Mrs. Spires, the baby farmer, and her husband about
whether this means putting the baby up for adoption or letting them kill
the child, Esther tries to escape Mr. Spires's strong physical grasp.

> "Help, help, murder!" Esther screamed. Before the brute could seize
> her she slipped past, but before she could scream again he laid hand
> on her at the door. Esther thought her last moment had come. "Let
> 'er go, let 'er go!" cried Mrs. Spires. . . . "We don't want the perlice in
> 'ere." . . . With a growl the man loosed his hold, and feeling herself
> free Esther rushed into the area and up the wooden steps. (158)

Esther's resistance here recalls actions described earlier in the novel, which
suggest that Esther often takes action when she believes she is in physical
danger. At one point Esther's mother, who is pregnant with her fifth child
at the same time Esther is pregnant with her son, tells Esther that her husband, Esther's stepfather, has been beating her. We learn that Esther, too,
has been his victim in the past but resisted his violence. "It was only the
other day," Esther's mother says, "just as I was attending to his dinner—it
was a nice piece of steak, and it looked so nice that I cut off a weeny piece
to taste. . . . 'Well, then, taste that,' he says, and strikes me clean between
the eyes" (97). To this Esther replies, "You was always too soft with him,
mother; he never touched me since I dashed the hot water in his face"
(97).

While Esther does not face physical abuse with either William or Fred,
there are times when she uses physical action, especially turning away, to
resist their attempts to categorize her. In response to this categorization, a
more subtle form of controlling women, Esther adopts a strategy of resistance that can be linked to her reaction to the overt violence of her stepfather. When William returns and tries to convince Esther not to marry
Fred and to live with him instead, she resents that she must "fall" once
again just to support her child. When William reaches for her arm, in an
attempt to convince her he will give up gambling if she moves in, she pulls
away, combining resistance through spoken word and action. "'Don't
touch me,' she said surlily, and drew back a step with an air of resolution
that made [William] doubt if he would be able to persuade her" (235).

Then, when Fred confronts Esther at Derby Day, she resists his judgments about her marriage to William by ending the conversation when she wishes and by "mov[ing] away" before he can convince her to leave William and come back to him (281). Further, when Fred comes to William's public-house to warn Esther that the police are going to charge William with selling bets in the bar, she again ends the conversation when she tires of Fred's judgments, "turn[ing] her face from him" to show her resistance (304).

Interestingly, Esther's resistance through physical action encompasses a variety of specific ways women are subjugated—violence against them, violence against their children, the subtle but dangerous judgments placed on those who do not fit the norm, the implementation of a class system that prevents them from individual agency, etc.—and the breadth of her resistance is impressive. It is not surprising, given this breadth, that Esther's last action in the book—returning to Woodview after William's death in order to avoid going to the workhouse—is an action taken not only out of necessity but also for her own pleasure. Realizing she must do some work to support herself and her son, now almost a man but still not old enough to support himself entirely, Esther chooses to go into service in a house she loves and with a mistress she adores. With Mrs. Barfield, Esther is able to transcend the role of servant, for "the two women came to live more and more like friends and less like mistress and maid" (388). Ultimately, Esther seems very satisfied with her life, and she expresses the view that her life's work—supporting her son—has been important. "She was only conscious that she had accomplished her woman's work—she had brought him up to a man's estate; and that was her sufficient reward" (394).

While Esther's comment that "woman's work" has been a "sufficient reward" seems somewhat self-abnegating, we can forgive Esther's self-abnegation because we recognize the limitations class status puts on her ability to move out of woman's work. Also, we recognize that her work is more physically demanding than the work of middle-class women, who run their households without getting their hands dirty. Esther's reward has been hard-earned, and, had she been born a decade or two later and into even a lower-middle-class rather than a working-class family, she might very well have become the young professional woman of the 1890s, working in the public sphere as a typewriter girl rather than in the private sphere as a domestic servant. Esther is a hard worker, and so her comment about being satisfied with her "woman's work" carries a level of authenticity not always associated with the phrase.

In constructing Esther's character, Moore achieved the feminist ideal, and after receiving praise from feminist periodicals in the wake of *Esther Waters's* publication, Moore took the necessary steps to ensure his literary reputation, a goal of particular importance to him. To that end, he made

revisions to the novel to make it more "English," changes indicating he
was trying to capitalize on his success in writing a book that was less nat-
uralistic and more in tune with the softer form of realism preferred by the
British.[5] He also made marketing decisions emphasizing the woman-
centered approach of *Esther Waters*. He negotiated with T. Werner Laurie
for a "fine" edition of the novel in 1920, and this negotiation highlights
Moore's affinity for women and books, especially as aesthetic objects that
could transform a man's way of looking at the world. Finally, he wrote a
woman-centered preface to accompany the 1932 American edition of the
novel, in which Esther returns as an apparition and exerts control over
Moore's writing process.

The letters from Moore to Laurie regarding the 1920 edition reveal
the author's persistence in negotiations as well as his desire to assure his
literary reputation through the woman-centered novel. In this particular
set of letters, Moore's concern over the *appearance* of the edition ties
books and women together as fine, aesthetic objects, objects Moore associated with literary reputation. In letters written in 1918 and 1919,
Moore repeatedly mentions a proposal for a "fine" edition of *Esther
Waters,* stating in 1918, "I do not pretend to be as good a judge as you in
these matters but I cannot rid myself [of] the belief that an expensive edition of *Esther Waters* would find subscribers" (Moore, *Transition* 384),
and in 1919, "I wonder if you could see your way to an expensive edition
of *Esther Waters*. I think there would be a demand. But the paper? How
much will there be left after *Avowals* is printed? Not enough for *Esther
Waters* but there might be enough for a small edition of *The Lake*. Will
there?" (414–15). Already, Moore sees on the horizon a whole collection
of "fine" editions which would spring from the *Esther Waters* project and
eventually be produced in a uniform edition by Heinemann. By 1920,
discussion of details—what typeface they would use, how the corrections
on the proofs were to be done, and how many free copies of the edition
Moore would receive—dominates Moore's letters to Laurie. In a letter
dated April 21, 1920, Moore claims to "never interfere in any business
matters," but he has ample advice for Laurie on how to obtain permission to use type from another edition, as well as advice on whom they
should hire to do the corrections (461). He is concerned that the typeface will not look appropriate for a fine edition, but he finally agrees to
let Laurie and Pawling, who have the type from a past edition, "wrangle"
with each other (464).

While there are no apparent comments on the typeface used in the better edition of *Esther Waters* in Moore's letters to Laurie after the edition
appears, Moore was extremely disappointed that the paper had been cut
instead of being left with rough edges. In a letter dated October 3, 1920,

Moore claims that "*Esther Waters* is in appearance a mere enlargement of the ordinary 6/ or 7/6 novel," and he asks that the pages of *Héloïse and Abélard* be "rough like the edges of *Avowals* and not chopped like the edges of *Esther Waters*" (480). Moore then launches into a lengthy discussion of the problems a publisher encounters: he "sympathizes" with Laurie's troubles but refuses to let his sympathy excuse the appearance of the edition. "I keep my eyes fixed on the ultimate success of the whole series," Moore writes, suggesting he has far more invested than simply the commercial success of one book:

> It is therefore necessary for me to come to an understanding with you regarding this new question—the rough edges. . . . I know it is very difficult to get the paper but almost any other plan would be better than to offer the public *Héloïse and Abélard* in form that would be practically *Esther Waters* over again. On points of this kind I think my opinion is worth consideration for my whole life have [*sic*] been given to questions of taste. (480)

Moore's emphasis on "taste" here accentuates his philosophy on how lasting literary success might be achieved via the woman-centered novel, since "taste" suggests an appreciation of the book akin to the appreciation of a woman.

For Moore, the aesthetic pleasure of a woman and the aesthetic pleasure of the book are closely wedded, and he often uses a woman-as-book, book-as-woman trope in his writing. This trope first appears toward the beginning of *Confessions of a Young Man,* when Moore writes of the experience, at age eleven, of hearing his parents speak of, and then reading himself, Mary Elizabeth Braddon's *Lady Audley's Secret.* Braddon's novel evokes for Moore "echo-augury," a term he borrows from Thomas De Quincey and uses to describe the moment when one hears, among the many "cries" that fill one's head, a more "persistent" cry one follows faithfully. This persistent cry is like a "voice of conscience" which pulls a person out of a "perplexed state" and gives him or her direction, and for Moore this cry is often associated with the feminine (49–50, 76, 233). Further, in *Confessions,* Moore writes of women and books as similar entities: living, breathing, vital. "Books are like individuals," he says, "you know at once if they are going to create a sense within the sense, to fever, to madden you in blood and brain, or if they will merely leave you indifferent, or irritable, having unpleasantly disturbed sweet musings as might a draught from an open window. Many are the reasons for love, but I confess I only love woman or book, when it is as a voice of conscience, never heard before, heard suddenly, a voice I am at once endearingly intimate with" (76).

Moore's claim in his letter to Laurie that he has devoted his "whole life" to the issue of "taste" shows the degree to which he craved literary success and the extent to which he defined literary success via his love for women. Although Moore's letters to Laurie are almost always strictly business-oriented, with little mention of the "womanliness" of books, the letter from October 3, 1920 is one in which the connection between books and women seems to seep in most thoroughly. By far the longest letter in this series from Moore to Laurie, and the most personal in tone, it continues this way:

> I have no knowledge why you ordered the chopping of *Esther Waters*
> but I assume there were reasons; it could not have been natural pref-
> erence on your part for I found you by no means *in love* with *Esther
> Waters,* when the first copies came in. . . . [I]t may be that the thick
> paper folds into a slightly larger book . . . and that the pages were
> chopped to equalize the size; if that was the reason I think that it was
> a bad one and that it would be better to issue *Héloïse and Abélard* in
> a slightly larger form unchopped. You will not think that I am rais-
> ing difficulties that need not have been raised I am sure of that. You
> have not forgotten that I am responsible for the *shapeliness* of these
> books. (Moore, *Transition* 480, my emphasis)

Here, the words "in love" and "shapeliness" stand out, for they are not typical of the language Moore uses when writing to Laurie, and they reveal the investment Moore has in books as both living entities and aesthetic objects that will ensure his literary reputation after his death. Throughout this letter Moore asserts that he is above mere commercial success and is striving for long-lasting artistic success and that a book's appearance (much like a woman's appearance) goes a long way toward ensuring the success of the book and its author.

Additional evidence of Moore's attempt to achieve lasting literary success via the woman-centered novel can be seen in the woman-centered preface to the 1932 American edition of *Esther Waters*. This preface, titled "A Colloquy: George Moore and Esther Waters," is a dialogue between the author and his female character: Esther appears as an apparition, who urges Moore not to write the preface, for she believes that Moore is no longer in control of his creation. This preface illustrates well Moore's deep investment in his female characters and his use of the woman-as-book, book-as-woman trope to invest *Esther Waters* with the power to influence the future of his career.

Moore begins the preface by complaining about writer's block, which has become so extreme that he throws away twenty drafts of the preface which the publisher Liveright has required him to write for the new edition. Finally, after much frustration, Esther comes to him, and a debate over the power of the author versus the power of his books ensues. Employing the woman-as-book, book-as-woman trope, *Esther Waters*-the-book and Esther-as-living-person are conflated, and, of the moment Esther appears, Moore writes:

> I heard the noiseless approach of a new thought. On velvet pads it moves out of the subconsciousness; a moment more and it will begin to speak its message; and it was whilst I was thinking that nothing could befall which would restore me to my lost faith in life that I heard my visitor proclaim her mission:
> I have come here to defend my life.
> Thy life? cried I.
> Every living thing hath the right to defend the life given it to live. (viii)

In this moment, *Esther Waters*-the-book has become Esther-as-living-person, a "living thing" who has the right to defend her own life, and she immediately questions Moore's assumptions about his power as her creator. When Moore wonders whether a book can "live"—"Given it to live, I repeated, amazed at hearing a book speak so clearly" (vix)—Esther responds, "I was thine in the beginning, but as soon as a book is written all right passes from the author to the book itself" (vix). Here, Esther indicates she believes she holds the power to influence others, and she iterates this power when she says there can be "no doubt" that the book has a longer life than the author, suggesting that it is the book that will determine the author's literary reputation after death. "A man's life is brief," she says, "a book's life may be prolonged century after century" (vix). Furthermore, the book should be the one to determine the extent of an author's revisions to the text. When Moore says to Esther, "I have revised thee many times without protest," she replies, "Thy revisions were limited to the smoothing out of a rugged sentence, and not wishing to seem unfilial in thine eyes, I let thee have thy way with me as a dandy might allow his valet to remove a speck from his embroidered waistcoat, but beware! any larger license I cannot permit" (vix). Finally, as the preface comes to a close, Esther iterates once more the power of the book to control the author's actions. To Moore's protest that Esther "hast lost trust" in the one who created her, she responds:

> That question has already been debated. . . . To debate it again would be superfluous. Thou hast suffered enough in the last month [from

trying to write the preface] and I would save thee further mental suffering if I may. Return to thy stories and leave Liveright to his own
devices. And I beg of thee, if I should have occasion to visit thee
again, that thou wilt, out of mere courtesy, refrain from the word
"Prefacer." I have little liking for that word. (x)

Ultimately, Moore writes a preface in which he imagines his most successful book with immense power, the power not only to determine the degree
of revisions performed by the author but also the reputation of the book
and the author beyond his own lifetime.

That Moore crafted this preface at the end of his life, when he was most
concerned about his literary reputation and how it would hold up once he
was no longer living, indicates his awareness of the power of the woman-
centered novel, especially the New Woman novel so favored by the
woman's press of the 1890s. Aware that his experimentation with literary
style in the 1880s and 1890s had created a lack of consistency in his work
but that his engagement with gender issues in the 1890s via *Esther Waters*
had improved his literary reputation, Moore chose the novel most likely
to ensure his reputation beyond his lifetime and capitalized on its success.
Through the "fine" edition of 1920 and the 1932 woman-centered preface, *Esther Waters* became Moore's female helpmate as he tried to write
himself into the British literary tradition. For Moore, reaching the summit of Parnassus mattered most, and only the woman-centered novel
could take him there.

While Moore's concern about his literary reputation can be traced quite
easily through letters and nonfiction writings, Henrietta Stannard's concern about her reputation is more ambiguous. The archival resources for
Stannard are limited, but available resources show that Stannard was fairly comfortable with her position as a commercially popular author and
was not particularly concerned about fame beyond her own lifetime,
though she took the position of women writers as a whole quite seriously.
The letters used by Oliver Bainbridge in his biography of Stannard, *John
Strange Winter: A Volume of Personal Record* (1916), and those in the
Society of Authors archive at the British Library, present a woman who
perceived herself as already established in the literary community and who
did not see her commercial popularity as an obstacle to literary success.
After all, she had the support of John Ruskin, who told the public he
believed that Stannard was "the author to whom we owe the most finished
and faithful rendering ever yet given of the character of the British soldier"

(Bainbridge 80). Further, she saw herself on par with other women writers, such as Marie Corelli, whose novel *The Sorrows of Satan* (1895) made her one of the more popular writers of the late-Victorian period (Bainbridge 96–102).

Stannard expected a certain degree of respect from those in the literary community, and when she felt she was not being respected, she voiced her feelings without hesitation. For example, when she heard that Corelli was angry over the rumor that Stannard had urged a journalist to "write against" Corelli, she confronted Corelli, and the two women ended up in a fairly ferocious quarrel (Bainbridge 101). The same year, 1901, Stannard temporarily resigned from the Society of Authors, an action based on where she and her husband were seated at the society's annual dinner, though she withdrew her resignation once she received an apology (Stannard, Letter Book no page). Her actions in both cases suggest that Stannard expected a certain level of privilege within the literary community, which she believed she already had earned by the 1890s, but she generally seemed happy to bask in this already-earned reputation rather than trying to change the public's perception of her, as Moore tried to do for himself.

While there are times when Stannard takes the issue of literary reputation seriously—as when she believed that women writers were unfairly excluded from the community—when she writes about her own authorial position, she seems intent on mocking the process of establishing literary reputation. For example, in an essay written for a collection about authors' first publications, Stannard tells of her earliest experiences with writing in a straightforward but light-hearted tone. Detailing how her first book was a story put together on "the floor of the nursery room" when she was a child, Stannard jokes that she is relieved no one ever recovered this piece, as has happened to some authors ("Cavalry" 239–40). She maintains this light-hearted tone as she describes her entry into professional writing. After she starts writing for the *The Family Herald* under the pseudonym Violet Whyte, she characterizes herself as someone who thought more of her writing than she should have and who needed to be reminded of this fact. "I was very young then," states Stannard, "and thought a great deal of my pretty bits of writing and those seductive scraps of moralising, against which Mr. Stevens [her editor] was always warning me" (240). Certainly, Stannard emphasizes her own struggles as an author in telling the story of her first book, including the "long haggle over terms" she endured while working with Chatto and Windus on *Cavalry Life* (252), but the tone she uses is distinctly different from that of Moore, who always maintained a thoroughly serious attitude when discussing the obstacles he faced in becoming a great artist. Stannard does note her accomplishments by indi-

cating she received a "rattling good notice" from the *The Saturday Review*
for her work on *Calvary Life*, but her discussion remains easy and unpre-
tentious. At the end of "My First Book," she returns to the jovial tone with
which she began the piece, stating she hopes she never again will have to
go through the "cold sweat" induced by looking at that first review (255).

Stannard mocks the process of publication even more fully in her novel
Confessions of a Publisher, Being the Autobiography of Abel Drinkwater
(1888), in which she tells the story of a publisher who manipulates
authors in order to make a profit. Drinkwater, who has worked his way up
from a clerk in a publishing company to the operator of the company,
agrees to publish a dreadful manuscript by a rich young woman named
Margery, but he insists that she pay for a portion of the publication herself. This act of greed on Drinkwater's part leads to his being blackmailed
by a hack writer, who has fixed up the manuscript in order to make it
respectable. The entire story is prefaced with a "Warning" from Stannard,
which states, "Abel Drinkwater has been sketched from odds and ends of
gossip which have come to my ears, and if any gentleman in the publishing world finds the portrait faithful enough to say: 'That is meant for
me'—I can only protest that I am truly sorry for that person, and would
beg him, for his own sake, not to think of putting so unbecoming a cap
upon his head" (3).

Though the emphasis of the story is on Drinkwater's interest in turning a profit, the story does point out the one issue regarding literary reputation upon which Stannard always was serious: the position of women
in the literary market. In presenting Margery as a woman who has been
fooled into paying for publication, Stannard exposes the manipulation of
amateur women writers in the market place.[6] Stannard certainly was aware
of the role that gender played in the literary market, and she consistently
argued for the acceptance and fair treatment of women writers. She especially encouraged the Society of Authors to take up the cause of women
writers: in 1889 she wrote a letter to Walter Besant, Secretary of the
Society, in which she named specific women he should recruit as members
of the society (Stannard, Miscellaneous Letters no page), and she pushed
for the election of women as officers in the society in 1896 (Anonymous,
"Society of Authors" 224). She also was central in the formation of the
Writers' Club, which she and other women writers established after being
excluded from the Society of Authors Club, a controversy which deserves
more detailed discussion, since it highlights the tension between male and
female authors at the *fin de siècle* and the way this tension might have
influenced how women writers, including Stannard, thought about their
place in the literary tradition.

When, in December 1890, Besant suggested in the pages of the soci-

ety's journal, *The Author,* that the society form an Authors' Club, a small-
er social club within the society, it was evident that the society's male members feared the admittance of women into the club. While Besant made it
clear that any club sponsored by the society should include its female as
well as its male members, in the spirit of acceptance exhibited by the
Albemarle Club (Besant, "News and Notes" 200–201), when members of
the society responded to Besant's call for feedback on the project, the male
members objected to the presence of women in the club. As Besant states
in his summary of the voting, "The ladies who voted for a Club did not
raise a word against the admission of men, but many of the men, speaking
for a club, urged strongly upon us the necessity of excluding ladies"
("Notes and News" 252). Although Besant himself seems to have recognized that it would be unfair to exclude women from the club, he and a
subcommittee of six other men ultimately decided that the club would be
for men only, with women admitted on Wednesday afternoons and for
special events (Anonymous, "Authors' Club" 85–86). As a result, Stannard
and other women writers started the Writers' Club, which provided a space
for women writers to gather (Anonymous, "Ladies' Club" 134). An
announcement about the opening of the club in Stannard's own periodical, founded in 1891 as *Golden Gates* and later called *Winter's Weekly* and
Winter's Magazine, highlights the planned services of the club: "good substantial refreshments," a "silent room" in which members would be able to
"work in peace," and ample space for women writers to "see their friends,
read the papers, and rest after doing business in the great centres of publishing" (Stannard, "Editor's Thoughts" [14 Nov. 1891] 19).

In addition to working for the acceptance of women as literary profes-
sionals, Stannard took a firm stance when male authors denigrated the
work of women writers, especially women journalists, which was a matter
of great debate in periodicals in the 1890s. Though this debate over the
increase of women journalists and what it meant for men in the field was
discussed in a variety of publications, Stannard's statements about the
debate appear in *Golden Gates.* In the "Editor's Thoughts" column for
February 13, 1892, Stannard relays a conversation overheard at the opening of the Writers' Club, to which male friends of the members were invited. "Pretty crowd of women this," one male journalist was overheard saying to another, whose reply was: "Yes; all taking our work away from us"
(242). To this gibe about women in journalism, Stannard replies in her
column:

> I only wish that I had happened to hear this myself—I would have
> promised these clever gentlemen that any of their sex who could take
> our respective places away from us would be more than welcome to

them—at least, I can speak for myself. To me it is deplorable that there should be this grudging spirit on the part of some men, who seem to think it hard that men should have to work for women, and yet who object to the women earning a living for themselves. (242)

Stannard then suggests that perhaps women are taking work away from men in journalism because women are better at it, and she reminds readers that in other professions, such as the milliner profession, men are replacing women as the main proprietors of the product. Clearly, Stannard was prepared to defend women writers and their work, and *Golden Gates* provided a forum in which she could make her opinions known.

Around the same time she responded to the women-in-journalism debate, Stannard also took issue with another article that denigrated women's writing by suggesting they should act only as traditional female helpmates to male authors. "On Literary Collaboration," which ran in the March 1, 1892 issue of *The Author* and was written by Walter Besant, advises every literary man to find a young woman who will help him develop his characters but will not demand payment for her help, a strong contrast to those female helpmates I envision for Moore and Stannard in this chapter. Arguing that "[w]oman does not create, but she receives, moulds, and develops," Besant articulates his vision of woman as "man's best partner" rather than independent inventor (328). Stannard responded strongly to this argument in her March 19, 1892 *Golden Gates* editorial column, stating, "One would not have expected that Mr. Walter Besant, who is supposed to be as full of chivalry as he is generally full of common sense, would have let his latest advice to young authors appear in the full light of day" (338). Stannard then quotes Besant's comments about the necessity for male authors to find female collaborators and refutes his statement that women do not create. She argues that one can easily match the three best male novelists (Scott, Thackeray, and Dickens, in her opinion) with three superb female novelists: Gaskell, Charlotte Brontë, and Eliot. These women, says Stannard, are as "realist" in their depiction of human life as are the male novelists, and this is what makes them great writers (338).

Although Stannard did not talk about her own literary reputation directly, it is clear from her comments about the great women writers of the nineteenth century that she understood the issues surrounding canonization, particularly that gender was one of the factors affecting this process. Still, Stannard seems to have overlooked her own reputation beyond the *fin de siècle,* since recognizing this aspect of her career might have led her to more fully embrace the feminist realist aesthetic. While Stannard did engage feminism in the 1890s, she did so primarily through her work as a journalist rather than as a writer of fiction. Further, since she held moderate views on women's issues, she could not embrace certain aspects of feminism, especially suffrage, and this likely influenced her ability to embrace the feminist realist aesthetic, since the emphasis on making one's voice heard through voting is deeply connected to at least one of the three aspects of woman's agency emphasized in this aesthetic.

Nevertheless, it is important to acknowledge the ways in which Stannard did engage feminism because this knowledge can inform our reading of *A Blameless Woman,* the novel by Stannard that most fully addresses women's issues. Stannard clearly established a moderate position on gender issues in her magazine *Golden Gates* when she responded to both conservative and liberal feminists writing about gender issues. First, she, like Caird, responded to Eliza Lynn Linton's "The Wild Women as Social Insurgents," which had appeared in the periodical *The Nineteenth Century* as part of a series of articles critiquing the New Woman. In her February 27, 1892 editor's column, Stannard writes that while she values Linton as an author and a friend, she takes issue with Linton's new statements about "the girl of the period," which Linton had first addressed in her 1868 article on the topic (282). Stannard objects to Linton's characterization of the modern girl as one who "talks about 'oof,'" or money, since she is not sure whether this type of girl actually exists. Writes Stannard: "I know many hundreds of women and girls of all sorts and conditions. . . . I have never, never once heard the word 'oof' from the lips of any women" (282). In questioning Linton's conclusions about the modern girl, Stannard leaves room for a more complex understanding of gender issues at the *fin de siècle* than Linton does.

Yet Stannard also rejects some of the ideas of liberal feminists, including those of Florence Fenwick Miller. In her March 5, 1892 editorial column, Stannard engages Fenwick Miller and her essay "Women as Workers at Home," which asserts that women who work at home often are the equivalent of unpaid domestic help. While she thinks that the essay is "brilliant and vivid," she disagrees with the idea that women cannot do domestic labor out of love (298). "[I]n all *real* marriages," Stannard writes, "the money question does not come in between husband and wife. What belongs to the one should and generally does belong to the other, and there ought not be any question of 'paying' for the wife's work" (299). Further, Stannard points out that if the wife were to be paid, the husband also could insist that the wife always work, regardless of her health. Eventually, Stannard argues, "the debit and credit system would effectually ruin the romance and beauty of marriage" (299). Again, Stannard seems to be taking a moderate position, and, interestingly, at the end of her discussion of Fenwick Miller's essay, she compares Fenwick Miller to Linton, stating that what she finds in common in the two women is the tendency to abuse one group of people or another. Further, she believes that this approach of abusing certain groups is typical of the "modern reform" movement. She writes:

> Mrs. Lynn Linton abuses the women, and Mrs. Fenwick Miller abuses the men. These two brilliant women are but representatives of many who follow in the footsteps, even if afar off. Well might the men turn round and abuse us as a whole. But they don't—no, they are generous and chivalrous towards us in literature, or perhaps I should more clearly say in their pen; and therefore may we not take it as a fairly established fact that the generality of men don't want to humiliate their wives, and that they do not believe that the modern girl is a pestilential creature who is ruthlessly dragging the whole world down to perdition? (299)

Stannard exaggerates her own position a bit here, since there are other instances in her editorial writing where she suggests that men *do* abuse women in their writing, but she clearly wants to carve out a moderate position in a debate often deeply split along the lines of "conservative" and "liberal."

As a moderate, Stannard often takes up issues that might be deemed as fairly safe in comparison to agitating for political reform, but when she takes up these issues, she does so with vigor. For example, in 1893 she established the League of the Silver Cord, which focused on the social factors influencing alcoholism in women and which aimed to curb easy access to liquor. In one of the early articles about this issue, "Grocers' Licenses and Secret Drinking," published with an accompanying pledge form for readers to fill out and join the league, Stannard argues that when women drink excessively, the rest of the family is affected, but the problem can be stopped by boycotting the source of the problem: the grocers who sell the alcohol and make it easily accessible to women who may drink because of "trouble, physical failings, or hereditary inclination" (262). This cause indicates Stannard's commitment to helping women whose lives were difficult due to social demands, especially their family responsibilities.

Stannard also takes up the cause of practical, if not rational, dress for women, and, through the pages of *Golden Gates* and other periodicals, she organized the Anti-Crinoline League, which argued against the return of the crinoline in women's dress and boasted 15,000 members less than two months after its founding (Stannard, "Outside Edge" 49). In one of the many articles that appeared in *Golden Gates* regarding this issue, "Death in Our Skirts," Stannard rails against the enormous skirts, saying that they make women "look ridiculous, vulgar, inelegant, and ungraceful" (51). Speaking of the woman who wears the crinoline, Stannard writes, "She knows that the men, from one end of the world to the other, will laugh at her, jeer at her, sneer at her. She knows that they will hold up her 'cage' as a reason why she should not have the vote, as good evidence of her incapacity to manage her own business, and of her unfitness to be the companion and helpmeet and equal of man" (51). In other words, if women accept the return of the crinoline, they accept their subordination to men on many different levels, including (interestingly) the vote.

Stannard did make a mark in the feminist community, albeit one based on "moderate" views, so the lack of attention to her fiction from feminist periodicals is somewhat surprising. *Shafts* and *The Woman's Herald* did run articles about Stannard's Anti-Crinoline League (Anonymous, "How the World Moves" 188; Stannard, "Outside Edge" 49–50), and *The Woman's Herald* ran articles about some of her other causes, such as women's drinking (Anonymous, "Notes and Comments" [22 Oct. 1892] 5). *The Woman's Herald* even interviewed Stannard twice for the front-page feature, but these articles seem to focus more on Stannard's person than her writing. The 1889 interview does discuss her fiction briefly and characterizes it as focusing on "ordinary" people, "in whom she is able to discover a generosity and a pathos which would remain hidden to a casual observer," but there is no in-depth analysis of Stannard's technique, except a brief description of it as "unsentimental" (Anonymous, "Interview: Winter" 1). Further, significant time is spent on Stannard's family history and marriage: her husband is praised because he "has devoted most of his time to helping his wife in the minor details of her literary work," and Stannard is praised for her ability to take care of her children, despite the stereotype that "literary women do not devote much thought to domestic affairs" (1).

The focus on family history is typical of the front-page features that ran in *The Woman's Herald*, but in comparison to the interviews with other women writers, such as Grand or Caird, there is more emphasis on personal life here. Such emphasis suggests that *Shafts* and *The Woman's Herald* perceived Stannard as a writer to be taken less seriously, perhaps because her fiction was of the popular variety but also perhaps because she took a moderate rather than liberal stance on women's issues. In its short notice about Stannard's work on the crinoline, *Shafts* characterizes the issue as unworthy of attention, since the writer doubts that the crinoline will actually return to women's fashion. The writer praises "Miss Florence Balgarnie," who has written "a very sensible letter" to *The Daily Chronicle* on the topic. "Like ourselves," the writer states, "she believes there is nothing in it. She has too much faith in womanhood to believe that they who 'within these latter years have escaped from so much of the bondage of the past, will again hand themselves over bodily into slavery'" (Anonymous, "How the World" 188). This characterization suggests that Stannard had selected a frivolous issue to support and even accepted the notion that women were silly enough to buy into the craze. In fact, Stannard did believe that many women were not rational; one of the reasons she opposed suffrage was her belief that many women were not ready for the responsibility accompanying it. In an editorial column in *Golden Gates* titled "Fashion and Feathers," which takes up the issue of using bird feathers to adorn women's clothing, Stannard argues that it is the women who adorn their clothes with bird feathers who justify denying women the right to vote. These women are "easily-led dolls" who are "so unable and so unwilling to think and act for themselves" that they cannot be trusted with making important decisions for the country ("Editor's Thoughts: Fashion" 69). Interestingly, Stannard draws directly on the feminist ideal of thinking, speaking, and acting in her comments here, indicating she did value individual liberty for women, even if she did not support the suffrage movement.

Still, while Stannard's choices about which causes to support may not have pleased liberal feminists, Stannard did undergo a transition in her writing in the mid-1890s when she published *A Blameless Woman,* a novel Ann Ardis has described as an "open-ended challenge to the traditional romance plot and the Victorian 'pattern' of the good woman" (*New Woman* 81). *A Blameless Woman* does not fulfill the feminist realist aesthetic to the degree Moore's *Esther Waters* does, but it does highlight the consciousness of a woman who fears recrimination for her "fallen" status, despite her lack of intent in falling. Further, it shows how she resists the typical guilt borne by women labeled as fallen, even if she does not change societal views regarding guilt, as Esther does in Moore's novel.

The novel focuses on Margaret North, a young woman who marries a Russian prince, Paul Dolgouroff, and moves to Berlin with him, only to learn two years later he staged the ceremony and is actually married to another woman. Though Dolgouroff begs Margaret to stay with him, she immediately seeks out help from the Russian embassy, which informs her that their marriage license is simply an agreement for Dolgouroff to support her on £2000 per year. When Margaret realizes her "fallen" state, the look on her face immediately reveals her horror, and the representative at the embassy says, "I fear this has been a blow to you" (44). Still, Margaret remains resilient. When the Russian ambassador worries that Margaret will kill herself because of the shame associated with her fall, Margaret tells him there is no need to worry: she has her own money and can take care of herself. "No, sir, I shall not kill myself—I promise you that," she says as she leaves the embassy. Having established herself as a woman who will not be ruined by her fall, Margaret returns to England, where she hopes to be able to live in a culture that still stigmatizes the fallen woman, even if she is not to blame for her situation. Certainly, Margaret struggles, since she still loves Dolgouroff and feels that her only option is to hide her love for him. Still, she manages to resist cultural norms that label her as "fallen" to at least some degree, and she achieves this resistance through the three methods of expressing agency detailed by the feminist periodicals: consciousness, spoken word, and action.

Margaret's consciousness, the strongest of the three methods of asserting agency in the novel, receives immediate attention upon her return to England, since the narrator begins chapter 9, appropriately titled "The Burden of Life," with emphasis on the need to think about one's position in life. States the narrator:

> There are some situations in life, which, looked at from a distance, you would feel it would be impossible for you to go through. If anybody had represented to Margaret North that the time would come when she would part, without a word of farewell, from Prince Dolgouroff, that she would go back to Blankhampton and take up her life of emptiness there without shedding so much as a single tear, she would have said that it would be impossible. And yet, when we are in such a time of tribulation, there is no help for us, and we must only get through it as best we can. (58)

While Margaret does not feel the impact of what has happened to her yet (since, as the narrator says, "one does not feel a cut with a razor until some little time has gone by" [58]), she does feel it by the end of chapter 9, when she locks herself in her room to read Dolgouroff's farewell letter, in which he professes his love for her and apologizes for what has happened (60). Upon reading Dolgouroff's letter, Margaret reflects on how her fall will change her life. She imagines she will be alone for the rest of her life, and, while this is difficult to accept, she musters the strength to reply to Dolgouroff and tell him she will never write to him again (64–65).

Margaret's distress over losing Dolgouroff and her self-sacrificial promise to herself to never see him again seem like stock conventions of the sentimental romance. Initially, it seems as if Margaret holds fairly traditional ideas about her fallenness, since a second letter from Dolgouroff prompts a reply in which Margaret, refusing to live "in adultery," turns down Dolgouroff's plea that she return to him (79). Further, Margaret refuses to marry a suitor from her early years, Max Stewart, by telling him she is not "a marrying girl" (106). Yet she is eventually convinced to marry Stewart, and at this point some less conventional ideas about fallenness begin to emerge, indicating that perhaps Stannard is moving away from the traditional romance as Ardis suggests. Recognizing she lacked the information needed make an informed decision when she married Dolgouroff, Margaret decides to keep her past a secret from Stewart, but out of the conviction she has done nothing wrong rather than out of shame. Again, the narrator takes readers inside Margaret's consciousness at this point:

> Somehow the thought of confiding everything to Stewart never occurred to her. In truth, I do not think that many women, placed in Margaret North's circumstance, would have thought it necessary or wise to reveal the whole story of their past, of such a past. . . . She did not feel either that she was doing any wrong to Stewart, in not telling him anything. If she had sinned, the whole situation would have been different; but she had been wholly innocent and after she had found out the truth, she had not remained under the roof of the man who had betrayed her even an hour longer than was necessary, or even possible, for her to take herself away from it. (143)

While Margaret's plan to keep her secret might been seen as less than ideal from the feminist realist perspective, since she does nothing to help change the lives of other stigmatized women, Margaret makes the best use of the options she believes she has, including those actions based on absence (silence) rather than presence (speaking out). Still, Margaret is not as strong as Meredith's Diana or Carinthia (who more fully explore actions based on both absence and presence) or Moore's Esther Waters (who chooses to reject the label "fallen" publicly rather than privately), and it is clear that Margaret suffers as a result of her silence. Once engaged to Stewart, the narrator tells us, "Margaret North could not be said to possess any mind of her own. It seemed to her many times that Stewart took possession of her, body and soul" (150). Despite Stewart's possession of her, Margaret cannot let go of her love for Dolgouroff, and this love seems to represent a rejection of the label "fallen." When Margaret burns the relics from their relationship, she retains one lock of his hair (164), and when she and Stewart are married, she sees Dolgouroff's image in front of her rather than Stewart (166). These moments indicate that while Margaret is ready to "shut the door with a resolute hand upon the past" (165), she will not forget Dolgouroff, since her love for him was not wrong in her mind.

Again, the novel relies on a sentimental and even sensational plot, and a feminist realist critic likely would object to this movement away from realistic representation of modern women's lives, but it is true that a read-

er with feminist sensibilities, then and now, can recognize the value of representing the problems associated with suffering in silence. The reviewers
for *Shafts* and *The Woman's Herald* did not reject exposure of the difficult
conditions women faced and the ways in which these conditions might
prevent women from asserting agency, but reviewers did prefer novels bal-
ancing such exposure with positive alternatives, as in Grand's *Heavenly
Twins,* where Evadne's and Edith's failures to assert agency are balanced
with Angelica's more successful endeavors.

Still, Margaret does make some progress in moving out of silence and
into resistance via spoken word. Once her twenty-year-old adopted daughter Effie begins to investigate Margaret's past after ten years of marriage to
Stewart, Margaret can no longer take a passive approach to hiding her "fall-
en" status. When Effie figures out that Margaret knows a Russian Count
named Zelenberg, who is visiting the area, she assumes that Margaret and
Zelenberg had an affair while Margaret lived in Berlin. Concerned that
Effie will learn her secret, Margaret begins to resist through speech and
action. When Effie slyly mentions Margaret's time in Berlin, Margaret is
taken aback by her statement, and her face exhibits a "sudden startling pal-
lor," but she quickly regains her composure, is able to reply to Effie's questions, and even convinces Effie she must have misunderstood. First, she
acts ignorant of Zelenberg's connection to Berlin, stating, "Oh! has he
lived in Berlin?" (228), and to Effie's statement that she did not know that
Margaret's time in Berlin was a "secret," Margaret replies, "My dear child,
you must have taken leave of your senses. What could have put any such
idea into your head? A secret! Who said anything about a secret!" (229).
The result of this interchange, which seems to be controlled by Margaret,
is that Effie believes she has "made a blunder," and Margaret believes she
has put an end to Effie's curiosity.

Yet Effie's curiosity only grows, and once it becomes clear that
Zelenberg will marry Effie and become part of the family, Margaret
resolves to take action and get Effie out of the house (232). Though it
could be argued that Margaret is not working directly against cultural
norms which support the subordination of women but rather is simply trying to protect her secret, protection of the secret represents something
more important to Margaret: the ability to live freely. As long as no one
knows that Margaret is a "fallen" woman, she can live freely, whereas once
people know her secret, her sense of autonomy, a key concept in the discussion of agency, will be diminished, if not destroyed. In fact, when
Margaret does not feel threatened by exposure of her secret, the narrator
tells us, she "breathed more freely, and grew more like her old bright self"
(234). At times Margaret feels so much at ease that she gives up the notion
of getting Effie out of the house (235), but when Dolgouroff suddenly

comes to visit Zelenberg and tries to pursue a relationship with Margaret, Margaret is put back on the defensive, since she fears exposure once again.

Still, Margaret allows Dolgouroff to call at her home, in part because she thinks that doing so will make Effie and others *less* suspicious about her past. As such, Margaret's lack of resistance to Dolgouroff's presence should not be taken as a sign of lack of agency on Margaret's part but as an indication that she is making calculated decisions about her interactions with him. When Dolgouroff begs Margaret to receive him at the house, she considers her options and makes the decision she thinks is best: to admit him and act as though he is "an ordinary acquaintance" (242). Still, it is difficult for Margaret to pretend that Dolgouroff is an ordinary acquaintance, and it takes a great degree of self-control on her part to accomplish this. At one point, when Dolgouroff has stayed at the house much longer than Margaret expected, she begins "to dread lest her strength and self-control would give out and that she would distinguish herself either by fainting or by going off into a fit of raging hysterics" (245). Nevertheless, Margaret maintains her self-control, and at the end of the night she is able to reflect on "what course would be best for her to adopt in the immediate future" (247). In other words, Margaret remains active in her assertion of agency, even though many of her actions are based on silence rather than speaking out.

Eventually, Effie figures out that it is Dolgouroff Margaret loves, not Zelenberg, and she gathers the evidence needed to prove that Margaret and Dolgouroff lived together in Berlin. After Stewart threatens to cut off his support of Effie, due to the tension she has created, Effie reveals she can prove that Margaret and Dolgouroff had an affair (330). Stewart takes it upon himself to look for evidence and finds a love letter from Dolgouroff to Margaret (333), so he leaves for London, where he will meet with his lawyers and file for divorce (336–37). Though Margaret accepts Stewart's judgment that she has disgraced him, and while she even forgives Effie for her role in telling her secret, she does resist cultural norms that support the subordination of women by labeling them as fallen. She says to Effie, "The world will condemn me, but the world is not always right" (340). Further, when Stewart decides to divorce Margaret, she gives testimony indicating her innocence, and she refuses to go back to Dolgouroff, whose wife has died and who is now free to marry Margaret, if only she will accept him. Still, it is her commitment to her children that makes Margaret go through the divorce proceedings and reject Dolgouroff's offer to take her away with him, so it seems that Margaret's assertion of agency is not entirely consistent. Further, the novel ends with Margaret remarrying Dolgouroff, after a thoroughly sentimental moment in which Dolgouroff offers to take her away and the narrator comments, "So Margaret let pass the last scene in the drama of her life's story come to pass! She who, from the first awful hour of discovering the truth, had lived for her honour before all else, gave up the struggle to prove herself to be the pure soul that she was, she fought no more against the inevitable, but passed away out of her own country followed by the tender wishes of only one of all the friends of her brilliant married life" (351).

Margaret's return to Dolgouroff does appear to trump her earlier efforts to assert agency, but it is important to put her action in context and to acknowledge the choices reasonably available to her at the end of the novel. There is nothing in the novel to suggest that it is set late enough in the century for Margaret to make a living as a single professional woman, so her choices are likely limited, with remarriage as perhaps the only viable option for her. Also, it is important to acknowledge that Stannard supplements Margaret's action of marrying Dolgouroff with commentary from Margaret's friend, Laura Escourt. At the end of the novel, upon leaving the wedding, Laura praises Margaret for the resistance she has put up to cultural norms that support her subordination: "When I think of that dear saint . . . when I remember her sweet face, her patience with Max [Stewart], her dignity, her tact, her pure and wholesome mind, and compare her with that brainless thing at Claverhouse [Stewart's new wife], it makes me ill. Margaret's whole life was a protest against what the two men who loved her forced her against her will into being" (351–52). Still, we must acknowledge that neither *Shafts* nor *The Woman's Herald* reviewed the novel, suggesting that not only did Stannard's sentimental ending trump Margaret's earlier assertions of agency but even Laura Escourt's praise could not balance out the strong emphasis on a "happily-ever-after" ending. In the end Stannard did not make as much use of her female helpmate as she might have, perhaps because she could not let go of the literary style that had made her so commercially popular and perhaps because her moderate politics, which included the belief that women might sometimes sacrifice for love, had interfered with her ability to write a novel that would be seen as successful under the feminist realist aesthetic.

Two years after the publication of *A Blameless Woman, The Woman's Herald* did feature Stannard in one of its front-page interviews, and the paper's characterization of her as an author is almost exactly the same as it was in 1889, when it previously featured her. In this 1896 interview, written by Florence Fenwick Miller, Stannard is again described primarily through her person rather than through her writing. While the article begins with emphasis on the success Stannard gained with the publication of *Bootles' Baby,* and while Fenwick Miller characterizes Stannard's writing as possessing a "staying power," there is no in-depth analysis of her works nor any mention of *A Blameless Woman,* a novel Fenwick Miller might have found compelling had Stannard not reverted to the sentimental ending. As was the case in the 1889 interview, there is a significant amount of emphasis on Stannard's family life: her husband is praised again for his willingness to help Stannard with the business aspect of her work, and readers are given an update about the Stannards' growing family, since they had just delivered a new baby (Miller, "Character" 65–66).

Although the feminist periodicals did not review *A Blameless Woman,* the novel seems to have received a good reception by other periodicals, according to excerpts of the reviews used as advertisements in the back of Stannard's 1898 novel *In the Same Regiment.* The reviewer for the periodical *Truth* tells readers, "You certainly should read 'A Blameless Woman,'" and the reviewer for *Public Opinion* argues that *A Blameless Woman* is "[t]he ablest novel this talented authoress has yet produced" (no page). In addition, the reviewers for *The Daily Graphic* and *Citizen* highlight the literary quality of the book, writing, "It is a very simple, direct tragedy, skilfully worked out, thoroughly interesting," and "John Strange Winter may well be proud of a book which combines such as good plot with such fine human characterization," respectively. The reviewer for the *Sheffield Telegraph* also focuses on the novel's literary quality but combines this discussion with mention of the novel's contribution to the fallen woman genre: "The new word that might be said about the woman with a past, but which no one imagined could be invented, has been said with exquisite pathos and the charm of true womanliness by 'John Strange Winter.' . . . It has been the novelist's art to kindle these events into a beautiful story." Finally, reviewers for *The Realm* and *The Lady* argue that the novel will sustain Stannard's reputation, which the reviewer for *The Lady* feared was being hurt by "overproduction":

> Some among John Strange Winter's legion of admirers may, of late years, experienced a fear that she was erring on the side of overproduction, as book after book was written by her prolific pen; but her latest novel sets all such doubts at rest for the present. "A Blameless Woman" is decidedly the best work she has yet given us, not even excepting the ever-delightful "Bootles' Baby," with which she won her first laurels.

The Realm confirms the perseverance of Stannard's reputation when its reviewer writes: "'A Blameless Woman' is an honest straightforward love story, and will ensure a continuation of Mrs. Stannard's well-earned reputation" (no page).

This positive reception by the mainstream press perhaps is another indication that Stannard had not engaged the feminist realist aesthetic as fully as she might have but had remained closer to her already-established sentimental literary style. In fact, Stannard continued to write in a senti-mental vein through the 1890s and after the turn of the century. She did address certain aspects of gender in some of her novels—such as the prob-lem of arranged marriages in *The Peacemakers* (1898)—but she continued to do so in her own moderate, rather than liberal, fashion. And she con-tinued to pump out commercially successful novels at a consistent rate; she published three or four novels per year through 1904, when her produc-tion slowed considerably.

While Stannard herself seemed unconcerned with her literary reputa-tion beyond her lifetime, Oliver Bainbridge took it upon himself to try to ensure that Stannard would be remembered into the twentieth century with the publication of *John Strange Winter: A Volume of Personal Record* in 1916. Yet he relies both on Stannard's earlier sentimental fiction and on her personality in his attempt to solidify this literary reputation. His biog-raphy contains chapters focusing on various aspects of her personality, such as "Mrs. Stannard's Love of Animals," which focuses on her tendency to adopt stray cats, to the degree that her neighbors automatically saw her house as a depository for such strays; "Mrs. Stannard's Courage," which highlights her interventions in public disturbances, such as a drunk man beating his wife; "Mrs. Stannard's Charities," which discusses her work with ill people, especially "incurable" children; and "Mrs. Stannard Goes into Trade," which tells how, after the publishers of her magazine *Golden Gates* went bankrupt, Stannard turned to marketing lotions in order to pay off her debt. This focus on her personality, rather than her writing, assumes the same sort of established reputation Stannard herself supposed and it seems to have done little to improve her literary reputation.

Still, there is a chapter titled "Mrs. Stannard as an Author" in the biog-raphy, which describes Stannard's writing process and some of her literary achievements, especially *Bootles' Baby*. There also is a chapter on the Anti-Crinoline League, which positively portrays Stannard's work on this issue, and a chapter titled "Man vs. Woman," which focuses on Stannard's reply to an article about women in *The Daily Chronicle*. However, neither of these chapters includes any mention of *A Blameless Woman*. The book ends on a fairly sentimental note, with a chapter titled "Mrs. Stannard Crosses the Silent Ocean," which describes the last days of Stannard's life and her death, characterized by Bainbridge as the crossing of the "Silent Ocean in the swift-sailing canoe to the Spirit Land," where she could only be happi-er, having "escaped from her suffering" and having "acquired a sacred dig-nity" (162). In writing this "personal record," an appropriate label for his book because it relies more heavily on anecdotal information than formal biography, Bainbridge presents a view of Stannard that might make readers like her as person and see her as a worthy contributor to society, but not necessarily see her as a serious author. Ultimately, his focus on the niceties of Stannard's personality contributes to her sentimental reputation rather than promoting her to a higher status within the literary community based on her work.

In the end Stannard was not as concerned about literary reputation beyond one's own lifetime as Moore was, and, since she did not see this process as important, she did not need her female helpmate, *A Blameless Woman,* as desperately as Moore needed *Esther Waters* to ensure his journey to the summit of Mount Parnassus. Had Moore not taken specific steps to emphasize his achievement with *Esther Waters,* he might be less well-remembered today. While his reputation has waxed and waned throughout the twentieth century, his current place in the literary canon can be attributed in part to *Esther Waters* and its focus on the issue of woman's agency, which was the central concept in the feminist realist aesthetic of the 1890s. While Stannard made her own contribution to the *fin-de-siècle* discussion of woman's agency by valuing and defending the place of women writers in the literary market, she felt secure with her own position as a writer, even if it amounted to commercial success rather than the literary success that would gain an author a place in the British masculinist tradition. Certainly, the exclusion of women writers from certain aspects of the late-Victorian marketplace influenced how they perceived themselves within the literary tradition and likely made them less fixated on long-term literary reputation. Still, had Stannard more fully used her female helpmate, *A Blameless Woman,* to embrace the feminist realist aesthetic, she might be a more central figure in the current recovery of women writers. Nevertheless, Stannard's attempt to embrace the aesthetic, albeit incomplete, should be recognized, since our own twenty-first-century feminist aesthetic must remain as flexible as possible. Like feminists of the 1890s, we should continue to value the central principles of the aesthetic—expression of agency through consciousness, spoken word, and action—but we should also recognize that women's attempts to assert agency were shaped by cultural conditions and were not always as successful as we might wish.

Engaging and Shaping Modernism

The feminist realist aesthetic incorporated, in varying degrees, by the authors in this study contributed significantly to the debate over realism at the *fin de siècle* by advocating serious consideration of the representation of woman's agency. By laying out specific principles for Hardy's idea in "Candour in English Fiction" (1890)—the idea that "the relations of the sexes" should be represented in literature—feminist periodicals created a progressive yet flexible standard for late-Victorian authors to emulate. This standard praised authors for incorporating any of the three methods—consciousness, spoken word, and action—but saw the latter two as springing from the first. This new aesthetic acknowledged consciousness and the narrative strategy of internal perspective more fully than previous realist aesthetics had. In fact, in an article titled "Is the Present Increase in Women Authors a Gain to Literature?," which appeared in *Shafts* in 1894, the author of the article identified the ability to write about the "inner life" rather than outward detail as the "modern tone in literature" (240).

The emphasis on inner life, especially the inner lives of women, helped push the development of the novel toward a modernist aesthetic at the *fin de siècle*. Once woman's consciousness was represented in the novel, it was a quick step to the thought-oriented aesthetic of the modernist novel. While the transition from Victorianism to modernism has typically been attributed to the use of antirealist narrative strategies by late-Victorian authors, antirealist strategies should not receive sole credit, since the transition is more fluid than such a theory suggests. Rather, this transition should be attributed equally to the impulse by late-Victorian authors not only to work within the realist tradition but also to transform it, as authors who adopted the feminist realist aesthetic did. By acknowledging the influence of feminist realism in the development of the novel, we enhance our understanding of the multiple sources for the modernist novel. It is not only the antirealists who encouraged the transition from Victorianism to modernism but also those authors who engaged and incorporated feminist realism at the *fin de siècle.*

As I laid out in the introduction to this study, recent discussions of nineteenth-century British realism have tried to expand our understanding of the term beyond the traditional definition of highly detailed, external description of society, a definition that ignores the inner workings of the mind as well as the experiences of women. Still, as this study has also shown, the traditional definition of realism, which shaped the assumptions of much of the literary criticism produced in the nineteenth century, collided with competing definitions of the term, especially in the latter part of the century. Authors encountered new variations of realism, such as French naturalism and psychological realism, and as part of their encounters with these variations, they developed their own form, "New Realism," of which Hardy was the main proponent. The New Realists, which tended to be male-dominated and included Meredith and Moore, distanced themselves from the naturalists, especially Zola, by placing less emphasis on a strongly animalistic approach to representation of people and their actions. However, they shared with the naturalists an interest in "the relations of the sexes" as a way to capture the reality of human experience. Likewise, they shared similarities with psychological realists, such as Henry James, who emphasized woman's consciousness as a legitimate subject for fiction in novels such as *The Portrait of a Lady* (1881). Still, they were not disciples of James, since they did not focus as intently on representing the interior thoughts of characters as he did.

At the same time as male authors were developing the New Realism, women writers were constructing their own form of "new" realism—the New Woman novel, which illustrated contemporary cultural conditions for gender relations and advocated alternative roles for women. Ultimately, a dialogue—sometimes friendly, sometimes combative—emerged between the New Realists and the New Woman novelists, and both male and female authors engaged feminist realism through this dialogue. As I have already discussed, some recent critics want to emphasize the differences between male and female authors of the 1890s in order to make the point that the transition from Victorianism to modernism depended primarily on women writers because they supposedly could depict women's experiences better than male authors could and because they were responsible for certain late-century literary innovations usually attributed to male authors. However, pitting male and female authors against each other creates a history of the novel that does not fully account for the way in which the feminist realist aesthetic and the woman's press actually shaped modernism. The woman's press was inclusive of male authors but also emphasized the contributions of women writers to create its own mini-canon of authors who would go on to shape modernism, even if they did not become as well known as the typically recognized modernists, such as Joyce and Woolf.

In writing about the works of successful authors, regardless of gender, the woman's press of the 1890s made a significant contribution to the development of modernism: a specific literary aesthetic that allowed authors to stretch the boundaries of realism in ways even other late-century variations on realism did not. By engaging the feminist realist aesthetic, Sarah Grand highlighted the role of consciousness in assertions of agency by female characters who faced difficult marriages and unfulfilling lives because they were restricted to the domestic sphere, while Thomas Hardy depicted women who had increased awareness of their cultural conditions but could not translate that awareness into feminist speech or action. George Gissing and Mona Caird successfully employed dialogue to show women using spoken word to resist the traditional expectations for romantic relationships between men and women. George Meredith illustrated the wide variety of actions possible for women in difficult situations, and Ménie Dowie pushed the possibilities for action and marked the limits of the feminist aesthetic. Finally, George Moore and Henrietta Stannard took different approaches to the issue of literary reputation and, as a result, engaged the feminist realist aesthetic with varying degrees of success.

Further, through its commitment to reviewing novels that successfully depicted woman's agency, the woman's press gave male authors a venue for feedback on their work not provided by the mainstream press. It is clear that many male authors wanted a better understanding of women readers, since some of them commented on women who were reading their novels, and the woman's press provided this opportunity. For women writers the woman's press provided a venue for recognition of their work, especially when they felt misunderstood or were ignored by the mainstream press. Many women writers were aware of the bias against them in the literary community, and the woman's press provided a space for them to hear positive messages about working literary women. Finally, the woman's press worked to combat misconceptions about the modern woman. If readers of the period had looked only at the mainstream press's representation of the modern woman, who was usually presented as a caricature (the opinionated, bicycle-riding, smoking New Woman), they might very well have had a negative impression of this figure. But, as presented in the pages of *Shafts* and *The Woman's Herald*, this figure is not the flat caricature suggested by the mainstream press. She is a well-rounded person with admirable professional goals and dedication to the cause of changing the cultural conditions for women.

These important contributions of the woman's press remain significant today, possibly more so than in the past, because knowledge of the woman's press can shape our own views of literary history. Few bibliographies of authors' works produced in the twentieth century include reviews written by the woman's press, and our judgment of the reception of male authors has been skewed, just as the judgments of late-nineteenth-century readers were skewed by the mainstream press of the day. Even recent work on women writers, which does account for reviews found in the woman's press, does not acknowledge as fully as it might the consistent literary aesthetic found in this press. Highlighting the role of this aesthetic should change our views about the development of the novel, which has been distorted because too much emphasis has been placed on other late-century literary movements and not enough attention has been paid to feminist realism.

Ultimately, both male and female authors of the 1890s broke with tradition while still relying on previous narrative techniques, and, as this study has shown, both put increased emphasis on woman's consciousness, the key element in terms of the transition from Victorianism to modernism. After their engagement with the feminist realist aesthetic in the 1890s, many of these authors engaged modernism in works which they produced after those discussed in this study were written. Still, as they engaged modernism, it always was with some awareness of the realist tradition that had come before. Hardy, for example, turned away from the novel and wrote poetry, a genre that seemed to allow for the more subjective, personal experience that had emerged through the feminist realist aesthetic and was moving to a new level in the modernist period. In poems such as "The Darkling Thrush" (1900), Hardy's fascination with the bleakness of human existence and the effect on the psyche is evident in the "I" narrator, who recognizes the passing of the old century and the "fervourless" state of himself and "every spirit upon earth" (Hardy, *Complete Poems* 150). While there is new hope as the century turns, as exemplified by the singing thrush, the narrator remains untouched by this hope: "Some blessed Hope, whereof he knew / . . . I was unaware" (150). In highlighting this skepticism, Hardy anticipates what would become the modernist mentality, especially after World War I. Yet even after World War I the tension between hope and hopelessness remains, and, in "I Looked Up from My Writing" (1917), Hardy highlights this tension by focusing on an encounter between the "I" narrator, who wants to write a book, and the moon, which questions how the narrator can write "In a world of such a kind," where men are killed in battle (551).

Sarah Grand, too, engaged modernism in *Adnam's Orchard* (1912) and *The Winged Victory* (1916), the first two parts of her unfinished trilogy about social problems, including eugenics, at the turn of the century. According to Teresa Mangum, these two novels touch on the "psychic" and "spiritual" aspects of modern life (193), and *The Winged Victory* is particularly modernist. Writes Mangum: "The darkness and futility of *The Winged Victory* are unprecedented in Grand's earlier work, and, if the texture and tone of the novel are Victorian, the ambience is Modernist" (211). Certainly, the events of the novel are bleak: the climax of the story features the main character, Ella Banks, murdering one of the men who have pursued her romantically. Further, Ella learns that the love of her life, Lord Melton, actually is her brother, and the man who has been providing for her financially and caring for her emotionally is her father.

In addition to exploring these bleak events, Grand continues the focus on consciousness, the quality that made her work from the 1890s protomodernist. In fact, the novel begins with a quotation emphasizing consciousness from Edward Carpenter's *A Visit to Guani*: "When the noise of the workshop is over and mallet and plane laid aside, the faint sounds come through the window . . . intuitions, perceptions, which though partaking in some degree of the character and thought, spring from ultimately different conditions, and are the forerunners of a changed consciousness" (vi). The story soon turns to the increased consciousness of Ella, a lacemaker who spends much of her time working but also has ample time to reflect on her condition and the condition of other lacemakers. Ella recognizes that her own position is more privileged than that of other lacemakers (a Duke and Duchess support her), but it also is a lonely existence, since she is housed in London and cannot see the many she loves. Still, Ella is determined to improve her situation, so she reasons, "She decided to be grateful, but without being compliant. . . . It was understood, of course, that she should do her duty by the commercial part of the [lacemaking] enterprise; but, apart from that she had her own object and would make for it direct . . . to make the most of her many advantages" (32).

This reflection illustrates the attention given to Ella's internal perspective in the novel, primarily through realist narrative techniques, but Grand also pushes the boundaries of realist narration by following this reflection with one which is more thoroughly modernist, since the flow of words more closely resembles stream-of-consciousness. "Following upon this determination [to make the most of her advantages], her spirits rose to the height from which it is a joy to look. She opened the window and leant out. With the opening of the window she let in a muffled roar, like the roar of the sea in a shell. It was as if she held London to her ear and listened— London, the city joyous of her dreams!" (32). Already the narrative contains a stream-of-consciousness quality—in the repetitive phrase "muffled roar, like the roar of the sea in a shell"—but it becomes increasingly modernist as Ella's thoughts continue:

> A band passed in the distance playing a rollicking march, and her heart, throbbing to the throbbing of the drum, swelled high with hope. Then there were the feet—pattering feet coming, coming, coming from every direction; and going, going, going again, in every direction. The feet were most strange and exciting to her unaccustomed ear—footfalls of such numbers of people as it was hard to believe existed, each pursuing an object, and what object? Perhaps that great glow in the sky was the glory to which they were hurrying, to bathe in it, and from which they were returning all radiant and fresh. Joy was the predominant note to Ella's ear. Only the fulness of life appealed to her at the moment, with an ecstatic sense of well-being. Those feet! those feet! messenger feet! *How beautiful upon the mountains are the feet of him that bringeth good tidings.* . . . They were coming into her life, those feet, bringing her joy! (32)

Though the narrative soon returns to a more realist vein, there are forays into modernist technique throughout the novel, as when Ella reflects on the power that lacemaking has to change the world in the chapter titled "Ella's Retrospect" and when mystical descriptions of nature dominate in the chapter titled "Ella's Intellect Wars Against Spiritual Influences." Finally, we see the modernist effect when Ella, having left England after killing Brastaby, returns "an altered woman," and her thoughts run on about what she has done: "She was torn by the horror of bloodshed, torn by that suggestion of the Duke's that she had been in no danger, which made the deed unjustifiable—though she knew better! She knew better! . . . It was awful to have taken a man's life, but the wretch, the wretch— Oh, she wanted to kill him over and over and over again!—Yet she did not want him to be dead" (511). Ultimately, Grand remains within the realist tradition, but her interest in woman's consciousness helps her push the narrative technique into the realm of modernism.

Like Grand, Mona Caird explores the psychic and the spiritual in the works she published in the late 1890s and after the turn of the century: *The Pathway of the Gods* (1898), *The Stones of Sacrifice* (1916), and *The Great Wave* (1931), which John Sutherland believes is "exalted and visionary, a full blown expression of the mysticism latent in all Caird's writing" (100). Through this mysticism, Caird explores the connection between past, present, and future, a connection which gives her work a protomodernist quality, since the "great" modernists also incorporated nonlinear approaches to time. For example, in *The Pathway of the Gods,* Caird emphasizes the past by highlighting how images from the Golden Age of Italy pervade the thoughts of the main character, an artist named Julian, but she connects these images from the past to the present and the future by having Julian use them as a way to process what is happening in his life at the moment and what he expects to happen in the future. Still focused on the place of the New Woman in society, Caird develops the connection between past, present, and future primarily through Julian's relationship with a woman named Anna, a love from Julian's past whom he believes is much like him, since they both are "waifs and strays . . . more or less out of touch with their own people" (19).

Eventually, Anna and Julian are reunited in Italy, but Julian, who represents *fin-de-siècle* aestheticism, doubts whether Anna, who represents the New Woman, can be a true companion to him, since he is not sure whether she shares his "worship of the eternal Spirit of Beauty" (211). While the novel ends with a vision of Anna as one of the Christians sacrificed in Rome, an image which has served as inspiration for Julian throughout the novel and which suggests that Anna does have the commitment Julian seeks, the novel also ends with Anna's female competitor, Clutha, overseeing the sacrifice. Ann Heilman, in *New Woman Strategies: Sarah Grand, Olive Schreiner, Mona Caird* (2004), has pointed out that Julian's vision of Anna throughout the novel is highly mythologized and that his glorification of Clutha over Anna at the end of the story suggests he cannot accept the New Woman. In fact, writes Heilmann, any "straightforward reading of the ending as an invocation of a new dawn in human relations becomes destabilised" (177). Ultimately, Caird uses mythology, particularly the movement between past, present, and future, to critique the return of patriarchy in *fin-de-siècle* ideologies, especially aestheticism, but she also anticipates modernism via her experimentation with time.

Caird's use of mysticism to experiment with time yet critique patriarchy also is present in *The Stones of Sacrifice,* where several of the main characters congregate at the Standing Stones, Stonehenge-like configurations in Scotland, and discuss the connections between human sacrifices in the past and present-day philosophies about sacrifice, including the sacrifice of women and animals. Like *Pathway of the Gods,* this novel critiques patriarchy by making the protagonist, Alpin Dalrymple, a New Man and his love interest, Claudia, a New Woman. The two marry but maintain an "individualistic marriage" in which each is free to do as he or she pleases (383). Further, they establish a group called the "Alternatives," which advocates replacing the "negative idea of sacrifice" with the "positive living substitute of sympathy," which functions in turn as a "glorious substitute for crucifixion" (384). At the end of the novel, Alpin, Claudia, and friends

return to the Standing Stones, where Alpin, who has become especially
devoted to preventing the sacrifice of animals, realizes he must continue
working toward a harmonious world, where the norm is "love and pity for
all not merely for a favoured handful" (455). The most upbeat of the three
novels that Caird wrote as the century turned, *Stones of Sacrifice* suggests
there can be positive change. As Heilmann explains, the novel indicates
how the progressive "sexual politics of the Alternatives yield immediate
positive results," and the novel ends with a "vision of a society in which
human, animal and natural worlds are at peace" (198).

In *The Great Wave*, Caird's last novel and the one most thoroughly
influenced by the historical events of the modernist period, the author's
interest in mysticism plays itself out by focusing on Grierson Elliott, a
young man who rejects his family's penchant for war and becomes an
experimenter, drawing inspiration from a fourteenth-century alchemist
who worked in the same attic-laboratory he inhabits. The novel focuses on
Grierson's increasing consciousness about the world and his place in it,
and Grierson's interest in the past comes into contact with real issues of
the present, especially the possible onset of war between the British and
the Germans. Grierson's strong opposition to war shapes the decisions he
makes about his experiments and even causes him to abandon them at one
point, when it becomes clear that his scientific knowledge may end up in
the hands of those who want to go to war. Still, Grierson eventually
returns to his work believing that he can do something to improve the
lives of humans while they struggle against inevitable defeat.

In keeping with Caird's interest in the place of the New Woman in
society, Grierson's female partner, Nora Geddon, a New Woman because
she is Grierson's intellectual equal, plays an important role in the novel's
storyline. Claiming that "the only man she could bring herself to marry
would be one who had a rooted objection to matrimony" (297), Nora
befriends Grierson, falls in love with him, and becomes part of his intimate circle of advisors who help him decide how to use his scientific innovations and help him protect his innovations from those who might use
them to destroy humanity. In fact, without Nora, Grierson's innovations
would have fallen into the hands of his war-hungry antagonist, Waldheim.
Via Nora, Caird continues to explore feminist issues even as she is engaging other issues central to turn-of-the-century culture, confirming
Heilmann's opinion that Caird's novels "consistently drew attention to the
close interrelationship between sex/gender discourses and the prevailing
ideological structures of the system" (199). Although Caird's literary technique in these novels is not as protomodernist as Grand's technique is in
the work she produced after the turn of the century, her experimentation
with time does have a protomodernist effect. Further, her critique of mod-

ern life and her construction of a different kind of world based on specific gender politics indicate that Caird did engage the important issues of early-twentieth-century culture.

Finally, George Moore engaged new literary styles in the work he produced in the late 1890s and after the turn of the century and, in doing so, helped to shape modernism. Influenced by William Butler Yeats, whom Moore admired for his involvement in the Irish revival movement, he constructed plots revolving around religious women in *Evelyn Innes* (1898) and *Sister Teresa* (1901) to move from the realist style that characterized *Esther Waters* to a more symbolist literary style. In *Evelyn Innes,* for example, a musically inclined young woman struggles to reconcile the traditional religious values taught to her by her parents with the agnostic values of her lover, Owen Asher. Not only does Evelyn becomes a symbol for this struggle between religion and agnosticism, but also the discourse of music becomes a method for discussing love and sexuality, which is a key element in Evelyn's spiritual struggle. Like Caird's, Moore's narrative technique is not as protomodernist as Grand's, but his use of symbolism creates a protomodernist effect.

Evelyn Innes creates a strong link to the works Moore produced after the turn of the century, since Evelyn seems to symbolize Moore's own struggle with traditional Catholicism and agnosticism. Moore returned to Ireland in 1901, in part because he sensed that Ireland was about to become artistically exciting and he wanted to participate in Yeats's revival movement (Frazier 273–75), but he struggled with the continuing influence of Catholicism in his home country. In works such as *The Untilled Field* (1903) and *The Lake* (1905), both of which take Ireland as their subject matter, Moore's symbolist technique emerges once again. "In the Clay," one of the stories included in *The Untilled Field,* explores the same tension between religion and agnosticism Moore explores in *Evelyn Innes* via the story of the sculptor, Rodney, whose freedom from the repressive religious atmosphere in Ireland is ensured only by the production of religious iconography because it will provide the funds needed to leave Ireland. The story focuses on Rodney's production of a statue of the Virgin Mary and Child, which is destroyed by two boys who overhear a priest bemoaning the fact that the artist used a nude model to create the statue, and the symbolism of all the women in the story, not just the Virgin Mary, is strong. Rodney's charwoman is larger than life—she functions as the bearer of the bad news about the statue—and Lucy, the young woman who models for Rodney and wants to travel to Paris with him after his misfortune, serves as a symbol for the choice between Rodney's freedom and the responsibility that would come from taking her with him. Finally, the statue itself acts as the strongest symbolist element in the story, since it symbolizes the irony of Rodney's situation in Ireland and his struggle to come to terms with the fact that in order to leave Ireland and its repressive atmosphere, he must participate in the system he despises. Ultimately, he believes "there can be no renaissance" in Ireland in terms of art unless there is "religious revolt" (27), and this attitude seems to reflect Moore's own paradoxes about life in Ireland.

In *The Lake*, Moore again employs a symbolist approach to comment on Irish life, especially the stifling effect of religious Ireland and the freedom associated with leaving Ireland and living abroad. In the novel Father Oliver, a somewhat open-minded priest, becomes entranced by a parishioner, Rose Leicester, who leaves Ireland for England and then Italy after she is shunned by Oliver himself for her "fallen" status. Over time, Oliver realizes he is not seeking Rose so much as he is seeking "life," and at the end of the novel he swims across the lake near his parish, with the plan of making his parishioners think that he has drowned when in fact he has gone to New York to start a new life. Both Rose and the lake function as strong symbolic elements, and Moore's tendency to idealize women—a habit I discussed in chapter 4—is evident. While Moore's narrative technique is not as radical as modernist stream-of-consciousness, his technique is strongly subjective, since the novel is built upon the very personal letters Oliver writes to Rose. Further, both Rose and Oliver explore the wanderings of their minds in these letters, and such exploration suggests that Moore's novel anticipates the subjective narratives of the better-known modernists. As Robert Welch, in "Moore's Way Back: *The Untilled Field* and *The Lake*" (1982), says of Moore's work in *The Lake*: "[I]n opening fiction up to the shifting uncertainties of consciousness, he was attempting something new in literary narrative" (43).

Ultimately, many of the authors in this study engaged modernism at the turn of the century, but the feminist aesthetic they employed in the 1890s had already facilitated their own engagement and the engagement of others with this emerging style. Still, we cannot claim that the move from Victorianism to modernism necessarily results in more fully feminist representations in the modernist period. In fact, modernism often produces *less*-feminist representations because modernist writers focus so thoroughly on consciousness that the three-step process of asserting agency seen in the feminist realist ideal is left behind. A brief look at James Joyce's *Ulysses* (1922) and Virginia Woolf's *Mrs. Dalloway* (1925) can help us see why modernist texts did not necessarily result in successful representations according to the feminist realist aesthetic. This exercise more importantly helps us see that late-Victorian authors who incorporated this aesthetic did anticipate the move to more emphasis on consciousness in modernist texts.

While critics disagree about whether Molly Bloom is liberated at the close of Joyce's *Ulysses,* Joyce puts strong emphasis on Molly's heightened consciousness and accords her the narrative space needed to explore this consciousness by ending the novel with her monologue. Within the monologue, her account of her daily life, which has sometimes been seen as the "drudgery" of the traditional housewife (Unkeless 151), gives readers access to a point of view not highlighted in Bloom's narrative, and Molly's final exclamations of "yes," sometimes read as sexual liberation (Pearce 56–57), suggest a liberation also of thought and feeling. Still, the emphasis on consciousness limits what Joyce can do with the two other methods of asserting agency. Even if Molly were intent on changing the conditions of her marriage, as the "yes" exclamations might suggest, there is no room for assertion of agency through speech or action at the end of the novel.

The same is true in *Mrs. Dalloway,* where the emphasis again is on consciousness rather than speech or action. As Clarissa journeys through a day of party planning for her upper-class family and friends, her internal perspective acquaints readers with her early life as a more carefree woman, with her and others' struggles to survive World War I, and with the ways in which the demands of her present life as the wife of a government figure seem to have contributed to her physical illness and emotional fragility. While there is some room for assessing Clarissa's resistance to cultural conditions, since toward the end of her party she must decide whether to remain in her own inner world or return to her party, the outcome—her return to the party—does not bode well when placed next to the feminist realist aesthetic, since it seems as if Clarissa has done little to change the cultural expectations for women.

Still, this is not to say that Clarissa Dalloway and Molly Bloom are wholly negative representations of the modern woman. The emphasis on internal perspective allows for development of highly complex interior lives of female characters, and this development allows for exposure of the cultural conditions that prevent characters such as Clarissa and Molly from asserting agency. In Clarissa's case, the overwhelming emphasis on class status among her circle of friends, and the way in which notions of "respectability" dictate how individuals can express emotions, limit Clarissa. In Molly's case, the conventional values of Bloom make it difficult for Molly to be liberated outside her own mind. The modernist emphasis on consciousness illustrates the complexity of women's emotional lives, even if literature of the period does not meet the feminist realist ideal.

Ultimately, this study advocates a more open view of realism and a more complex view of the relationship between Victorianism and modernism. A return to George Levine's call for a more open understanding of realism (which I discussed at the beginning of this book) is appropriate, since as Levine reminds us, our thinking about the function of realism tends to be unnecessarily narrow. As Levine argues, realism is not an effort to avoid the indeterminacy of human experience (and, hence, a form of literature antithetical to modernism) but a method of actively engaging the issue of indeterminacy by struggling to reconcile "the monstrous" with the more "civilized" lives nineteenth-century people thought they should be living. Although Levine does not discuss the male and female authors in this study, with the exception of Hardy, it seems to me that for male and female writers of the 1890s, the monstrous is embodied in the debate over representation of "the relations of the sexes," since gender relations, especially the changes in these relations at the *fin de siècle,* were certainly perceived as monstrous by more traditional Victorians. The "truth" about the relations of the sexes—that they cannot be adequately represented by realism of the mid-century but only once realism is redefined, as it was by the New Realists, the New Woman novelists, and the late-Victorian woman's press—shows the limits of the genre when defined too narrowly. In engaging the relations of the sexes, even through the realist tradition, male and female novelists of the 1890s highlight "the monstrous" and make it central to the representation of human experience, and the late-Victorian woman's press recognized this. It is, then, the very act of working within the mainstream tradition, and transforming it into something new, that makes the efforts of authors who engaged the feminist realist aesthetic so effective. As much as antirealist narrative strategies may have contributed to the development of modernism, variations of realism, especially feminist realism, were equally important in this significant shift in literary style.

Notes

Notes to Introduction

1. John Kucich, in "Curious Dualities: *The Heavenly Twins* (1983) and Sarah Grand's Belated Modernist Aesthetics" (1996), uses the term "feminist realism" to describe a literary style common among the New Woman novelists, who demanded feminist "truth" and exhibited a certain amount of contempt for art because of their interest in feminist principles. Clearly, my use of the term is different—and more along the lines of Jennifer Phegley's use of it in *Educating the Proper Woman Reader: Victorian Family Literary Magazines and the Cultural Health of the Nation* (2004). Both Phegley and I are more confident about the accomplishments of feminist realism, though Phegley's focus is on its presence in 1860s rather than 1890s feminist periodicals. As a result, our definitions of the term differ somewhat, since the feminist literary aesthetic changes during this thirty-year gap, but we both use the term "feminist realism" in a positive sense.

2. Thanks to James Phelan for his help in working through this model to shed light on the assertion of agency by fictional characters.

3. For more on internal perspective, see Gérard Genette's *Narrative Discourse* (1980), especially chapter 4 in which Genette introduces the concept of focalization, and James Phelan's *Living to Tell about It* (2005), especially chapter 3 which includes discussion of Genette's concept and the various responses to this concept by other narratologists.

4. More recently, Butler has articulated a more nuanced model of the subject and has addressed the issue of consciousness more directly in *The Psychic Life of Power: Theories of Subjection* (1997). Here, she seems to embrace a model that acknowledges opportunities for assertion of agency (i.e., Hegel's bondsman recognizing the objects of his labor as his own) but also recognizes the limitations on such agency (i.e., the bondsman also recognizes his own work in the signature of his lord upon his work) (36–37). Further, she more fully addresses the issue of conscience, one specific aspect of consciousness, via her analysis of the ideas of Nietzsche, Freud, Foucault, and Althusser. While she still emphasizes speech over thought, and her basic belief that the subject is already acted upon remains, she more thoroughly engages the role of consciousness in subject formation.

5. Michiel Heyns's *Expulsion and the Nineteenth-Century Novel: The Scapegoat in English Realist Fiction* (1994), for example, focuses on authors of the "Great Tradition" (Austen, Dickens, Eliot, Conrad, and James) and shows how works by these authors "support the status quo" but also shows how these works contain the means to "escape appropriation to the status quo" (49). Likewise, Katherine Kearns's *Nineteenth-Century Literary Realism* (1996) shows the contradictory aspects of realism; she argues that while realism is "an essentially pragmatic mode whose predication of character as something enacted, partially but inevitably, within the environmental restrictions is

designed to reveal an imperiled ecological system of soul and society," it also has "an alternative energy, perhaps in direct consequence of its shouldering of ethical and social responsibility, that is sufficient to destabilize the reformist agenda at hand" (1). In other words, while realism appears to uphold the dominant nineteenth-century perspective that reform could happen through a practical, material approach, it also engages a more mysterious side of life. Finally, Tom Lloyd's *Crises of Realism: Representing Experience in the British Novel, 1816–1910* (1997) follows Heyns and Kearns, arguing that novelists from Austen to E. M. Forster carved out a "realistic middle space," which both "unsettles and reassures its readers, for the reality it replicates inevitably is domesticated in the act of retelling" (9).

6. Fenwick Miller, for example, thought Somerset's purchase of the paper from Henrietta Müller in 1893 had been an attempt to prevent competition in the woman's press, and she states this in a letter to the *Daily Chronicle*. However, Sibthorp thought Fenwick Miller had mistaken Somerset's motives, and she defends the "excellence" of the paper through its various editorial changes. But even she recognized that *The Woman's Herald* was a different paper under Somerset than it had been under Müller. In an article in the April 1898 *Shafts*, "Two Women's Papers," Sibthorp writes: "[I]t then became a Liberal organ, and so ceased to be absolutely a woman's paper" (78).

7. It is precisely for this reason that I have not included *The Englishwoman's Review* in this study. The periodical ran until 1910 and did review literature in the 1890s, including Sarah Grand's *The Heavenly Twins,* but it did not review most of the major novels of the decade, including those discussed in this book. Instead, it tended to review nonfiction on a wide range of topics (from the care of babies to how to paint to the qualities of proper English); reprints of works by earlier women writers (such as Mary Wollstonecraft's *Vindication of the Rights of Woman*); and other periodicals and short pamphlets. There simply are not enough reviews of prose fiction to discern a consistent literary aesthetic. Even the review of *The Heavenly Twins* is so short that it cannot cover the same range of issues raised in the periodicals I have included in this study.

8. It should be noted that Krout also was an admirer of George Gissing, though she did not write about him for *The Woman's Herald.* In December 1896, Krout sent Gissing a clipping of an article that she had written and that had appeared in a Chicago paper, *The Daily Inter Ocean.* Titled "Women's Kingdom: 'The Odd Women' and Its Influence in England," the article emphasizes the novel's popularity in England and details how Gissing realistically portrays the sufferings of single women with no income and little training to find work for themselves. While Krout does not address the issue of woman's agency or Gissing's representation of it directly in this article, she does draw attention to the connection between the lives of literary characters and lives of real-life women in England, as she devotes the latter part of the article to the real-life conditions of women in England and argues there is "no parallel situation" in the United States (16).

Notes to Chapter 1

1. Among those mainstream reviewers who criticized Hardy: Margaret Oliphant, whose criticism of *Jude* in *Blackwood's Edinburgh Magazine* enraged

Hardy; Mowbray Morris, whose comments about *Tess* in *The Quarterly Review* Hardy assessed as an example of the stagnant state of the reviewing apparatus; and, of course, the anonymous reviewer whose "attack" on *Tess* in *The Saturday Review* led Hardy to consider resigning his membership at the Savile Club, since he feared encountering the reviewer there (*Collected Letters* 2:105, 1:264–65, 2:252). Interestingly, all of these reviews have in common an emphasis on the "unnatural" story lines found in Hardy's work and his inability, as the reviewers saw it, to represent accurately characters as they would act in civilized society. This trend has relevance to the gender issues raised by Hardy in "Candour in English Fiction" because reviewers most often touched on the lack of natural actions of the central female characters, Tess Durbeyfield and Sue Bridehead. What these reviewers hoped for, it seems, were more traditional female characters rather than characters who reflected the changing times.

2. The controversy over Grand's depiction of syphilis is well documented, but what is less documented are the ways in which mainstream reviews marginalized Grand by characterizing her work as falling short of the realist ideal of the period and presenting degenerate characters instead of characters who would uphold respectable society. These reviews suggest that novels highlighting the relations of the sexes were outside the norm. For example, the review of *The Heavenly Twins* in *The Pall Mall Gazette,* which was so negative it sparked a heated discussion in more than one journal over the definition of realism being used by the critical establishment, states that while the "degenerate modern reader" may enjoy the book, the central character of the story, Evadne, is "the feminine conscience of modernity made flesh; too, too, solid flesh altogether" (Anonymous, "New Novels: According" 432).

Likewise, the reviewer for *The Critic* characterizes Grand as taking a Zolaesque approach to drawing characters and objects to the delineation of Angelica's character, claiming that it is a "mental strain" to "believe that a young married woman, the granddaughter of an English Duke, is in the habit of paying long visits at night, wearing her brother's clothes and passing for a boy" (Anonymous, "Heavenly" 437). This reviewer also argues that it is inappropriate for sexual standards to be the "central motive" for a novel "meant for general readers of both sexes" (437). Finally, in "The Strike of the Sex," William Barry takes a sarcastic tone, naming all the reasons people might like the novel (style, sentiment, tragedy) and refuting each one. Then Barry contrasts the novel to Ward's *Marcella,* which he believes is more "successful" because it does not close at a "psychological moment," follows the plot out to its logical end, and generally includes "a type closer to life than the grotesques and caricatures of 'The Heavenly Twins'" (452). This type of criticism, which masks dislike for the subject matter in discussion about literary style, is not unlike that used against Hardy to marginalize those writers who were taking on controversial subject matter.

3. While Lord Dawne disapproves of some of Ideala's actions, it cannot be said that he is unsympathetic to feminist principles. To Ideala, he argues that no person can "stand alone," separate from the rest of society, indicating that he may be supportive of a woman's movement that emphasizes collective action as well as individual transformation. "[W]e are all part of this great system," he tells Ideala. "[I]ndividuals must suffer, must even be sacrificed, for the good of the rest. When the sacrifice is voluntary, we call it noble" (165). Dawne uses this argument to try

to convince Ideala that it would be wrong to run away with Lorrimer. His argument might be seen as patriarchal rather than feminist, as Dawne does seem to have some romantic interest in Ideala, but Dawne never articulates (or acts on) his attraction to Ideala. So it is possible to read Dawne's perspective as feminist rather than patriarchal.

4. Mangum, for instance, argues that the shift from third-person narration to Galbraith's first-person narration toward the end of the novel "signals the dangers of unquestioningly accepting the authoritative male account of female experience" (118), and Ann Heilmann, in "Narrating the Hysteric: *Fin-de-Siècle* Medical Discourse and Sarah Grand's *The Heavenly Twins* (1893)" (2001), states that the "most disturbing reflection of her [Evadne's] disintegration is the fact that her voice and perspective are filtered through a male consciousness" (126).

5. For example, in "Writing against the 'Husband-Fiend': Syphilis and Male Sexual Vice in the New Woman Novel" (2000), Emma Liggins finds the ending to be too traditional, a "conventional happy ending" in which the "New Woman's radical potential is sapped by the pressures of conforming to conservative plotlines, as Evadne achieves her womanly ideal of house, children, and husband of her own" (187). While I agree that the open-ended nature of the ending leaves one wondering whether Evadne ever will be able to act independently (and become less dependent on Galbraith), Evadne's marriage to Galbraith seems less conventional than Liggins suggests, and her reading does not recognize the positive role some men might have in a woman's transformation.

6. For more on the problems that mainstream critics had with *The Beth Book,* see the anonymous reviews in *The Athenaeum* (Anonymous, "New Novels"), *The Spectator* (Anonymous, "Some New Novels"), and the *Review of Reviews* (Anonymous, "Some Books of the Month").

7. "Focalizer" is the term used by narratologists to refer to characters whose internal perspective is dominant in the narrative at a particular time. As shifts in vision from one character to another occur in the narration, the character identified as the focalizer also shifts.

8. On January 15, 1894, Hardy writes to Florence Henniker, "I am creeping on a little with the long story, and am beginning to get interested in my heroine as she takes shape and reality: though she is very nebulous at present" (2:47). Then, on August 12, 1895, he writes and says, "I am more interested in this Sue story than in any I have written" (2:84).

9. For more on the language of sympathy, see Audrey Jaffe, *Scenes of Sympathy: Identity and Representation in Victorian Fiction* (2000).

10. Oliphant's "conservatism" is complex, as evidenced by the fact that she also discusses Grand's *Ideala* in the same article and reviews it fairly favorably. Ann Heilmann, in "Mrs. Grundy's Rebellion: Margaret Oliphant between Orthodoxy and the New Woman" (1999), explains Oliphant's conservatism well by pointing out that she would not accept depictions of sex outside of marriage. This is how she could criticize Hardy's *Jude* but accept Grand's *Ideala,* since Ideala was tempted in her marriage but did not act on that temptation. Still, I recognize that Oliphant's position on women's rights is ambiguous, especially when one traces her own statements on the issue across her career. For more on this, see Heilmann as well as Merryn Williams's "Feminist or Antifeminist? Oliphant and the Woman Question" (1995). My characterization of Oliphant as "conservative" applies to

her reviews for *Blackwood's*, which, Heilmann emphasizes, was a periodical with Tory associations and edited by a conservative editor (218).

11. See, for example, Black's "The Need of Trade Unions for Working Women," which ran in the May 21, 1892 issue of *The Woman's Herald* and in which Black argues that working women would be better off if they belonged to trade unions as they would be able to exert enough pressure on employers to raise wages and make enough money to provide for themselves in old age. See also "The Servant Question," in which Black was interviewed by Sarah Tooley about the differences between the lives of factory girls and servant girls, and "Questions of the Day," in which Frances E. Willard interviewed Black about a variety of questions, including her opinion about modern fiction. Of the "sex novel," Black states, "I am glad to see women speaking out in this kind of novel, even when the ideas expressed are erroneous. It is well to bring to light even the false point of view on such questions, and I think women should undoubtedly say what they think. I feel it is to the general good that a woman should put into a novel her own thoughts" (Willard 130).

Notes to Chapter 2

1. See for example, *The Speaker*'s "Fiction," which characterizes the novel as more of an "essay in social ethics" than a novel (Anonymous, "Fiction" 417). Some of the reviews, including the one in *The Speaker*, do praise Gissing's efforts at tackling an important social issue, and the review in *The Pall Mall Gazette* even touches on Gissing's use of dialogue, saying that it distinguishes "good from bad realism" (Anonymous, "Reviews: *Odd*" 220). However, this review also seeks to separate *The Odd Women* from those New Woman novels in which the characters simply talk about social issues instead of living them (219).

2. Selig, in "A Sad Heart at the Late-Victorian Culture Market: George Gissing's *In the Year of the Jubilee*" (1969), argues that it is Gissing's negative view of popular culture that prevents Nancy from being the sustained focal point of the novel, as Gissing's preference for high culture over low leads him to condemn Nancy for her obsession with low culture and to praise Tarrant for his commitment to high culture. This turn, Selig believes, works against the sympathies of Gissing's readers, who expect Nancy to remain the central character in the novel. "Gissing spoils it," writes Selig, "by shifting the point of view from Nancy's perceptiveness to Tarrant's moral obtuseness. In the last sentence of Part 5, Chapter 5, we are told that Tarrant '. . . went home to a night of misery.' . . . Yet our interest is not in him, the lesser character, but in Nancy. What did she go home to? It is in Nancy that the human values of *Jubilee* reside" (719).

Sloan, in "The 'Worthy' Seducer: A Motif under Stress in George Gissing's *In the Year of the Jubilee*" (1985), and Harman, in "Going Public: Female Emancipation in George Gissing's *In the Year of the Jubilee*" (1992), also focus on Nancy's loss of power to Tarrant. Sloan does this by discussing Nancy in the role of the fallen woman: he argues that while the setting in middle-class Camberwell suggests that Nancy might experience freedom not afforded members of the working class, Nancy is portrayed as a "wanton" woman who should be judged for her displays of independence (357). Harman argues that while Nancy has the opportunity to gain freedom through the free union, the material conditions of her life prevent her from fully embracing this alternative to marriage. The free union,

Harman asserts, keeps intact individual freedom without forcing individuals into a position of isolation, and by proposing such an alternative Gissing suggests that Nancy has some degree of agency because her acquiescence to Tarrant's "free union" idea might be read as an act of self-control rather than submission (365). However, Harman believes that the actual conditions of Nancy's life in this alternative marriage do not match up with the theoretical ideal, making Nancy much less liberated than Rhoda Nunn of *The Odd Women,* who is able to achieve a psychological freedom through her more theoretical understanding of the free union (370).

In contrast to these critics, Constance Harsh, in "Gissing's *In the Year of the Jubilee* and the Epistemology of Resistance" (1994), reads the novel as a more successful representation of woman's agency. Correctly characterizing most criticism of Gissing's work as obsessively occupied with establishing a "stable authorial point of view" for Gissing through biographical information identifying him with his male characters, Harsh argues that in *Jubilee* we see how lack of narrative control actually functions to create space for the expression of agency by Nancy (854–55). Harsh identifies three ways in which Gissing makes Nancy the central character in the book, as central as Lionel Tarrant: (1) he thematically associates Nancy with modernity through her attendance at the Jubilee celebration, which suggests that she is capable of feminist revolt; (2) he builds her character through "free indirect discourse," which results in an "epistemology of resistance" on the part of Nancy; and (3) he depicts Nancy as essentially female, aware of "woman's biological destiny," which becomes a way for her to resist Lionel Tarrant's masculinist perspective. While I agree with Harsh that Nancy *initially* is more empowered than Selig, Sloan, and Harman believe, I disagree with the notion that Nancy's understanding of "woman's biological destiny" allows her to resist Tarrant toward the end of the novel. It seems to me that she accepts the idea of "biological destiny," and this prevents her from taking concrete action to change the material conditions of her life.

3. Florence Boos, in "A History of Their Own: Mona Caird, Frances Swiney, and *Fin de Siècle* Feminist Family History" (1998), examines the historicist and social constructionist views expressed by Caird in *The Morality of Marriage* (1897), and Ann Heilmann, in "Mona Caird (1854–1931): Wild Woman, New Woman, and Early Radical Feminist Critic of Marriage and Motherhood" (1996), discusses Caird's critique of motherhood in both her nonfiction essays and in *Daughters of Danaus*. Finally, Patricia Murphy, in "Controlling Women's Time: Regulatory Days and Historical Determinism in *The Daughters of Danaus*" (2001), considers Caird's critique of the Victorian expectation that women would spend their time fulfilling social duties and the frustration Hadria Fullerton feels when forced to do so. All three articles are helpful in terms of understanding the specific views expressed by characters in *The Daughters of Danaus,* who spend significant time debating issues surrounding women's individual liberty and, therefore, the opportunities to assert agency.

4. For more on this debate see Harry's Quilter's *Is Marriage a Failure?* (1888, rpt. 1984), a collection of some of the letters written by readers with commentary by Quilter, who was *The Daily Telegraph*'s theatre critic at the time. It is important to note that Quilter disagreed with much of what Caird believed about marriage, and one weakness of the collection is that he does not reprint her original article

but summarizes it in such a way that his bias against her is evident. In addition, Quilter included other resources on the matter, such as Eliza Lynn Linton's "The Philosophy of Marriage," in the collection, and his selection of sources also reveals his bias against Caird. He saw Linton's essay as a more "practical" view of the issues surrounding marriage and believed that her "brilliant" view balanced out Caird's more "vague and high falutin'" perspective (13–14).

5. Both of these organizations were founded by Elizabeth Wolstenholme Elmy, one of the more prominent figures in the suffrage movement. The latter was founded in response to a disagreement between Elmy and Florence Fenwick Miller, who also was prominent in the Women's Franchise League, over the fact Elmy had a paid position within the organization. Loyal to Elmy, Caird followed her to the Women's Emancipation Union (Crawford 90, 413, 713–20).

6. For accounts of specific debates held at the club, see the numerous anonymously authored articles in *Shafts* and *The Woman's Herald,* but especially Anonymous, "Pioneer Meetings," which describes debates about "The Nationalisation of the Land" and "Rational Dress," and Anonymous, "Debate at the Pioneer Club," which describes a debate over women's suffrage. Also see "The Pioneer Club," which highlights the fact women were learning something from attending the debates, especially how to "separate personal friendships from matters of principle" (Anonymous, "The Pioneer Club" Dec. 1893, 183). This suggests that the Pioneer Club, like Pearson's Men and Women's Club discussed below, valued "objective" debate.

7. The commitment to "objective" debate became a point of contention in the club; some of the women members were perceived by the male members as responding from an emotional perspective rather than an objective one. Henrietta Müller, founder of *The Woman's Herald,* for example, was perceived as departing from the scientific approach Pearson had set at the first club meeting (Bland 14). Another point of contention was the differing motives of the men and the women in the club. While many of the women cited a commitment to the women's movement as their reason for joining the club, some of the men, especially Pearson, had formed the club because they wanted to understand better the way women think, and this made some of the women feel as though they were objects of scrutiny (6–7).

8. Caird also cites Pearson's *Sex-Relations in Germany* in "Marriage" (190).

Notes to Chapter 3

1. The former is confirmed by the regular column, Anonymous, "What Liberal Women Are Doing," which features details of the everyday work done by women in the Women's Liberal Federation, and the latter is confirmed by other articles about women's unions, such as "Women Trade Unionists," which emphasizes that working-class women "are also awakening to the knowledge that they ought not to accept less [pay for the same work] than a man" (Anonymous, "Women Trade" 3).

2. Though neither *Shafts* nor *The Woman's Herald* reviewed *The Amazing Marriage,* Frances E. Ashwell wrote a six-part series, "George Meredith's Heroines," for the periodical *Great Thoughts* in 1896 and 1897. In her article

about Carinthia, which was the last in the series, Ashwell argues that while the women in Meredith's later novels are not as powerful as Diana or Rhoda Fleming, Carinthia is the strongest of the heroines Meredith created in the three novels he wrote in the 1890s (407). Ashwell also seems to have been a reader of *The Woman's Herald*; in August 1894 a Frances E. Ashwell wrote a letter to *The Woman's Herald* concerning "The Influence of the Feminine Novel." In this letter, Ashwell defends Meredith and Ibsen from the charge that they "write of an abnormal class who are unnatural, in so far as they repress the angel in the animal" (124) and argues, to the contrary, that these two writers exhibit the "healthy-body-healthy-mind view of human well-being," in which the angel is made to "illumine" and "purge" the animal, since "real progress" is dependent on the two types working in unison (124).

3. For more on caricatures of the New Woman, see Angelique Richardson and Chris Willis's "Introduction" to *The New Woman in Fiction and in Fact: Fin-de-Siècle Feminisms* (2001).

4. Here I depart from Richardson, who in *Love and Eugenics in the Late Nineteenth Century: Rational Reproduction and the New Woman* (2003), as well as in the articles "'People Talk a Lot of Nonsense about Heredity': Mona Caird and Anti-Eugenic Feminism" (2001) and "The Eugenization of Love: Sarah Grand and the Morality of Genealogy" (2000), argues that Grand was writing from a eugenicist point of view in *The Heavenly Twins*. I generally agree with Richardson's assessment of Grand, but her argument about eugenics in Grand's work relies too heavily on Grand's post-1900 nonfiction to suggest that her earlier fictional work, especially *The Heavenly Twins,* contained eugenicist ideas.

5. That seems to be the light in which *The Woman's Herald* and *Shafts* interpreted Grand's *The Heavenly Twins.* In *The Woman's Herald's* review of the novel, the reviewer discusses the "double standard" for sexual relations Grand was trying to dismantle. For the first time, says the reviewer, women have the chance to control their own futures, particularly when it comes to marriage, by asking questions such as, "Is any kind of a man good enough to be my husband?" and "Is any kind of man—provided he be respectable and well-to-do—good enough to be the father of my children?" Not necessarily, the reviewer suggests and goes on to say: "Either men must become as moral as women, or women will become as immoral as men" (Anonymous, "Marriage" 123). Certainly, this statement advocates social purity, but the reviewer never pushes these ideas to the point of eugenicism, since the key idea seems to be changing the morals of men rather than breeding a particular "race." In *Shafts,* Mary Fordham also articulates a social-purity view when discussing Grand's novel in an article titled "Knowledge Is Power," claiming, "We want one and the same moral code for men and women; not one for one sex and one for the other. We want to see equality between men and women, and this can only be secured by the elevation of the man, not by the degradation of the woman. Men, no less than women, must lead pure lives before marriage, and afterwards remain true to one wife" (137). Again, the emphasis is on changing the moral behavior of men rather than encouraging women to engage what would come to be called "race motherhood."

6. In addition to the articles by Smith and Courtney, articles about Meredith's female characters appeared in the periodicals *Woman* and *Great Thoughts,* neither

of which was explicitly feminist but both of which hired feminist writers to write about Meredith. Clementina Black authored "Women Under Victoria: Women in the Literature of the Reign," which ran in *Woman* in May 1897, and Frances E. Ashwell authored the six-part series "George Meredith's Heroines" in *Great Thoughts* in 1896 and 1897.

7. The essays in *The Lady* were part of the magazine's weekly literary competitions and were written by "average" people under pseudonyms such as "Amaryllis," "Broad Arrow," "Mustard Seed," and "Rotha." The competitors were given specific topics each week, in this case, "Write an analytical essay on the women in George Meredith's 'Diana of the Crossways.'" Interestingly, the winners "Rotha" and "Mustard Seed," as well as the judge of these essays, "Hypatia," comment on Diana's actions. Hypatia wonders whether Diana's actions can be forgiven, writing, "It is impossible not to love Diana—perhaps we love her most when we feel most inclined to blame her, save only when she performed the only deliberately dishonourable action of her life, and sold the secret Dacier confided in her" (Anonymous, "Lady Literary" .172). Rotha addresses the issue less directly but seems to indicate she would have a hard time forgiving Diana for selling Dacier's secret. While she claims that Meredith helps readers sympathize with Diana at this point in the novel, she also emphasizes Diana's faults and ends her essay with the statement, "Through the women of his book Meredith conveys the teaching that lack of feeling is not a virtue, that the truly good woman is not she who does not know, but she who stoutly resists temptation" (172). Mustard Seed, on the other hand, seems thoroughly capable of forgiving Diana: "'True, she errs, but in her own grand way,' and she errs in exactly the way in which a woman of Diana's warm heart and vivid imagination would do. . . . She has nothing of the coquette in her, albeit she once verges terribly near it, but that is when she is striving to keep Redworth's love at bay" (172).

8. Bedford draws special attention to Diana's beauty not only in his individual portrait of her but also in the introduction of the book, when he writes that "of all the Meredith heroines, [Diana] is the only one possessed of beauty on strictly classical lines" (18). While attention to Diana's beauty and clothing, and the decision to paint portraits of Meredith's heroines in the first place, might be seen as tempering Meredith's feminist tendencies, a closer examination of the book shows that Bedford wants to play up, rather than diminish, the connection between Meredith and feminism. Bedford's introduction, divided into sections with specific headings, begins with the section "George Meredith's Allegiance to Feminism," and many, though not all, of the other headings pick up on themes evident in feminist criticism of the 1890s. There is a section "Their Gift of Brains," which includes Diana's wit as one of its examples of Meredith's commitment to portraying women as intelligent (22), and a section "Friendship between his Women," which includes reference to Diana and Emma's friendship, characterized by Bedford as the "most outstanding" of Meredith's female friendships (29).

Notes to Chapter 4

1. Moore also used the image of Parnassus in "Cheap Tripping to Parnassus" (1886), which exposes the corruption of achieving success via the story of Julien, owner of the studio Moore attended while living in Paris, and in "The Decline of

the Drama" (1921), in which Moore writes about the frustration of theatre critics upon seeing the work of playwrights who seem not to have lived up to the expectations set by drama of the 1890s, when it seemed as though "Ibsen had hit upon a dramatic road that would lead every body to Parnassus who cared to go there" (1). In both of these cases, Moore uses the image in a somewhat derogatory manner, yet he discusses his own association with Parnassus in strictly positive terms.

2. Among those critics who have revised Watt are John Richetti (*Popular Fiction Before Richardson: Narrative Patterns 1700–1739,* 1969, rep. 1992), Nancy K. Miller (*The Heroine's Text: Readings in the French and English Novel, 1722–1782,* 1980), Michael McKeon (*The Origins of the English Novel, 1600–1740,* 1987), Nancy Armstrong (*Desire and Domestic Fiction: A Political History of the Novel,* 1987), Margaret Anne Doody (*The True Story of the Novel,* 1996), and Josephine Donovan (*Women and the Rise of the Novel, 1405–1726,* 1999). While Richetti and McKeon have done much to question Watt's omission of a discussion of the romance in his account, most useful to my work here are the studies by Miller, Armstrong, Doody, and Donovan. Their studies address directly the masculinist assumptions of a traditional history of the novel (Miller and Armstrong) and the overlooked contributions of early women novelists (Doody and Donovan). These revisions to the history of the novel make clear the strong investment nineteenth-century male authors had in building and sustaining a masculinist tradition.

3. Moore's hatred for Hardy is well known, with his most negative comment appearing in his 1917 revision of *Confessions of a Young Man* (1888), where he writes, "I read Mr. Hardy despite his name. It prejudiced me against him from the first; a name so trivial as Thomas Hardy cannot, I said, foreshadow a great talent; and 'Far from the Madding Crowd' discovered the fact to me that Mr. Hardy was but one of George Eliot's miscarriages" (211). Moore iterated his poor opinion of Hardy in *Conversations in Ebury Street* (1924), where he again contrasts Hardy to Eliot by stating that Eliot would explore the various motives of Angel Clare in the confession scene in *Tess of the d'Urbervilles,* hearing Tess's confession, whereas Hardy avoids such exploration, a result of his "lack of invention," or "brain paralysis" (122). Hardy returned the favor on his deathbed in 1928, when he composed a scathing epitaph for Moore: "'No mortal man beneath the sky / Can write such English as can I / They say it holds no thought my own / What then, such beauty (perfection) is not known.' / Heap dustbins on him: / They'll not meet / The apex of his self conceit" (Hardy, *Complete Poems* 954).

4. Of the process, Moore states that after deciding on Alice's profession, the writing of sentimental stories, he "passed in review all the women I know who took part in the world's work; I remembered some five or six who collectively were a realization of the character which, in vague and fragmentary outline, I had already conceived. I thought of these women long and anxiously[;] I recalled looks, words, and gestures; I raked together every half-forgotten memory; I considered the main structure of each temperament; and I took note of special peculiarities; over and over again I pulled these women to pieces like toys, and strove to build something of my own out of the pile of virtues and vices that lay before me" (279–80).

5. To make the book even more "English" than it already was, Moore added the subtitle "An English Story" to Heinemann's regular third edition, and he

added a dedication to his friend T. W. Rolleston, which replaced the original dedication to Moore's brother, Maurice (Gilcher 46). In this new dedication, Moore emphasized that Rolleston was an Irishman who could "always love Ireland without hating England" and that he respected Rolleston for this, a statement that confirms Moore's interest in appearing friendly to the English. These "English" revisions are included in the fine edition of 1920, as well as in the 1932 edition with the woman-centered preface I discuss later in this chapter.

6. This issue also was taken up in the Society of Authors' periodical *The Author*, which Stannard received as part of her membership in the Society. In 1890 *The Author* highlighted "A Hard Case," in which a young woman had been ripped off by a publisher, who convinced her to pay for lessons in writing and the publication of her book, which did not sell a single copy (Anonymous, "Hard Case" 8).

Bibliography

Anderson, Amanda. *Tainted Souls and Painted Faces: The Rhetoric of Fallenness in Victorian Culture.* Ithaca: Cornell University Press, 1993.

Anonymous. "Authors' Club." The Author (1 Aug. 1891): 85–86.

———. "A Book of the Hour: *The Morality of Marriage*." *The Woman's Signal* (25 Aug. 1898): 115–17.

———. "Correspondence: Re 'The Heavenly Twins.'" *Shafts* (Nov. 1893): 167.

———. "Debate at the Pioneer Club." *The Woman's Herald* (25 May 1893): 211.

———. "Extinct Monsters: Muriel Dowie on 'Woman Adventurers.'" *The Woman's Herald* (29 June 1893): 297.

———. "Fiction." *The Speaker* (14 Oct. 1893): 417–18.

———. "Gallia." *The Saturday Review* (23 Mar. 1895): 383.

———. "A Hard Case." *The Author* (15 May 1890): 8–9.

———. "The Heavenly Twins." *The Critic* (7 Oct. 1893): 219–20. Rpt. in Heilmann, *Journalistic* 435–37.

———. "How the World Moves." *Shafts* (21 Jan. 1893): 188.

———. "Influential Lives: Mrs. Matilda Sharpe and Her Schools." *Shafts* (3 Nov. 1893): 3–4.

———. "Interview: John Strange Winter." *Women's Penny Paper* (29 June 1889): 1.

———. "Interview: Mrs. Mona Caird." *Women's Penny Paper* (28 June 1890): 421–22.

———. "Is the Present Increase in Women Authors a Gain to Literature?" *Shafts* (Apr. 1894): 230–31.

———. "Ladies' Club." The Author (1 Oct. 1891): 134.

———. "The Lady Journalists." *Today's Woman* (22 June 1895): 17.

———. "'The Lady' Literary Society." *The Lady* (1 Feb. 1900): 172.

———. "Literature of the Month: *Emilia in England*." *The Victoria Magazine* (June 1864): 184–85.

———. "Marriage and the Modern Woman: or, the Story of the Heavenly Twins." *The Woman's Herald* (13 Apr. 1893): 123–24; "Marriage and the Modern Woman; Tom Jones as Husband." *The Woman's Herald* (20 Apr. 1893): 140–41; "The Story of Evadne." *The Woman's Herald* (27 Apr. 1893): 155; "The Story of Evadne." *The Woman's Herald* (11 May 1893): 186.

———. "New Novels: The Beth Book." *The Athenaeum* (27 Nov. 1897): 743–44. Rpt. in Heilmann, *Journalistic* 474.

———. "New Novels. According to Sample: Heavenly!" [Review of *The Heavenly Twins*.] *The Pall Mall Gazette* (3 Apr. 1893): 3. Rpt. in Heilmann, *Journalistic* 432–33.

———. "Notes." *Golden Gates* (19 Nov. 1892): 449.

————. "Notes and Comments." *The Woman's Herald* (22 Oct. 1892): 4–5.

————. "Novels." *The Guardian* (3 Apr. 1895): 510.

————. "Our Library Table: *Ideala: a Study from Life.*" *The Woman's Herald* (12 Oct. 1893): 537.

————. "Our Policy." *Women's Penny Paper* (27 Oct. 1888): 1.

————. "Pioneer Club." *Shafts* (Mar. 1893): 12.

————. "Pioneer Club." *Shafts* (Dec. 1893): 183.

————. "Pioneer Meetings." *Shafts* (3 Dec. 1892): 73.

————. "Pioneer Club Records." *Shafts* (May 1894): 251.

————. "Present-Day Women Novelists." *The Woman's Herald* (17 Sept. 1892): 3–4.

————. Review of *Tess of the d'Urbervilles. The Saturday Review* (16 Jan. 1892): 73–74. Rpt. in Cox 188–90.

————. "Reviews." *The Englishwoman's Review* (15 Jan. 1891): 61.

————. "Reviews: 'The Heavenly Twins.' By Sara[h] Grand." *Shafts* (25 Feb. 1893): 268.

————. "Reviews and Notices." *The Englishwoman's Review* (17 Jan. 1894): 52.

————. "Reviews: *The Odd Women.*" *The Pall Mall Gazette* (May 1893): 4. Rpt. in *Gissing: The Critical Heritage.* Ed. Pierre Coustillas and Colin Patridge. London: Routledge and Kegan Paul, 1972. 220–21.

————. "Reviews: *The Wing of Azrael.*" *Women's Penny Paper* (25 May 1889): 10.

————. "Sarah Grand: A Study." *The Woman's Herald* (17 Aug. 1893): 401.

————. "Society of Authors." *The Author* (1 Feb. 1896): 223–25.

————. "Some Books of the Month." [Review of *The Beth Book.*] *The Review of Reviews* 16 (1897): 618–22. Rpt. in Heilmann, *Journalistic* 459–66.

————. "Some New Novels." [Review of *The Beth Book.*] *The Spectator* (13 Nov. 1897): 691–92. Rpt. in Heilmann, *Journalistic* 467.

————. "A Study in Average Women." *The Woman's Herald* (22 June 1893): 281–82.

————. "Thoughts about Books: *The Morality of Marriage.*" *Shafts* (Feb./Mar. 1895): 24–27.

————. "Two Women Who Write." *The Woman's Herald* (6 July 1893): 309.

————. "Typewriting as an Employment for Women." *Shafts* (3 Nov. 1893): 11.

————. "Unsigned Review." [Rev. of *Diana of the Crossways.*] *The Pall Mall Gazette* (28 Mar. 1885). Rpt. in Williams 265–68.

————. "Weight in Sex." *The Woman's Signal* (29 Aug. 1895): 131.

————. "What Liberal Women Are Doing." *The Woman's Herald* (11 June 1892): 8.

————. "What the Girl Says." *Shafts* (3 Nov. 1892): 5.

————. "A Woman's View of George Meredith's Heroines." *The Woman's Herald* (28 Dec. 1893): 710.

————. "Women Trade Unionists." *The Woman's Herald* (17 Sept. 1892): 3.

Ardis, Ann. *Modernism and Cultural Conflict, 1880–1922.* Cambridge: Cambridge University Press, 2002.

————. *New Women, New Novels: Feminism and Early Modernism.* New Brunswick, NJ: Rutgers University Press, 1990.

Armstrong, Nancy. *Desire and Domestic Fiction: A Political History of the Novel.* New York: Oxford University Press, 1987.

Ashwell, Frances E. "George Meredith's Heroines: I.—Lucy Desborough." *Great Thoughts* (3 Oct. 1896): 3–4; "II.—Rhoda Fleming." *Great Thoughts* (14 Nov. 1896): 107–8; "III.—Emilia Alessandra Belloni." *Great Thoughts* (26 Dec. 1896): 215–16; "IV.—Diana of the Crossways." *Great Thoughts* (30 Jan. 1897): 271–72; "V.—Clara Middleton." *Great Thoughts* (6 Mar. 1897): 351–52; "VI.—Carinthia Jane." *Great Thoughts* (27 Mar. 1897): 407–8.

———. Letter to the editor: "The Influence of the Feminine Novel." *The Woman's Signal* (23 Aug. 1894): 124.

"Aurora." "Between the Lights: The Woman's Writers' Dinner." *The Woman's Signal* (13 June 1895): 384.

Bainbridge, Oliver. *John Strange Winter: A Volume of Personal Record.* London: East and West, Ltd., 1916.

Bakhtin, Mikhail. "Discourse in the Novel." *The Dialogic Imagination: Four Essays.* Ed. Michael Holquist. Trans. Caryl Emerson and Michael Holquist. Austin: University of Texas Press, 1981. 259–422.

Barry, William. "The Strike of the Sex." *The Quarterly Review* 179 (1894): 295–305. Rpt. in Heilmann, *Journalistic* 443–53.

Bedford, Herbert. *The Heroines of George Meredith.* Banbury: Hodder and Stoughton/Henry Stone and Son, Ltd., 1914.

Beer, Gillian. "*The Amazing Marriage:* A Study in Contraries." In *Meredith: A Change of Masks,* Gillian Beer. London: University of London/Athlone Press, 1970. 168–81.

———. "*Diana of the Crossways:* The Novelist in the Novel." In *Meredith: A Change of Masks,* Gillian Beer. London: University of London/Athlone Press, 1970. 140–67.

Bertrandias, Bernadette. "Jeux de focalisation et problematique de la figuration dans *Tess.*" *Cahiers victoriens et éduoardians* 27 (Apr. 1988): 141–48.

Besant, Walter. "On Literary Collaboration." *The Author* (1 Mar. 1892): 328.

———. "News and Notes." *The Author* (15 Dec. 1890): 200–201.

———. "Notes and News." *The Author* (16 Feb. 1891): 252.

Black, Clementina. "Literature: The Odd Women." *The Illustrated London News* (5 Aug. 1893): 155. Rpt. in *Gissing: The Critical Heritage.* Ed. Pierre Coustillas and Colin Patridge. London: Routledge and Kegan Paul, 1972. 222–24.

———. "The Need of Trade Unions for Working Women." *The Woman's Herald* (21 May 1892): 6–7.

———. Review of *Tess of the d'Urbervilles. The Illustrated London News* (9 Jan. 1892): 50. Rpt. in Cox 186–87.

———. "Women under Victoria: Women in the Literature of the Reign." *Woman* (5 May 1897): 10–11.

Bland, Lucy. *Banishing the Beast: English Feminism and Sexual Morality 1885–1914.* New York: Penguin, 1995.

Boos, Florence. "A History of Their Own: Mona Caird, Frances Swiney, and *Fin de Siècle* Feminist Family History." *Contesting the Master Narrative: Essays in Social History.* Ed. Jeffrey Cox and Shelton Stromquist. Iowa City: University of Iowa Press, 1998. 69–92.

Butler, Judith. "Contingent Foundations: Feminism and the Question of 'Postmodernism.'" *Feminists Theorize the Political.* Ed. Butler and Joan W. Scott. New York: Routledge, 1992. 3–21.

————. *The Psychic Life of Power: Theories in Subjection.* Stanford: Stanford University Press, 1997.

Caird, Mona. *The Daughters of Danaus.* 1894. New York: Feminist Press at City University of New York, 1989.

————. "A Defence of the So-Called Wild Women." *The Nineteenth Century* 31 (May 1892): 811–29.

————. "The Duel of the Sexes—A Comment." *The Fortnightly Review* 84 (1905): 107–28.

————. *The Great Wave.* London: Wishart and Co., 1931.

————. "The Ideal Marriage." *The Westminster Review* 130 (1888): 617–36.

————. "Marriage." *The Westminster Review* 130 (1888): 186–201.

————. "Mrs. Mona Caird on Women's Suffrage: Part I." *Women's Penny Paper* (10 May 1890): 340.

————. "Mrs. Mona Caird on Women's Suffrage: Part II." *Women's Penny Paper* (17 May 1890): 350.

————. *The Pathway of the Gods.* London: Skeffington and Son, 1898.

————. "Phases of Human Development." *The Morality of Marriage and Other Essays on the Status of Women.* London: George Redway, 1897.

————. "Preface." *The Wing of Azrael.* London: Trubner, 1889.

————. *The Stones of Sacrifice.* London: Simpkin, Marshall, Hamilton, Kent and Co. Ltd., 1915.

Courtney, W. L. "George Meredith's Heroines." *The Daily Telegraph* (21 July 1897): 12.

Cox, R. G., ed. *Thomas Hardy: The Critical Heritage.* New York: Barnes and Noble, 1970.

Crawford, Elizabeth. *The Women's Suffrage Movement: A Reference Guide, 1866–1928.* London: University College London Press, 1999.

Cunningham, Gail. *The New Woman and the Victorian Novel.* London: Macmillan, 1978.

Dickins, F. V. Rev. of *Diana of the Crossways. The Spectator* (18 Apr. 1885). Rpt. in Williams 270–74.

"Dole." "Mr. George Meredith on Women's Status." *Shafts* (3 Nov. 1892): 8.

Donovan, Josephine. *Women and the Rise of the Novel, 1405–1726.* New York: St. Martin's Press, 1999.

Doody, Margaret Anne. *The True Story of the Novel.* New Brunswick, NJ: Rutgers University Press, 1996.

Doughan, David and Denise Sanchez. *Feminist Periodicals, 1855–1984: An Annotated Critical Bibliography of British, Irish, Commonwealth and International Titles.* Washington Square, NY: New York University Press, 1987.

Doughty, Terri. "Sarah Grand's *The Beth Book:* The New Woman and the Ideology of the Romance Ending." *Anxious Power: Reading, Writing, and Ambivalence in Narrative by Women.* Ed. Carol J. Singly and Susan Elizabeth Sweeney. Albany: State University of New York Press, 1993. 185–96.

Dowie, Ménie Muriel. *Gallia.* 1895. Ed. Helen Small. London: J. M. Dent/Everyman, 1995.

————. *A Girl in the Karpathians.* 1891. New York: Cassell, no date.

————. *Women Adventurers.* London: T. Fisher Unwin, 1893.

Flint, Kate. *The Woman Reader 1837–1914.* Oxford: Clarendon Press, 1993.

Fordham, Mary. "Knowledge Is Power." *Shafts* (Sept. 1893): 137.

Forman, Maurice Buxton. *Meredithiana, Being a Supplement to the Bibliography of Meredith.* New York: Haskell House Publishers Ltd., 1971.

Foucault, Michel. *The Archaeology of Knowledge.* 1969. Trans. A. M. Sheridan Smith. New York: Pantheon/Random House, 1972.

———. *Discipline and Punish: The Birth of the Prison.* 1978. Trans. Alan Sheridan. New York: Random House, 1995.

Fraser, Hilary, Stephanie Green, and Judith Johnston. *Gender and the Victorian Periodical.* Cambridge: Cambridge University Press, 2003.

Frazier, Adrian. *George Moore, 1852–1933.* New Haven: Yale University Press, 2000.

Genette, Gérard. *Narrative Discourse: An Essay in Method.* Trans. Jane E. Lewin. Ithaca: Cornell University Press, 1980.

Gerber, Helmut E. "Introduction." *George Moore on Parnassus: Letters (1900–1933) to Secretaries, Publishers, Printers, Agents, Literati, Friends, and Acquaintances.* Newark: University of Delaware Press, 1988. 21–80.

Gerber, Helmut E. and W. Eugene Davis, eds. *Thomas Hardy: An Annotated Bibliography of Writings about Him.* DeKalb: University of Illinois Press, 1973.

Gilcher, Edwin. *A Bibliography of George Moore.* DeKalb: Northern Illinois University Press, 1970.

Gissing, George. *The Collected Letters of George Gissing.* Ed. Paul F. Mattheisen, Arthur C. Young, and Pierre Coustillas. Athens: Ohio University Press, 1994.

———. *In the Year of the Jubilee.* 1894. Intro. John Halperin. London: Hogarth Press, 1987.

———. *The Nether World.* 1889. Ed. Stephen Gill. Oxford World's Classics Ser. Oxford: Oxford University Press, 1992.

———. *The Odd Women.* 1893. Intro. Elaine Showalter. New York: Penguin, 1983.

———. *The Unclassed.* 1884. Ed. Jacob Korg. Brighton: Harvester Press, 1983.

Gosse, Edmund. "Review of *The Amazing Marriage.*" *St. James's Gazette* (Nov. 1895). Rpt. in Williams 429–31.

Grand, Sarah [Frances McFall]. *Adnam's Orchard.* London: Heinemann, 1912.

———. *The Beth Book.* 1897. Intro. Sally Mitchell. Bristol: Thoemmes Press, 1994.

———. "On Clubs and the Question of Intelligence." *The Woman at Home* 9 (Sept. 1900): 839–42. Rpt. in Heilmann, *Journalistic* 94–99.

———. "Foreword." *The Heavenly Twins.* 1923 ed. London: Heinemann, 1923. v–xvi. Rpt. in Heilmann, *Journalistic* 397–408.

———. *The Heavenly Twins.* New York: Cassell, 1893.

———. *Ideala.* 1888. New York: Optimus, no date.

———. "Letter to the Editor." *The Daily Chronicle* (3 May 1894): 3.

———. "Marriage Questions in Fiction: The Standpoint of a Typical Modern Woman." *The Fortnightly Review* (Mar. 1898): 378–89. Rpt. in Heilmann, *Journalistic* 77–91.

———. "The Modern Girl." *The North American Review* 158 (1894): 706–14. Rpt. in Heilmann, *Journalistic* 36–44.

———. "The Modern Young Man." *The Temple Magazine* (1898): 883–86. Rpt. in Heilmann, *Journalistic* 58–63.

————. "The New Aspect of the Woman Question." *The North American Review* 158 (1894): 271–76. Rpt. in Heilmann, *Journalistic* 29–35.

————. "Preface." *Our Manifold Nature: Stories from Life*. 1894. Short Story Index Reprint Ser. Freeport, NY: Books for Libraries Press, 1969. iii–v.

————. *The Winged Victory*. New York: D. Appleton and Co., 1916.

Hardy, Barbara. *"Lord Ormont and His Aminta* and *The Amazing Marriage."* *Meredith Now: Some Critical Essays*. Ed. Ian Fletcher. London: Routledge, 1971. 295–312.

Hardy, Thomas. "Candour in English Fiction." *The New Review* 2 (Jan. 1890): 6–21.

————. *The Collected Letters of Thomas Hardy*. Ed. Richard Little Purdy and Michael Millgate. Oxford: Clarendon Press, 1978–84.

————. *The Complete Poems of Thomas Hardy*. Ed. James Gibson. New York: Macmillan Publishing Co., 1978.

————. *Jude the Obscure*. 1895. Ed. and Intro. C. H. Sisson. New York: Penguin, 1985.

————. *Tess of the d'Urbervilles*. 1891. Ed. John Paul Riquelme. Boston: Bedford, 1998.

Harman, Barbara Leah. "Going Public: Female Emancipation in George Gissing's *In the Year of the Jubilee.*" *Texas Studies in Literature and Language* 34 (1992): 347–74.

Harsh, Constance. "Gissing's *In the Year of the Jubilee* and the Epistemology of Resistance." *Studies in English Literature, 1500–1900* 34 (1994): 853–75.

Haweis, M[ary] E[liza]. "Foreword." *A Flame of Fire*. London: Hurst and Blackett, 1897.

————. "Review: *Tess of the d'Urbervilles.*" *The Woman's Herald* (13 Feb. 1892): 10.

Heilmann, Ann. "Mona Caird (1854–1931): Wild Woman, New Woman, and Early Radical Feminist Critic of Marriage and Motherhood." *Women's History Review* 5.1 (1996): 67–95.

————. "Mrs. Grundy's Rebellion: Margaret Oliphant between Orthodoxy and the New Woman." *Women's Writing* 6 (1999): 215–37.

————. "Narrating the Hysteric: *Fin-de-Siècle* Medical Discourse and Sarah Grand's *The Heavenly Twins* (1893)." *The New Woman in Fiction and in Fact: Fin-de-Siècle Feminisms*. Ed. Angelique Richardson and Chris Willis. New York: Palgrave, 2001. 123–35.

————. *New Woman Fiction: Women Writing First-Wave Feminism*. New York: St. Martin's Press, 2000.

————. *New Woman Strategies: Sarah Grand, Olive Schreiner, Mona Caird*. Manchester: Manchester University Press, 2004.

————, ed. *Journalistic Writings and Contemporary Reception*. Vol. 1, *Sex, Social Purity, and Sarah Grand*. Intro. Heilmann. London: Routledge, 2000.

Heilmann, Ann and Stephanie Forward, eds. *Selected Letters*. Vol. 2, *Sex, Social Purity, and Sarah Grand*. Transcribed, ed., and intro, Stephanie Forward. London: Routledge, 2000.

Heyns, Michiel. *Expulsion and the Nineteenth-Century Novel: The Scapegoat in English Realist Fiction*. Oxford: Clarendon Press, 1994.

Hone, Joseph. *The Life of George Moore*. New York: Macmillan, 1936.

Jaffe, Audrey. *Scenes of Sympathy: Identity and Representation in Victorian Fiction.* Ithaca: Cornell University Press, 2000.

James, Henry. *The Portrait of a Lady.* 1881. Ed. Nicola Bradbury. The World's Classics Ser. Oxford: Oxford University Press, 1995.

Joyce, James. *Ulysses.* 1922. Ed. Hans Walter Gabler with Wolfhard Steppe and Claus Melchior. New York: Random House/Vintage, 1986.

Kapteyn, Gertrude. "'Esther Waters' and What It Suggests." *Shafts* (May 1895): 24–26.

———. "Reviews: *Diana of the Crossways,* by George Meredith." *Shafts* (Nov. 1895): 109–11.

———. "Reviews: *Diana of the Crossways,* by George Meredith." *Shafts* (Dec. 1895): 125–26.

Kearns, Katherine. *Nineteenth-Century Literary Realism.* Cambridge: Cambridge University Press, 1996.

Kranidis, Rita. *Subversive Discourse: The Cultural Production of Late Victorian Feminist Novels.* New York: St. Martin's Press, 1995.

Krout, M[ary] H. "Woman's Kingdom: 'The Odd Women' and its Influence in England." *The Daily Inter Ocean* (7 Nov. 1896): 16.

———. "Women in Fiction." *The Woman's Herald* (21 Sept. 1893): 485.

———. "Women's Clubs." 1896. *A Looker-On in London.* 1899. http://www.victorianlondon.org/publications2/lookeron-9.htm. Accessed 1 Jan. 2004.

Kucich, John. "Curious Dualities: *The Heavenly Twins* (1893) and Sarah Grand's Belated Modernist Aesthetics." *The New Nineteenth Century: Feminist Readings of Underread Victorian Fiction.* Ed. Barbara Harman and Susan Meyer. New York: Garland, 1996. 195–204.

Langenfeld, Robert. *George Moore: An Annotated Secondary Bibliography of Writings about Him.* New York: AMS Press, 1987.

Ledger, Sally. *The New Woman: Fiction and Feminism at the Fin de Siècle.* New York: St. Martin's Press, 1997.

Ledger, Sally and Roger Luckhurst. *The Fin de Siècle: A Reader in Cultural History c. 1800–1900.* Oxford: Oxford University Press, 2000.

Levine, George. *The Realistic Imagination: English Fiction from Frankenstein to Lady Chatterley.* Chicago: University of Chicago Press, 1981.

Liggins, Emma. "Writing against the 'Husband-Fiend': Syphilis and Male Sexual Vice in the New Woman Novel." *Women's Writing* 7 (2000): 175–95.

Little, John Stanley. "George Meredith's Heroines." *The Woman's Herald* (9 Mar. 1893): 34.

Lloyd, Tom. *Crises of Realism: Representing Experience in the British Novel, 1816–1910.* Lewisburg: Bucknell University Press, 1997.

Mangum, Teresa. *Married, Middlebrow, and Militant: Sarah Grand and the New Woman Novel.* Ann Arbor: University of Michigan Press, 1998.

McKeon, Michael. *The Origins of the English Novel, 1600–1740.* Baltimore: Johns Hopkins University Press, 1987.

Meredith, George. *The Amazing Marriage.* Westminster: Archibald Constable and Co., 1895.

———. *Diana of the Crossways.* 1885. Intro. Lorna Sage. London: Virago, 1980.

———. *The Letters of George Meredith.* Ed. C. L. Cline. Oxford: Clarendon Press, 1970.

Miller, Florence Fenwick. "Books Worth Reading: Esther Waters." *The Woman's Signal* (3 May 1894): 296–97.

———. "Character Sketch: John Strange Winter." *The Woman's Signal* 30 Jan. 1896: 65–66.

Miller, Jane Eldridge. *Rebel Women: Feminism, Modernism, and the Edwardian Novel.* Chicago: University of Chicago Press, 1997.

Miller, Nancy K. *The Heroine's Text: Readings in the French and English Novel, 1722–1782.* New York: Columbia University Press, 1980.

Monkhouse, C. [William Cosmo]. Rev. of *Diana of the Crossways. The Saturday Review* (21 Mar. 1885). Rtp. in Williams 262–64.

Montefiore, Dora B. "Reviews: *Jude the Obscure*." *Shafts* (Feb. 1896): 12–13.

Moore, George. "Cheap Tripping to Parnassus." *The Bat* (26 Dec. 1886): 884–85.

———. "A Colloquy: George Moore and Esther Waters." *Esther Waters: An English Story.* New York: Liveright, 1932. vii–x.

———. *A Communication to My Friends.* England: The Nonesuch Press, 1933.

———. *Avowals.* London: Society for Irish Folk-lore, 1919.

———. *Confessions of a Young Man.* 1889. Ed. Susan Dick. Montreal: McGill-Queen's University Press, 1972.

———. *Conversations in Ebury Street.* New York: Boni and Liveright, 1924.

———. "The Decline of the Drama." *The Dial* Jan. 1921: 6–11.

———. "Defensio Pro Scriptus Meis." *Time: A Monthly Magazine* (Mar. 1887): 277–84.

———. *A Drama in Muslin.* 1886. Intro. James Plunkett. Belfast: Appletree Press, 1992.

———. *Esther Waters.* 1894. Ed. and Intro. David Skilton. Oxford: Oxford University Press, 1984.

———. *Evelyn Innes.* New York: D. Appleton and Co., 1898.

———. *George Moore in Transition: Letters to T. Fisher Unwin and Lena Milman, 1894–1910.* Ed. Helmut E. Gerber. Detroit: Wayne State University Press, 1968.

———. *Héloïse and Abélard.* London: Society for Irish Folk-lore, 1921.

———. "An Imaginary Conversation: Gosse and Moore." *The Fortnightly Review* (Nov. 1918; Jan. 1919): 772–85; 140–52.

———. *The Lake.* 1905. New York: Carroll and Graf Publishers, 1986.

———. *A Mere Accident.* London: Vizetelly and Co., 1887.

———. *A Modern Lover.* London: Tinsley Brothers, 1883.

———. *A Mummer's Wife.* London: Vizetelly and Co., 1885.

———. *Sister Teresa.* Philadelphia: J. B. Lippincott Co., 1901.

———. "Some Characteristics of English Fiction." *The North American Review* (April 1900): 504–17.

———. *The Untilled Field.* Philadelphia: J. B. Lippincott Co., 1903.

Morris, Mowbray. "Culture and Anarchy." *The Quarterly Review* (Apr. 1892): 319–26. Rpt. in Cox 214–20.

Murphy, Patricia. "Controlling Women's Time: Regulatory Days and Historical Determinism in *The Daughters of Danaus*." *Time Is of the Essence: Temporality, Gender, and the New Woman.* Albany: State University of New York Press, 2001. 151–88.

Nelson, Carolyn Christensen. *A New Woman Reader: Fiction, Articles, and Drama of the 1890s.* Peterborough, ON: Broadview Press, 2000.

Oliphant, Margaret. "The Anti-Marriage League." *Blackwood's Edinburgh Magazine* (Jan. 1896): 135–49.

———. "The Old Saloon." *Blackwood's Edinburgh Magazine* (Mar. 1892): 455–74.

———. Review of *The Adventures of Harry Richmond*. *Blackwood's Edinburgh Magazine* (June 1872). Rpt. in Williams 166.

———. Review of *The Egoist*. *Blackwood's* (Sept. 1880). Rpt. in Williams 236–40.

Pearce, Richard. "How Does Molly Bloom Look Through the Male Gaze?" *Molly Bloom: A Polylogue on "Penelope" and Cultural Studies*. Ed. Pearce. Madison: University of Wisconsin Press, 1994. 40–60.

Phegley, Jennifer. *Educating the Proper Woman Reader: Victorian Family Literary Magazines and the Cultural Health of the Nation*. Columbus: The Ohio State University Press, 2004.

Phelan, James. *Living to Tell about It: A Rhetoric and Ethics of Character Narration*. Ithaca: Cornell University Press, 2005.

Pykett, Lyn. "The Cause of Women and the Course of Fiction: The Case of Mona Caird." *Gender Roles and Sexuality in Victorian Literature*. Ed. Christopher Parker. Brookfield, VT: Ashgate, 1995. 128–42.

———. *Engendering Fictions: The English Novel in the Early Twentieth Century*. New York: St. Martin's Press, 1995.

Quilter, Harry, ed. *Is Marriage a Failure?* London: Swan Sonnenschein and Co., 1888. Rpt. New York: Garland Publishing, Inc., 1984.

Register, Cheri. "American Feminist Literary Criticism: A Bibliographical Introduction." *Feminist Literary Criticism: Explorations in Theory*. Ed. Josephine Donovan. Lexington: University Press of Kentucky, 1975. 1–28.

Richards, Grant. "Women Writers in '93." *The Woman's Signal* (11 Jan. 1894): 20.

Richardson, Angelique. "The Eugenization of Love: Sarah Grand and the Morality of Genealogy." *Victorian Studies* 42 (2000): 227–55.

———. *Love and Eugenics in the Late Nineteenth Century: Rational Reproduction and the New Woman*. Oxford: Oxford University Press, 2003.

———. "'People Talk a Lot of Nonsense about Heredity': Mona Caird and Anti-Eugenic Feminism." Richardson and Willis 183–211.

Richardson, Angelique and Chris Willis. "Introduction." Richardson and Willis 1–38.

Richardson, Angelique and Chris Willis, eds. *The New Woman in Fiction and in Fact: Fin de Siècle Feminisms*. New York: Palgrave, 2001.

Richetti, John. *Popular Fiction Before Richardson: Narrative Patterns 1700–1739*. 1969. Oxford: Clarendon Press, 1992.

Riley, Sam, ed. *Consumer Magazines of the British Isles*. Westport, CT: Greenwood Press, 1993.

Sadoff, Diane. "Looking at Tess: The Female Figure in Two Narrative Media." *The Sense of Sex: Feminist Perspectives on Hardy*. Ed. Higonnet. Urbana: University of Illinois Press, 1993. 149–71.

Schaffer, Talia. *The Forgotten Female Aesthetes: Literary Culture in Late-Victorian England*. Charlottesville: University Press of Virginia, 2000.

Schor, Naomi. *Breaking the Chain: Women, Theory, and French Realist Fiction*. New York: Columbia University Press, 1985.

Selig, Robert L. "A Sad Heart at the Late-Victorian Culture Market: George

Gissing's *In the Year of the Jubilee*." *Studies in English Literature, 1500–1900* 9 (1969): 703–20.

Sergeant, Adeline. "George Meredith's Views on Women by a Woman." *The Temple Bar* (June 1889): 207–13.

Shore, Arabella. "An Early Appreciation." *The British Quarterly Review* (Apr. 1879). Rpt. in Williams 192–201.

Showalter, Elaine. *A Literature of Their Own: British Women Novelists from Brontë to Lessing*. Princeton: Princeton University Press, 1977.

Sibthorp, Margaret. "Reviews: *The Daughters of Danaus*." *Shafts* (Apr.–July 1895): 5–7, 23–24, 39–41, 53–56.

———. "Two Women's Papers." *Shafts* (Apr. 1898): 77–79.

———. "What the Editor Means." *Shafts* (3 Nov. 1892): 8.

Silverman, Kaja. "History, Figuration and Female Subjectivity in 'Tess of the d'Urbervilles.'" *Novel* (Fall 1984): 5–28.

Sloan, John. "The 'Worthy' Seducer: A Motif under Stress in George Gissing's *In the Year of the Jubilee*." *English Literature in Transition* 28 (1985): 354–65. Rpt. in *George Gissing: The Cultural Challenge*, John Sloan. New York: St. Martin's Press, 1989. 129–40.

Smith, Garnet. "The Women of George Meredith." *Fortnightly Review* (May 1896): 775–90.

Stannard, Henrietta. [John Strange Winter.] *A Blameless Woman*. 1894. London: F. V. White, 1895.

———. *Bootles' Baby*. 1885. New York: Frank F. Lovell and Co., 1889.

———. "Cavalry Life." *My First Book*. Intro. Jerome K. Jerome. London: Chatto and Windus, 1894.

———. *Confessions of a Publisher, Being the Autobiography of Abel Drinkwater*. 1888. New York: Hurst and Co., 1892.

———. "Death in Our Skirts." *Winter's Magazine* (21 Jan. 1893): 51–52.

———. "Editor's Thoughts." *Golden Gates* (14 Nov. 1891): 19.

———. "Editor's Thoughts." *Winter's Weekly* (5 Mar. 1892): 298–300.

———. "Editor's Thoughts." *Winter's Weekly* (13 Feb. 1892): 242–43.

———. "Editor's Thoughts." *Winter's Weekly* (19 Mar. 1892): 338–39.

———. "Editor's Thoughts: Fashion and Feathers." *Winter's Magazine* (2 Dec. 1893): 69–70.

———. "Editor's Thoughts: The Girl of This Period." *Winter's Weekly* (27 Feb. 1892): 282–83.

———. "Grocers' Licenses and Secret Drinking: The League of the Silver Cord." *Winter's Magazine* (8 Apr. 1893): 262–63.

———. *In the Same Regiment and Other Stories*. London: F. V. White, 1898.

———. Letter Book, 1901. Ms. 57090. Society of Authors Archive. British Lib., London.

———. Miscellaneous Letters, 1889. Ms. 56865. Society of Authors Archive. British Lib., London.

———. "The Outside Edge: A Word to Butterflies and Others." *The Woman's Herald* (16 Mar. 1893): 49–50.

Sutherland, John. *The Stanford Companion to Victorian Fiction*. Stanford; Stanford University Press, 1989.

Tooley, Sarah A. "The Servant Question." *The Woman's Signal* (31 Jan. 1895): 66–67.

Unkeless, Elaine. "The Conventional Molly Bloom." *Women in Joyce*. Ed. Suzette Henke and Unkeless. Urbana: University of Illinois Press, 1982. 150–68.

Ward, Edith. "Shafts of Thought." *Shafts* (3 Nov. 1892): 2.

Watt, Ian. *The Rise of the Novel: Studies in Defoe, Richardson, and Fielding.* Berkeley: University of California Press, 1957.

Welch, Robert. "Moore's Way Back: *The Untilled Field* and *The Lake*." In *The Way Back: George Moore's* The Untilled Field and The Lake. Ed. Welch. Totowa, NJ: Barnes and Noble Books, 1982. 29–44.

Willard, Frances E. "Questions of the Day." *The Woman's Signal* (29 Aug. 1895): 129–31.

Williams, Ioan. *Meredith: The Critical Heritage.* New York: Barnes and Noble, 1971.

Williams, Merryn. "Feminist or Antifeminist? Oliphant and the Woman Question." *Margaret Oliphant: Critical Essays on a Gentle Subversive.* Ed. D. J. Trela. Selinsgrove: Susquehanna University Press, 1995. 165–80.

Wilt, Judith. "The Meredithian Subplot." In *The Readable People of George Meredith,* Judith Wilt. Princeton: Princeton University Press, 1975. 51–80.

———. "The Survival of Romance." In *The Readable People of George Meredith,* Judith Wilt. Princeton: Princeton University Press, 1975. 210–40.

Woolf, Virginia. *Mrs. Dalloway.* 1925. New York: Harcourt Brace Jovanovich/Harvest, 1985.

Young, Eva. "Moral Teaching for Children." *Shafts* (Jan./Feb. 1895): 370–71.

Index